KNIGHT CAPRON LIBRARY
LYNCHBURG COLLEGE
LYNCHBURG, VIRGINIA 24501

WITHDRAWN

ROBERTSON DAVIES
(1913–   )
Photograph courtesy of SRAMEK GRAFIK

Robertson Davies

By Michael Peterman

Trent University

Twayne Publishers
A Division of G.K. Hall & Co. • *Boston*

Robertson Davies

Michael Peterman

Copyright © 1986 by G.K. Hall & Co.
All Rights Reserved
Published by Twayne Publishers
A Division of G.K. Hall & Co.
70 Lincoln Street
Boston, Massachusetts 02111

Copyediting supervised by Lewis DeSimone
Book production by Marne Sultz
Book design by Barbara Anderson

Typeset in 11 pt. Garamond
by Modern Graphics, Inc., Weymouth, Massachusetts

Printed on permanent/durable acid-free paper
and bound in the United States of America

Library of Congress Cataloging in Publication Data
Peterman, Michael.
   Robertson Davies.

   (Twayne's world authors series ; TWAS 780. Canadian literature)
   Bibliography: p. 169
   Includes index.
   1. Davies, Robertson, 1913-   —Criticism and
interpretation.   I. Title.   II. Series: Twayne's world authors series ; TWAS
780.   III. Series: Twayne's world authors series. Canadian literature.
PR9199.3.D3Z79   1986   813'.54   86–12105
ISBN 0–8057–6629–4

Contents

About the Author
Preface
Acknowledgments
Chronology

    Chapter One
    Robertson Davies:
    Man of Letters as Artist   1

    Chapter Two
    Samuel Marchbanks   17

    Chapter Three
    The Bewitchments of Simplification:
    Robertson Davies's Early Plays   35

    Chapter Four
    The Theater As Temple:
    Robertson Davies's Later Plays   56

    Chapter Five
    The Salterton Novels   81

    Chapter Six
    The Deptford Trilogy:
    Passwords to the Duke's Realm   114

    Chapter Seven
    The Rebel Angels:
    Spelunking on Parnassus   154

Notes and References   160
Selected Bibliography   169
Index   176

About the Author

Michael Peterman is professor of English at Trent University in Peterborough, Ontario. Educated at Princeton and the University of Toronto, he has been at Trent since 1972. He is senior tutor at Lady Eaton College and editor of the *Journal of Canadian Studies*.

Professor Peterman has published articles on Edith Wharton, Robertson Davies, Willa Cather, W. O. Mitchell, Sara Jeannette Duncan, Susanna Moodie, and Catharine Parr Traill. His monograph on Susanna Moodie appeared in volume 1, Fiction Series of *Canadian Writers and Their Works* (Essays in Canadian Writing Press, 1983). With Carl Ballstadt and Elizabeth Hopkins, he has published *Susanna Moodie: Letters of a Lifetime* (University of Toronto Press, 1985) and is working on a companion volume of the letters of Catharine Parr Traill.

Preface

The question—"What kind of man is Robertson Davies?"—belongs properly to the biographer. While this study touches on the experiences and shape of Davies's life, especially in chapter 1, its concern is to present him as many-sided writer; in short, as man of letters. In a career approaching six decades the Ontario boy who wrote his first newspaper article at age ten has evolved into a literary figure of many parts. Now in his seventies he may seem to some younger writers "a novelistic Matthew Arnold";[1] however, few Canadian writers of the present day are so widely praised and so much in demand, both at home and abroad.

Since about 1960 Canada has been enjoying a conspicuous cultural awakening that has found expression in most aspects of literature and the fine arts. Robertson Davies has ridden the crest of this wave, enjoying acclaim as a novelist and social critic of the first rank, but it is essential to recognize that it is a wave he had much to do with stimulating. At a time when these energies were struggling to be born, his journalistic pieces and plays of the 1940s and 1950s brought him national recognition both as a comic writer and as a trenchant observer of Canadian culture. It was not unusual for reviewers of his early books to declare him the outstanding humorist or playwright in the country.

With the English publication of *The Table Talk of Samuel Marchbanks* and with English and American publication of his Salterton novels *(Tempest-Tost, Leaven of Malice,* and *A Mixture of Frailties)* in the 1950s, his reputation expanded. Today in the afterglow of the very successful Deptford trilogy *(Fifth Business, The Manticore,* and *World of Wonders)* not only is there greater awareness of his breadth and seriousness as a writer but his fame has expanded considerably. *Fifth Business* has, for instance, been translated into French, Polish, Swedish, Spanish, German, Finnish, Danish, Norwegian, and Portuguese. *The Rebel Angels* (1981), which is the basis for a third trilogy, was hailed by Anthony Burgess as one of the best novels of recent decades.[2] In a *Newsweek* feature entitled "The Inventor of Gods," Jean Strouse notes that *Fifth Business* "made readers south of the Canadian border snap to attention." With successive novels she adds, "Davies has become something of a cult figure" in the United States, though she allows that, even with *The Rebel Angels,* "his name is not yet a household word here."[3] The recently published sequel, *What's Bred in the Bone* (1985), has, however, already outstripped *The Rebel Angels* in popularity.

The aim of this study is in the first instance to introduce readers, especially those beyond Canada, to the range and significance of Davies's work as journalist, playwright, and novelist. The regrettable consequence is that it has been necessary to reduce attention to his academic studies, particularly of nineteenth-century theater *(The Mirror of Nature),* of theater in Canada *(The Well-Tempered Critic),* his book reviewing *(A Voice from the Attic* and *The Enthusiasms of Robertson Davies),* his skills as an essayist *(One Half of Robertson Davies),* his studies of Stephen Leacock, and his ghost stories *(High Spirits).* At the same time, commentary on *The Rebel Angels* is limited to the brief concluding chapter. As the first of a new series of novels it will, I am confident, provoke the kind of fresh debate and interest that is better addressed in response to the entire work rather than its initial part.

The major concern of the study is to investigate Davies's sustaining theme, the importance of self in modern life. From Samuel Marchbanks and the first plays, the struggle of the ego to deal with delimiting forces, to assert itself forcefully and flamboyantly, to gather knowledge not only in response to one's curiosity about life but also for the purpose of knowing more than others, to feel more deeply about life and to grapple with those feelings—these tendencies are consistent in his entire corpus. What the Anglican priest, Simon Darcourt, says in *The Rebel Angels* might stand for most of Davies's protagonists:

> I wanted to give all the time I could spare to saving my own soul, and I wanted to do work that gave me a little time for that greater work. [Some might] call me selfish. But am I? I am hard at the great task with the person who lies nearest and who is most amenable to my best efforts, and perhaps by example I may persuade a few others to do the same.[4]

Darcourt's vocation suggests the distance Davies has traveled from the 1940s in his increasingly concentrated concern with self. What Carl Jung called the process of "individuation" provides a kind of general goal for many of Davies's characters, but it is individuation

Preface

of a highly particularized stamp. Davies's later novels are increasingly preoccupied with the distinction between egotism and egoism, between selfishness and enlightened self-interest in men of special prominence, be they intellectuals, artists, or priests. The egoism of the hero figure—and Davies's novels and plays are seldom without heroes who are egoists—dominates his work. It is an egoism that he shows to be hard and harrowingly won. His characters typically have much to battle against. Domineering parents, threatening rivals, culturally imposed attitudes, and debilitating circumstances conspire to constrain native gusto and inhibit healthy selfhood in his sensitive protagonists. Battles rage around them on the social and psychological levels. Browbeating, advantage taking, jockeying for position, and playing upon the weaknesses of others come to seem the normal course of behavior. Inequity of power in a hostile world is everywhere apparent. The vulnerable ego must learn how to survive and to assert its own specialness in its own terms.

Survival, self-knowledge, and self-assertion distinguish Davies's heroes. The degree of that assertiveness and self-recognition increases with the author's experience and confidence. At the same time, his commitment to the comic mode and the pattern of romance continues to dovetail effectively with his underlying certainty that, whatever the pain, the worthwhile individual is capable of making his own way. The hero may even come to enjoy the luxury of the revenge he desires upon those cruel or insensitive beings who, seeing only a dull cocoon, have no sense that it disguises a butterfly of rare beauty.

Michael Peterman

Trent University

Acknowledgments

This study owes its greatest debt to Professor Gordon Roper, formerly chairman of the English department, Trinity College, University of Toronto, and currently professor emeritus, Trent University. A long-time friend of Robertson Davies, Professor Roper had undertaken the Twayne study when ill health forced him to relinquish the assignment. In asking me to take over he gave me a free hand to devise the kind of study I felt suitable, even as he stood by ready to listen to my ideas and to advise me—always wisely—concerning excesses, oversights, and infelicities. Thus, though the book began with him, owes much to him, and is, in deep affection, dedicated to him, it must bear the stamp of my views in all aspects.

Others have been very helpful. To Judith Skelton Grant, who read Chapter 1 for factual accuracy, to my Trent colleagues, Robert Chambers and James Neufeld, and especially to Zailig Pollock, who closely read the entire text, to Robert Lecker, Lewis DeSimone, and Anne Jones at G. K. Hall, and to the many others, including Robert Finch, Desmond Neill, Moira Whalon, and Douglas Lochhead, who shared some of their impressions of Davies with me, I offer my thanks. Nor can I forget Robertson Davies himself who generously found time to answer certain of my questions. I would also like to thank Tina Merchant, Dorothy Mutter, Gabrielle Lacroix, and particularly Launi Merrett, who typed various parts of the manuscript. Finally my fullest gratitude must be to my family, Cara, Robbie, and Jessica, for their unwavering interest and support.

An abbreviated version of chapters 3 and 4 appeared as "Bewitchments of Simplification," in *Canadian Drama* 7, no. 2 (1981):94–109.

Chronology

1913 Robertson Davies born in Thamesville, Ontario, 28 August.
1919 Family moves to Renfrew, Ontario.
1924 Visits Europe, England, and Wales with his parents.
1926 Rupert Davies purchases the *Kingston British Whig;* family moves to Kingston, Ontario.
1928–1932 Attends Upper Canada College in Toronto; edits the *College Times* in 1931–1932.
1932–1935 Attends Queen's University as a special student; writes for Queen's student magazine and acts with the Queen's University Drama Guild.
1935 Rupert Davies purchases the *Peterborough Examiner.*
1935–1938 Studies at Balliol College, Oxford, earning B.Litt.; active in the Oxford University Dramatic Society.
1938–1939 Joins Old Vic Company in London at Tyrone Guthrie's invitation.
1939 *Shakespeare's Boy Actors.*
1940 Marries Brenda Mathews and returns to Canada; joins staff of *Saturday Night* in Toronto; first daughter, Miranda, born.
1942 *Shakespeare for Young Players;* moves to Peterborough, Ontario, as editor of the *Peterborough Examiner;* second daughter, Jennifer, born; Rupert Davies appointed to the Canadian senate.
1943 Begins "The Diary of Samuel Marchbanks" as a weekly column.
1944 Completes *The King Who Could Not Dream.*
1946 Formally appointed vice-president and publisher of the *Peterborough Examiner.*
1947 *Overlaid* wins an Ottawa Drama League Workshop contest; *The Diary of Samuel Marchbanks;* active in

ROBERTSON DAVIES

founding the Peterborough Little Theatre; completes *King Phoenix;* third daughter, Rosamond, born.

1948 *Overlaid: A Comedy;* writes *Fortune, My Foe; Eros at Breakfast* awarded "Best Canadian Play" at the Dominion Drama Festival; mother dies in Kingston.

1949 *Eros at Breakfast and Other Plays; The Table Talk of Samuel Marchbanks; Fortune, My Foe;* wins awards as author and director at the Dominion Drama Festival.

1950 *At My Heart's Core;* Rupert Davies marries Margaret Esther McAdoo.

1951 *Tempest-Tost;* writes "The Theatre: A Dialogue on the State of the Theatre in Canada" for Vincent Massey's Canadian Royal Commission (the Massey Report) investigating national development in the arts in Canada.

1952 *A Masque of Aesop.*

1953 *Renown at Stratford. A Record of the Shakespeare Festival in Canada, 1953,* written with Tyrone Guthrie; elected governor, Board of Directors of the Stratford Festival (to 1971); begins "Books" column for the *Toronto Star.*

1954 *Leaven of Malice; Twice Have the Trumpets Sounded,* coauthored with Tyrone Guthrie; writes *A Jig for the Gypsy* for the Crest Theatre (Toronto); brother Fred dies in an accident in Bermuda.

1955 *A Jig for the Gypsy: Thrice the Brinded Cat Hath Mew'd,* coauthored with Tyrone Guthrie, Boyd Neel, and Tanya Moisewitsch; writes *Hunting Stuart* for the Crest Theatre; awarded the Stephen Leacock Medal for humor (1954) for *Leaven of Malice.*

1956 Davies's *The Lost Scene from "The Merry Wives of Windsor"* used in Guthrie's 1956 Stratford production; writes *General Confession* for the Crest Theatre.

1957 Wrote introduction to Leacock's *Literary Lapses.*

1958 *A Mixture of Frailties.*

1960 *A Voice from the Attic;* begins weekly column, "A Writer's Diary," for the *Toronto Star* and other papers (to June 1962); appointed visiting professor of English, Trinity College, University of Toronto; dramatizes *Leaven of Malice* as *Love and Libel* for the Theatre Guild of New York.

1961 Appointed first master of Massey College (University of Toronto) by Vincent Massey; appointed professor of English by University College, University of Toronto; awarded the Lorne Pierce Medal by the Royal Society of Canada for his contribution to Canadian literature.

1962 Resigns as editor of the *Peterborough Examiner*.

1963 *A Masque of Mr. Punch;* Massey College opens.

1964 Appointed first Edgar Stone Lecturer in Dramatic Literature, the University of Toronto.

1966 Writes one act of, and does the continuity for, the Canadian Centennial Spectacle slated for 1 July 1967.

1967 *Marchbanks' Almanack;* elected fellow of the Royal Society of Canada; Rupert Davies dies; the *Peterborough Examiner* sold.

1968 *Four Favourite Plays.*

1970 *Fifth Business; Stephen Leacock;* edits *Feast of Stephen: An Anthology of Some of the Less Familiar Writings of Stephen Leacock.*

1972 *The Manticore; Hunting Stuart and Other Plays,* ed. Brian Parker; appointed Companion of the Order of Canada.

1973 Wins Governor-General's Award for Fiction for *The Manticore;* readapts *Leaven of Malice* for the University of Toronto Drama Centre's production.

1974 Writes *Brothers in the Black Art* for the CBC.

1975 *World of Wonders; Question Time;* coauthors *The Revels History of Drama in English.* Vol. 6, 1750–1880.

1977 *One Half of Robertson Davies: Provocative Pronouncements on a Wide Range of Topics; Pontiac and the Green Man* performed in Toronto.

1979 *The Enthusiasms of Robertson Davies,* ed. Judith Skelton Grant.

1980 The Deptford trilogy dramatized by CBC radio; elected

the first Canadian honorary member of the American Academy and Institute of Arts and Letters.

1981 *The Rebel Angels; The Well-Tempered Critic: One Man's View of Theatre and Letters in Canada,* ed. Judith Skelton Grant; appointed professor emeritus by the University of Toronto; retires as master of Massey College.

1982 *High Spirits.*

1983 *The Mirror of Nature* (based on the 1982 Alexander lectures, University of Toronto).

1984 Elected a fellow of the Royal Society of Literature; *High Spirits* awarded the best Anthology/Collection by the World Fantasy Association.

1985 *What's Bred in the Bone; The Papers of Samuel Marchbanks.*

Chapter One
Robertson Davies: Man of Letters as Artist
The Davies Family: Thamesville (1913–19) and Renfrew (1919–25)

In towns covering the breadth of rural early twentieth-century Ontario, William Robertson Davies received an unusual nurturing from unusual parents. What he has become and what he has written owe a great deal to the pressures he felt in those environments and the attitudes his parents made vital to him. Dramatist, internationally acclaimed novelist, journalist, editor, essayist, critic, theater historian, lecturer, professor, master of Massey College at the University of Toronto, Robertson Davies has his roots in his distinctive responses to Thamesville, Renfrew, and Kingston, Ontario. What Dunstan Ramsay retrospectively observes of Deptford, a town modelled upon Thamesville, applies to Davies himself: though "I . . . left Deptford in the flesh . . . I recognized that I never wholly left it in the spirit."[1]

On 28 August 1913, the third son and last child of Rupert and Florence MacKay Davies was born in Thamesville, a southwestern Ontario village midway between London, Ontario, and Detroit. In the voice of Samuel Marchbanks, Davies recalled those years and that community, details of which he would later use in the Deptford trilogy:

There it all was: the house in which I was born . . . , the church in which I sucked ghostly wisdom from the knees of several Sunday School teachers, the Tecumseth House Hotel, and—best of all—the Ferguson Opera House in which, at the age of three, I made my first appearance upon the stage as an Israelite child in an opera about Queen Esther. . . . I saw two houses which, as a child, I believed to be inhabited by witches, and The Pit—a dreadful Sheol on the edge of town, believed in my youth to be a favourite haunt of German spies, who doubtless wanted to blow up the local canning factory. I found this Sentimental Journey quite exhausting, and returned to London [Ontario] in the shaky condition of a man who has had a good long look at his past.[2]

As would be the case in Renfrew, it was not so much the town, from which Davies seems to have been detached to a noticeable degree, but the home that definitively shaped him. Both parents were powerful individuals. As Tyrone Guthrie observed in his introduction to Davies's first book of plays, "I have met his parents and testify, with sincere admiration, that both made an instantaneous impression of quite extraordinary force—forces that must either make or break a sensitive child. That they did not break this child is a great tribute to all parties. The grapple, largely but not wholly unconscious, with The Family patently underlies many of the ideas that emerge in these plays—notably it governs the concept of 'Canada', dear and formidable."[3] The observation has proved a shrewd one. The "grapple . . . with The Family" has been a persistent theme in Davies's writing, as *Leaven of Malice, A Mixture of Frailties, The Manticore,* and *The Rebel Angels* illustrate.

Rupert Davies (1879–1967), who was to become one of the most influential newspaper publishers in Canada, a prominent liberal, a Canadian senator, and a man of considerable wealth, was neither a Thamesville nor an Ontario man. He was a man from elsewhere on his way to somewhere else. Born in Wales, he emigrated with his family during the depression of the 1890s. Arriving in Brantford, Ontario, in 1894, he lived with his uncle, John Robertson, and found work as a printer's devil with the local paper. He would later signify his fondness for the Robertsons, a Scottish family of bookish and academic inclinations, in naming his third son after them. The Robertson family, incidentally, included a Marchbanks by marriage.

A hard-driving young man with a shrewd eye for opportunities, Rupert Davies bought the weekly *Thamesville Herald* and its printing shop in 1907. By then he was married and had two sons. His wife, of Scottish-Dutch descent, was the daughter of a Brantford contractor. Her family was pragmatic, tough minded, and serious. As Davies recalls,

My mother was moralistic, but she was not of a religious temper, and was indeed somewhat anti-clerical; one of her favorite books, which she read and re-read, was *Elmer Gantry*. I think this may have been because she

had been 'preached against' in the Methodist Church in her girlhood—
the parson named her with two other girls because they had been dancing,
which Methodism did not countenance. So she left that church and became
a Presbyterian, but never a very doctrinal one. She was quick to detect
and despise religious hypocrisy.[4]

Both parents were plentifully endowed with temperament. The father had the mercurial emotions of the Welsh, his high spirits often giving way to withdrawn moods. The mother put up with no nonsense; she was unyielding and sharp with forms of indulgence. Neither parent was disposed to accommodate himself to the level of comprehension or the moods of a child. Together they provided an environment in which tensions and severity lived side by side with larger views and a certainty of distinctiveness and worth. A late-born child, some ten years removed from his older brothers, Davies learned to tread carefully and respectfully amidst these forces.

In the unhurried days before motor cars and mass-produced entertainment, the Davies were active in Thamesville life and alert to the world beyond. Rupert Davies was choir leader of St. James Presbyterian Church; like Owen Griffiths in *Brothers in the Black Art*, he "invited beauty into his life" through music and amateur theater. He also arranged family excursions to Detroit to attend plays and operas. In addition, the Davies were avid readers. In his autobiographical essay, "A Rake for Reading," Robertson Davies recalls dipping into magazines like the *Atlantic Monthly, Scribner's,* the *Saturday Evening Post,* the *Strand, Pearson's,* and *Punch.* So regularly was he read to as a child that he did not learn to read until he was six. Hearing Kingsley's *The Heroes,* Hawthorne's *Tanglewood Tales,* and Grimm's *Fairy Tales* read by his parents "frightened me out of my wits," he recalled, "and marked me forever as a lover, and victim, of myth."[5]

Shortly after having turned down the local Liberal nomination, Rupert Davies bought the weekly *Renfrew Mercury* and moved his family across Ontario to that town of 3,000 in the lumbering and farming country north of Ottawa. He was not a man to be confined for long in a village.

In Renfrew, while his brothers went to the town Collegiate, young Robertson was obliged to attend the country school in the North Ward. These were unpleasant times for him. A newcomer and outsider, bookish and unathletic, he was terrorized by the rough-edged sons of Scottish farmers, and of French-Canadian and Polish factory workers. To them he was alien and uppity. To him they were crude, vicious ruffians who taunted him and forced him to fight for his life at recesses.

Memories of this difficult and stressful period remain powerful for Davies and continue to color his attitude toward the common man, be he rural and crude or urban and vulgar. "I know the common man and he is not what people think," he has asserted; "he is a mean-spirited, low-minded, perverse being who tortures animals and little boys."[6] Not surprisingly, Davies often identifies with the sensitive victims of such abuse, Paul Dempster's experiences being perhaps the most vivid instance in his fiction. He has not forgotten the kind of sadistic mentality that enjoyed charivaris and certain Masonic rituals of the sort that led to the suicide of Renfrew's dwarf tailor. Repelled yet fascinated, the young Davies was witness to schoolyard acts of malignancy, sadism, and crude sexuality. What he learned outside the classroom, either by experience or through newspaper gossip, seems to have impressed him more deeply—that is, on the level of feeling—than what he learned inside, at least during this formative period.

Formal learning, however, was very important to him. It was in the classroom that he flourished, though his skill in declaiming moral dialogues and dramatic poetry from the *Ontario Reader* likely fuelled the hostility of many of his less literate classmates. The clever son of one of the town's most distinguished men, he doubtless enjoyed his role as outstanding student and teacher's favorite. Like Dunstan Ramsay, he took delight in his stature as a wise child, a polymath. One was not a Davies without a sense of eminence.

Apart from the roughness of Renfrew and the personal force of his parents, the strongest influence on the growing boy was the written word. The family's panelled library reflected his parents' tastes. There he read *The Swiss Family Robinson, Robinson Crusoe, Gulliver's Travels, Little Women, Chums* magazine, and the Sherlock Holmes stories, while dabbling in Dickens, Twain, Leacock, Kipling and W. W. Jacobs. "All my life long," Davies would recall, "reading has been my great refuge and solace."[7] He still remembers the excitement of discovering an article on ventriloquism whereupon he first dedicated himself to acquiring the art of mystifying people.

The magical power of language—spoken and written—he sensed early. In his family, witty talk, astringent tastes, and superior gossip were valued. Favorite phrases from plays, books, or songs were often parodied or embroidered upon. His father enjoyed mimicking the genteel prose of sleepy small-town papers and sharing with the family curious local stories that didn't make it into print. At the same time, young Davies was regularly subjected to the charged rhythms of the King James Version. He heard them in his parents' speech, in the Biblical stories they read to him, and at St. Andrews Presbyterian church where his father was superintendent of the Sunday School.

He experienced the thrill of seeing his own words in print at an early age. Writing was a competence Rupert Davies expected of his children. He was not long in demanding proof of his late-born son, sending him at age ten to review for the *Renfrew Mercury* a slide lecture about Shakespeare's England. In phrases that suggest what David Staunton labels "The Plain Style," Robertson Davies recalls the attitude toward writing in his home:

We all wrote things. It was part of the day's work. . . . We never thought of it as a special kind of accomplishment. . . . You had to do it accurately and concisely because [my father] was extremely pernickety about that. He insisted on the journalistic integrity of getting the times, dates, names, offices right, because it meant a lot of trouble if you didn't. And no overwriting, no tricks. He was opposed to journalistic clichés. He was very funny at home. . . . He used to come and say "And who do you think is visiting beneath the parental roof this week-end?" because endlessly weekly newspapers reported such stuff. And my mother was rather ironic . . . because she had been trained as a secretary and she was weary of the style of business letters which began "Your esteemed favor of even date to hand and contents noted." So you grew up with a sense that that sort of thing was base.[8]

At ten Davies also came to know at firsthand something of the larger world. In 1924 his father, who later became president of the Canadian Press, organized a pilgrimage of Canadian newspapermen and their wives to Belgium, France, and the British Isles. They visited famous battlefields, were received by the French president and Marshall Foch, then went to England to meet many of the figures who were their icons during World War I. Among them were the Prince of Wales, Lloyd George, King George and Queen Mary, Winston Churchill, and their own countryman, Lord Beaverbrook. The Davies also visited Stratford and Rupert Davies's

Welshpool birthplace. The boy who returned to Renfrew came home with an enriched sense of his father's and his own specialness. He was beginning to measure the isolation and inwardness of provincial Canada. Likely he was also beginning to envision a larger destiny for himself.

Collegiate Years: Kingston (1925–32) and Upper Canada College (1928–32)

In 1925, Rupert Davies bought the struggling *Kingston British Whig* and moved his family to that city at the eastern end of Lake Ontario. His judgment was typically astute, his timing impeccable. Within a year he negotiated a merger with the rival *Standard* to form the *Kingston Whig-Standard* which he and his partner, Henry Muir, quickly transformed into the most influential paper between Toronto and Montreal.

Located on the site of a fort built to control access to the Great Lakes, Kingston was one of Ontario's oldest settlements. A garrison town and shipbuilding center, it had briefly been in the 1840s the capital of the Canadas; indeed, were it not so close to the American border it might have been the capital of the new Dominion in 1867. Rich in United Empire Loyalist and British connections, Kingston offered the Davies a society more hierarchical than that of most Ontario cities and a sense of tradition embodied in its cathedrals, military college, and Scottish-Presbyterian university, Queen's. Here at last was a social environment in which the family was not out of place.

Though Davies often satirized Kingston as Salterton, he felt a deep affection for the city, admiring the strong character its quaintness disguised. It kept "a good opinion of itself," had "a satisfying consciousness of past glories," "in a modest way ma[de] its own rules," and realized that "a little snobbery, like a little politeness, oils the wheel of daily life." It was not a city engrossed merely in economic realities. "One of the happy things about Salterton," he wrote in *Tempest-Tost*, "is that it is possible to work well and profitably there without having to carry one's work into the remotest crannies of social life" (12–13).

The Davies soon established themselves in Calderwood, a large house with expansive gardens not unlike Mr. Webster's in *Tempest-Tost*. In Kingston Davies began his high school studies while dipping regularly in the joys of traveling English and American repertory companies, local amateur theater, and the Kingston Public Library, where he sought out "adult" books using his father's card. Here too he experienced a numbness in studying mathematics that would plague his subsequent education. With an eye in part to helping him overcome this difficulty, his parents sent him in 1928 to Upper Canada College, the most prestigious and longest established of Toronto's private schools.

Though U.C.C. was an intimidating environment, Davies was quick to find his way. He acted in several Drama Club productions, and he broadened his experience of theater by using free time to attend the University of Toronto's Hart House Theatre (at least two school masters performed there)[9] and downtown houses where he saw the touring company of Sir John Martin-Harvey and such new American drama as Elmer Rice's *Street Scene* and Eugene O'Neill's *Strange Interlude*. He also abandoned his piano studies for musicology, thus deepening his knowledge and appreciation of that subject.

Testing his independence, Davies read more widely. "After fourteen," he recalled, "I really got into high gear. *The Old Wives' Tale* was a revelation, and so was *Mademoiselle de Maupin; . . . Antic Hay* [and] *Point Counter Point . . .* were landmarks for me. I read most of Shaw at school, which won me a quite unmerited reputation as a dangerous thinker; it was the plays and the jokes I liked, not the political argument. *The Way of All Flesh* was another violent explosion in my life."[10] Davies's own literary ventures also found recognition. In successive years he won the school's prize for best poem in the *College Times*. During his last year he edited the *College Times*, following in the steps of two figures he admired, Stephen Leacock and B. K. Sandwell.

University Years: Queen's (1932–35) and Oxford (1935–38)

After a summer in Wales, where his father bought Fronfraith Hall, Davies entered the second year of honours studies at Queen's as a special student. Because his mathematics had not improved at U.C.C., he had failed to matriculate. At Queen's he spent the next three years reading literature, drama, and history. While he continued to write for student outlets and imbibed the "strong moral doctrine that was implicit in all of [Queen's] teaching,"[11] it was as a man interested above all else in theater that his contemporaries recalled him. He had begun to dress and talk theatrically, seizing every opportunity to enjoy plays or to be involved in production. "Kingston," Davies recalls,

was a number one touring town. The companies that were on their way between Montreal and Toronto would do . . . a split-week between Brockville and Kingston. . . . That meant a lot of New York musical shows but a lot of other performances too. For instance, Martin-Harvey always included it in his tours, for it was a very good theatre town. . . . [W]hen I was at Queen's University, I was involved in the Kingston Drama Guild, an experience which I described—in part—in *Tempest-Tost*. Arthur Sutherland was president, I was director; our most ambitious production was an *Oedipus Rex*. Kingston had three amateur societies, the faculty group, a group made up of the townspeople, and a group made up mainly of military people. But they all were interchangeable; everybody acted around.[12]

Such was Robertson Davies's fascination with the theater that, after Queen's, he hoped to join an American or English company. The Depression, however, reduced his opportunities. As a "special student" he did not receive an undergraduate degree (despite a sound record); thus, his academic possibilities also were limited. But fortune in the powerful form of Rupert Davies soon intervened:

When I was in my third year my father was abroad, and I remember getting a night cable letter from him, saying "What would you think about going to Oxford? Let me know and I will look into it." . . . And it just occurred to him, I suppose, as he was driving through Oxford. . . . It had never occurred to me, for one thing, because I assumed it would be immensely expensive. So he went there and . . . was interviewed by the admissions tutor at Balliol, who said: "Well, ask your son to send us some records and we shall see." And off I went that Autumn.[13]

At Balliol, he discovered that Oxford offered several more highly developed ways of life than Queen's. In particular, like David Staunton in *The Manticore*, he was drawn to the scholarly excitement Oxford generated. His tutor was Mark Roy Ridley, editor of the "New Temple Shakespeare." He attended Sir Edmund Chambers's lectures on Shakespeare, lectures on methods of research by C. S. Lewis and on Anglo-Saxon by J. R. R. Tolkien. He enjoyed college life, the talk, and the freedom to read widely, exploring obscure corners of English literature and culture. It was not his way to remain a provincial on the periphery of Oxford life.

His passion for theater led him quickly to the Oxford Dramatic Society. One issue of the *Isis* described him as an undergraduate notable for his waistcoats and distinguished by his stage managing of consecutive O.U.D.S. productions of *Macbeth* and *Richard II*. Since the Dramatic Society's policy was to invite leading professionals to take part in its productions, Davies was able to work with some of Britain's most prominent actors and directors, among them John Gielgud, Vivien Leigh, Florence Kahn (through whom he met Max Beerbohm), Jack Hawkins, and Esmé Church (who invited Tyrone Guthrie to see a production she was directing). Davies played Malvolio, Sly, and Dogberry in various productions. Nevill Coghill, who directed Davies's dissertation, later recalled the young man's Malvolio at Oxford as an outstanding performance.

In his third year Davies read extensively in Elizabethan drama while preparing his thesis on Shakespeare's use of boy actors to play female roles. His treatment of the subject was so well received in the Oxford *Viva* that his examiners dismissed him after fifteen minutes, urging him to seek publication. Dents was quick to show an interest and in January 1939 *Shakespeare's Boy Actors* by W. Robertson Davies was released in London. The *Times Literary Supplement* reviewer, while noting some unevenness, praised it as "the most useful and comprehensive survey of the subject that has yet been attempted."[14]

London and the Old Vic: 1938-39

B.Litt. in hand, Davies joined a company touring the English provinces with Morna Stuart's play, *Traitor's Gate*. When it folded, he followed up an invitation to call on Tyrone Guthrie. The result was a junior role in the Old Vic that included minor acting roles, teaching theater history in the school, and editing scripts with Guthrie. He enjoyed the work thoroughly, putting in long hours at what he most wanted to do among the kind of talented and dedicated professionals he most admired.

While the outbreak of World War II shortened Davies's stay in England, his brief employment at the Old Vic had a profound effect on him in several ways. To be with the Old Vic was to be involved in an exciting theater company fast becoming recognized for its innovative Shakespearean productions. He discovered magical links to the past in Ben Webster, who told him stories of Henry Irving and his North American tours, and Esmé Percy, a fine Shavian actor, who had worked with Shaw and Sarah Bernhardt. He performed as a peer with many of English theater's great names. He expanded his experience of plays and productions. Perhaps also he realized, as Guthrie did, that "he had not outstanding gifts as an actor."[15] More importantly, under Guthrie's direction he began to investigate the applicability of Freud's psychological theories to Old Vic productions like *Hamlet* and to be drawn to Guthrie's passion for the wonderful, strange, and surprising.

When the Old Vic disbanded during Christmas 1939, Davies decided to return to Canada. He had volunteered for military service in England but had been turned down because of his eyesight. He did not, however, return alone. On 2 February 1940 he married a young Australian stage manager, Brenda Mathews, with whom he worked closely in his year with the company. "I have never done any other single thing that was so fateful for my happiness and well-being," notes Davies, adding that "we have all of our life together been enthusiastic advocates of marriage for people who deserve to be happy, and this is a much more numerous breed than pessimists suppose."[16] The future writer who would make the idea of marriage based on friendship and respect one of his enduring themes, sailed out of the dark English winter for Canada with his new wife, the zig-zagging blacked-out ship suggesting the uncertainty before him.

A Journalistic Career and *Saturday Night:* 1940–42

Soon after returning to Calderwood, Davies began contributing thrice weekly columns to his father's papers, the *Kingston Whig-Standard* and the *Peterborough Examiner*. The first, "Cap and Bells," appeared on 1 August 1940 under the byline Samuel Marchbanks. Promising a wide-ranging subject matter—"roving reporter, book reviewer, art, music and drama critic, trained snoop and funny man"—Marchbanks declared that his objective was that of the man who wears the cap and bells, "to amuse and entertain." The clown in Marchbanks was, however, slow to emerge from the serious family business of journalistic commentary and reviewing.

To be back under his parents' aegis was a situation not long to be tolerated. Davies again attempted to enlist but was rejected. He and his wife then looked to Toronto where he approached the *Globe & Mail* and *Saturday Night,* catching on with the latter as book editor, while Brenda Davies found occasional work with the drama department of CBC radio. She gave birth to their first daughter in December 1940, a month after her husband joined the magazine.

Saturday Night was the Canadian embodiment of the independent and liberal weekly journal. Under B. K. Sandwell's editorship it had a status not unlike that of the *New Statesman* in Britain. Davies has described Sandwell, an overlooked figure in Canadian cultural history, as a journalist in "the best tradition," wide-ranging in his tone and unpartisan in his interests. He was a model of the serious yet witty "liberal humanist" in Canada, attuned to and ready to editorialize upon "every aspect of Canadian life."[17]

Under Sandwell's guidance, Davies sharpened his journalistic skills. He contributed articles on theater, music, and ballet, along with reviews of books by established writers like Willa Cather, Ernest Hemingway, Virginia Woolf, and John Cowper Powys. A confident expression of his ideas and tastes was quick to emerge. He praised James Joyce's brilliant mind, criticized the dryness and self-consciousness of T. S. Eliot's sensibility, and dismissed Gertrude Stein as a blank. Declaring himself a reactionary in so far as literary experimentalism was concerned, he forthrightly declared "I would far rather read a novel by a man who was the possessor of an unusual and brilliant mind, but who was an indifferent novelist, than a perfectly carpentered piece of work by a man who was a skilled novelist but a person of undistinguished parts."[18] Though his bias was acknowledgeably more British than American, what mattered most to Davies were the spirit and curiosity of the authors he considered. He was also careful to pay special heed to Canadian material and to apply his standards exactingly to such work. That he had a fine eye for merit was apparent in his positive appraisals of two path-breaking Canadian novels of 1941—Hugh MacLennan's *Barometer Rising* and Sinclair Ross's *As for Me and My House.*

Peterborough and the *Examiner:* 1942–60

Early in March 1942 Davies left *Saturday Night* to become unofficial editor of the *Peterborough Examiner.* Eleven years later he would return to *Saturday Night,* conducting its "Books" column from 1953 to 1959, but, for nearly two decades, Peterborough became his home. In this small, provincial city of 30,000, thirty miles north of Lake Ontario, he launched his career as playwright and novelist and established himself as an outstanding newspaper editor.

From London and the Old Vic to the conservative and isolated milieu of Peterborough was a long leap. It demanded adjustments and masks. A bearded young man with an air of university life and the stage about him, an outsider in a community firmly set in its ways, Davies knew well to proceed cautiously as a public figure. Not surprisingly, it was in Peterborough that Samuel Marchbanks emerged full-blown. While Davies produced editorials and book reviews for the *Examiner,* the Puckish or Rabelaisian side of his temperament, the side that could not resist a joke, needed release. Marchbanks gave him that other voice. Years later in a clever essay, "The Double Life of Robertson Davies" by Samuel Marchbanks, Marchbanks basked in the distinction. Davies, he claimed, was a mild, featureless, uncontradictory fellow.

> He is fawningly courteous; I am forthright. He is mangled by self-doubt and self-criticism; I am untouched by these ridiculous ailments. He has a conscience as big as a grand piano; I have no more sense of obligation than a tomcat. He makes excuses for everybody and tries to be charitable; I know a boob or a phony when I see one and I see a great many. He is inclined to be moderate in pretty nearly everything; I regard moderation as a sign of physical or intellectual weakness. He is just about everything which I detest; I am everything which he fears and seeks to avoid.[19]

For nearly a decade, under a variety of headings, Davies produced the Marchbanks weekly column for the *Examiner,* the *Kingston Whig-Standard,* and other syndicated papers. The fruits of the popular Marchbanks diary, correspondence, and journal entries appeared in book form as *The Diary of Samuel Marchbanks* (1947), *The Table Talk of Samuel Marchbanks* (1949), and, belatedly, *Marchbanks' Almanack* (1967).

It was not long before Davies's love of theater found expression in Peterborough. He had published his first Canadian book, *Shakespeare for Young Players: A Junior Course* (1942), while still in Toronto. By 1944, with Marchbanks often commenting on his theater excursions, Davies was at work on two three-act plays in the romantic and melodramatic tradition of Irving and Martin-Harvey. Writing with the Old Vic company in mind, he had no luck in interesting John Gielgud or Sybil Thorndike in the scripts. Undaunted by these rejections, he turned to writing shorter plays for Canadian local theater groups like the Ottawa Drama League, while with Brenda he helped in the formation of the Peterborough Little Theatre.

In 1947 after its suspension during the war years the Dominion Drama Festival was regaining momentum in Canada. Robertson Davies's one-act plays, *Eros at Breakfast* and *Overlaid,* won awards as did his three-act play with a Kingston setting, *Fortune, My Foe.* Indeed, both *Eros at Breakfast* (in 1948) and *Fortune, My Foe* (in 1949) won the Sir Barry Jackson Trophy as the best production of a Canadian play. The latter also earned Davies the Gratien Gélinas prize as author of the best Canadian play. In 1949 Davies received the Festival's Louis Jouvet award for best direction with the Peterborough Little Theatre's production of *The Taming of the Shrew* in which his wife played Katharina. He would later serve briefly as one of the DDF's Directors.

Theatrically, these were busy years. Davies directed numerous Peterborough productions, accompanied the Ottawa Drama League's production of *Eros at Breakfast* to the Edinburgh Festival, helped in a short-lived attempt to establish a local professional company (the Peterborough Summer Theatre), and saw his first collection of plays published. Both *Fortune, My Foe* and *At My Heart's Core,* the latter written as a historical play for the city of Peterborough's centennial, were also soon published.

During the 1950s Davies remained deeply involved in theater on many fronts. For the Massey Report, he created a witty dialogue on the state of theater in Canada. As playwright and as friend of Tyrone Guthrie, he was engaged in some of the early discussions concerning a Canadian Shakespearean Festival, the site of which later fell to Stratford, Ontario. In 1953 he was elected as a governor and a member of the Festival's Board of Directors. Year by year he wrote a great deal about the Festival, publicizing its efforts and evaluating its achievements. With Guthrie, he put together books commemorating each of the Festival's first three seasons. For a 1956 production by Guthrie he wrote the missing scene of *The Merry Wives of Windsor.* His adaptation of Jonson's *Bartholomew Fair* was considered by Guthrie but not used.

The fifties indeed proved a high point for Davies's theatrical ambitions. From 1954 to 1957 he contributed three major plays to the Crest Theatre of Toronto, a company organized by Donald, Murray, and Barbara (Chilcott) Davis. The Crest performed *A Jig for the Gypsy* and *Hunting Stuart* but disappointed Davies by turning down his Casanova play, *General Confession,* when J. B. Priestley offered the Davises *A Glass Cage,* a play written expressly for them. More tantalizing and exasperating was the fate of the dramatization of Davies's novel *Leaven of Malice.* Aiming at Broadway, the New York Theater Guild bought the rights to the novel, hiring Tyrone Guthrie as director and Davies as script writer. It premiered at Toronto's Royal Alexandra Theatre in early November 1960, then moved on to Detroit and Boston. In New York, however, it lasted less than a week, leaving Davies not only disappointed but frustrated by the process of endless rewriting to suit contradictory requests.

It was in the same decade that Robertson Davies emerged as a novelist. He had told an interviewer in 1947 that if he failed to have his plays produced in England by the time he was forty, he would "turn to novels."[20] The remark is an index of Davies's ambition and resolve. Meeting his own schedule, he wrote *Tempest-Tost* (1951), *Leaven of Malice* (1954), and *A Mixture of Frailties* (1958), attracting a new and larger audience by means of his skills as a satirist, storyteller, and cultural critic. *Leaven of Malice,* in fact, earned him the Stephen Leacock Medal for humor in Canadian writing.

The University of Toronto and Massey College: 1960–85

While the last twenty-five years of Robertson Davies's life have been marked by energetic growth and productivity, they can be summarized succinctly. The sixties were generally a fallow time, if such an adjective can apply to so prolific a writer. His major book of the decade was an energetic reworking of material drawn in large part from previous book reviewing, particularly his *Saturday Night* column. Accepting Alfred Knopf's invitation—Knopf regarded him as the foremost reviewer of the day—Davies wove together *A Voice from the Attic* (1960), published a year later in England under the more informative title, *The Personal Art: Reading for Good Purpose.*

Academic and administrative matters took much of Davies's time in the early sixties. In 1960–61 he spent a year as visiting professor of English at Trinity College, the University of Toronto. He also produced a weekly column, "A Writer's Diary" (January 1960 to June 1962), for the *Toronto Star* and ten other papers. Not long after the abbreviated run of *Love and Libel,* he was tempted by another unusual offer. His wealthy friend, Vincent Massey, invited him to become the first master of the newly endowed Massey College, a residence for selected graduate students at the University of Toronto. Weary of daily journalism, Davies welcomed the opportunity to escape the sort of telephone call he felt was typical of small-city Ontario, the kind in which a person would ask "Are you the fella on the *Examiner?* Well, can you tell me when Winston Churchill was born?"[21]

Appointed both master of Massey College and professor of English at University College in 1963, Robertson Davies found himself making his new home amidst the scholars he had often satirized. Modelled on Oxford colleges, Massey seemed remote from the rest of the university, fostering an academic elitism uncharacteristic of the North American scene. As master, a position he held until he retired in 1981, he rode out the college's various storms, gathering about him an impressive group of senior fellows such as Northrop Frye, Donald Creighton, Douglas Le Pan, Gordon Roper, Claude Bissell, and Tuzo Wilson. He also made the college the home of the University of Toronto's Drama Centre. At the same time he continued to write on request for a variety of newspapers and periodicals. His enthusiasm for Stephen Leacock culminated in an excellent monograph in 1970.

The seventies, like the fifties, was a very productive decade. Davies's most acclaimed novel, *Fifth Business,* appeared in 1970, followed by *The Manticore* (1972) and *World of Wonders* (1975). *Question Time* (1975), one of three plays of the decade, was performed to mixed reviews at Toronto's St. Lawrence Centre. All four works reflect Davies's great interest in Carl Jung's writing. In the mid-1950s, somewhat disappointed in the reductiveness and sexual emphasis of Freud, he developed an enthusiasm for Jung, particularly Jung's commitment to individuation and his emphasis upon healthfulness. That interest, at first apparent in *General Confession* and *A Mixture of Frailties,* contributes significantly to the psychological boldness and allusive richness of the Deptford novels.

No slackening of energy has been apparent since Davies's retirement. A wealthy man who could, if he wished, have retired in leisure years ago, he remains hard at work and very much in demand as a speaker, reviewer, and writer of occasional pieces. The publication of his seventh and eighth novels, *The Rebel Angels* (1981) and *What's Bred in the Bone* (1985), signals a new phase of his work centered significantly in the university scene that has been his most recent, and likely his happiest, milieu. His collection of Massey College ghost stories, *High Spirits* (1982), the publication of his "Alexander Lectures" on nineteenth-century English theater under the title *The Mirror of Nature* (1983), and his recent Marchbanks collection, *The Papers of Samuel Marchbanks* (1985) offer rich evidence of that sustained productivity.

Robertson Davies clearly revels in each new evidence of his continued growth and recognition. He is among Canada's most honored writers, having received honorary degrees from more than ten universities. In addition, he is a fellow of the Royal Society of Canada (1967) and a companion of the Order of Canada (1972). Among his many awards are the Lorne Pierce Medal awarded by the Royal Society of Canada (1961) and the Governor-General's Award for Fiction for *The Manticore* (1972). In recent years he has also received considerable international recognition. In 1980 he became the first Canadian to be elected an honorary member of the American Academy and Institute of Arts and Letters. The Royal Society of Literature also welcomed him as an elected member in 1984.

Chapter Two
Samuel Marchbanks
A Flamboyant Among Drabs

A man needs three careers, observed Robertson Davies in addressing a University of Windsor audience in 1971. He spoke with certainty remembering that in the early 1940s, when he was employed by his father's newspaper, he had consciously sought to develop his writing abilities in other areas. One was playwrighting. The other, fed by his inclinations as humorist, pundit, and critic, he dovetailed with his journalistic obligations. This was the creation of Samuel Marchbanks. At first simply an alternative signature for Davies's regular book reviews, Marchbanks, as circumstances allowed, began to take on a personality and life of his own, to become, as various observers have noted, "a persona," "a fictional second self," or an *"alter ego."*[1] From 13 November 1943 until the spring of 1953, excepting the summer months, the weekly diary entries of Samuel Marchbanks appeared every Saturday on the *Peterborough Examiner*'s editorial page, in effect replacing one of Davies's regular book reviews.[2]

What Davies gained in Marchbanks was a freedom from the conventional restraints of book reviewing and civic-minded editorializing. He could be cantankerous, outspoken, ribald, sagacious, or silly, tailoring his mood and purpose to the situation and occasion. Years later in "The Double Life of Robertson Davies" Davies had Marchbanks coyly comment that, as an editor, "Davies was somewhat unorthodox"; he "believes that newspaper work should have a slightly disreputable flavor, and fears that ingrowing respectability may rob it of all its charm."[3] Such an outlook animates the diary. Its purpose was to brighten and stir up an editorial page of a responsible and respectable kind. It allowed Davies to entertain, goad, or challenge its readership. It freed him, without elaborate rationale, to write critically or whimsically about human folly in general and the limitations of the Canadian state of mind in particular. As such, Marchbanks was "Davies' first major fictional character."[4] He prefigures later, more elaborately drawn characters like Humphrey Cobbler, Dunstan Ramsay, and Simon Darcourt, whose attitudes and opinions, like those of Marchbanks, spring from cosmopolitan and individualistic premises.

The development of Marchbanks belongs to Peterborough, though as early as 1940 Davies was using pseudonyms such as Marchbanks and Amyas Pilgarlic (later a correspondent of Marchbanks) in signing reviews for his father's papers and for *Saturday Night*. A column entitled "Cap and Bells" (1 August 1940) and signed by Marchbanks gives an early indication that Davies would inevitably evolve some idiosyncratic and distinctive form of journalistic expression:

Why Cap and Bells? . . . [I]t is preferable that the name [of the column] should give a clue to its nature. . . . If [the columnist] is a Franklin P. Adams or a Christopher Morley he knows that his readers expect a literary or highbrow article every day. But the ordinary common or garden columnist who must combine the tasks of roving reporter, book reviewer, art, music and drama critic, trained snoop and funny man all in one must choose his title with care. . . .

The object of this column is to amuse and entertain. That has always been the job of the man who wears the cap and bells. But to amuse and entertain is not always to be funny; no one is more dreary than the man who is always funny.[5]

Book reviewing remained Marchbanks's main concern for three more years. After Davies was appointed editor of the *Examiner* (1942), however, and he and his wife had settled uneasily into Peterborough's stratified and conservative social environment, the first installment of Marchbanks's individualized ruminations, "About Keeping a Diary," appeared on Saturday, 13 November 1943. The initial entry, for Sunday, though beguilingly humble, was marked by an acute awareness of traditional and contemporary approaches:

I decided today that this column sticks too rigidly to book reviews and expository articles, and is in imminent danger of becoming ponderous; would it not be a good idea to keep a diary in it? After all, Mrs. Roosevelt has countless readers for "My Day.". . . [O]ne of the best diaries ever written was called "The Diary of A Nobody"; if one nobody can write a diary, another nobody can attempt it. . . . [M]ost of the diaries I have read have been written with a possible reader in mind; only Pepys wanted to be completely secret, and was consequently indiscreet in his revelations;

indiscretions make the best reading of all. But Mrs. Roosevelt and I are never indiscreet—at least, if we are, we have no intention of telling several thousand people about it.

Other first-week entries included a complaint about Canadian taxes on books ("Canada is probably one of the most philistine countries on the earth"), another about the aggressive salesmanship of Victory Loans on the radio by Private Lorne Greene, observations about a Charles Boyer movie and a disappointing play and comments on both Halloween and anti-Semitism. Such was the diverse pattern that would endure for a decade.

Much of the material was topical—the conditions of life during the war and in postwar Ontario, current movies, plays attended, new books, names in the news, and seasonal activities. Each weekly diary took a title and topic—"Diary of a Recluse," "Notes of a Idler," "Diary of a Happy Gourmet," "The Cult of Exercise," and "Diary of a Rusty Magician." Unity of theme, however, was seldom a concern. What mattered was the flexible, self-certain Marchbanks voice giving vent to its grievances, preoccupations, and enthusiasms.

As diary, the Marchbanks material has distinctive features. It has a specific audience in mind. Reacting disdainfully to the tastes of Hollywood magazines, Marchbanks asserts, "I write for a highly exclusive public, subtle and pernickety in its tastes, and they are not to be bamboozled by any such pretentious tripe."[6] Such an audience Davies would define more particularly as "a recognized clerkly caste"[7] or as "the clerisy," people who read books "for pleasure and with some pretension to taste," who have developed the "special knowledge" and "priestlike" sense of culture's value so as to maintain their convictions in the face of the modern world's leveling forces.[8] Whenever Marchbanks discusses matters of taste, culture, or individuality it is in this like-minded audience he places his trust. From them he expects a spirited empathy, a welcoming of his rhetoric and the kinds of distinctions he enjoys making.

In his preface to the revised edition of *The Diary of Samuel Marchbanks,* Marchbanks describes the book as "not a work of fiction, but of history—a record of the daily life of a Canadian during one of the early years of the Atomic Age."[9] Such a summary, however, tells little about the special properties of these diary items. In fact, the entries offer little sustained sense of historical, political, or economic events. Generally speaking, only cultural issues and immediate social concerns arouse Marchbanks's zeal for commentary. At the same time, the entries are personal and intimate in only a very specialized way. Self-revelation is so carefully screened that the reader cannot be sure, for instance, whether or not Marchbanks is married or has children (he appears to be a bachelor and the landlord of Marchbanks Towers, but he occasionally mentions his "dependents" and often performs fatherly duties for a child or children "of my acquaintance"). The members of his family he specifically mentions are always the subject of broad comedy. His uncle, the Reverend Hengist Marchbanks, former bishop of Baffinland and author of *Scatology and Eschatology,* is but one example.

As Marchbanks makes clear, indiscretion and self-revelation are not his aims. He can, in a delightful piece of tonal dexterity, suggest that "furnace-fried and garden-torn," he is not unlike Tolstoy and Gaugin in offering the record of a life "shot through and through with toil and anguish, disappointment and shame, frustration and denial" (D, 68). His diary, he asserts, is not meant to be "funny," but "[t]ragic, mystic, sublime, perhaps." "[O]nly a coarse and witty soul could find food for laughter here" (D, 69). Something of both extremes—the comic as well as the self-serious—is present in almost all the entries.

On the one hand, the entries are carefully designed to focus on domestic tribulations in a generalized and humorous rather than a personally revealing manner. The "real" people of Marchbanks's daily encounters are never identified. Davies neither satirizes nor celebrates particular individuals.[10] On the personal level, Marchbanks has a strong antipathy to unabashed self-revelation:

Was reading some of the letters of Edgar Allen Poe today, and they confirmed me in my belief that a man's private correspondence should never be published. He does not write his letters with a horde of snoopy strangers in mind, and he says things which he would never say for publication. Poe was a great literary artist . . . ; why publish letters in which he makes a fool of himself, drooling weakly to his child wife, and tearfully addressing his mother-in-law as "Dearest Muddy"? (D, 163)

There is a sharp distinction here between acceptable and unacceptable kinds of revelation—between what is written to be published and what is merely private indulgence. Such a distinction is central to the aesthetic propriety of Marchbanks and, more importantly, of

Davies himself. Where there is a lack of authorial detachment (hence control), where there is neither wit nor style distinguishing the presentation, one finds merely a pathetic representation, the aching sensibility "drooling weakly."

On the other hand, *The Diary of Samuel Marchbanks* is nothing if not a celebration of self in a world where, too often, the pressures to conform and to accept the mediocre, or democratic mean, serve to dull that spark. Beneath Marchbanks's hypochondriacal tendencies, his uneasiness with doctors and dentists, his ineptness in mathematics, his lack of coordination, his uneasiness in nature ("Nature," he notes, "seemed to have no special message to me" {D, 55]) and his "daily struggles with bureaucrats, tax-gatherers and uplifters" (D, 4), there is a firm residue of selfhood, a clear-visioned commitment to the sovereignty of self that provides a foundation for every observation and opinion. He sees himself as an elusive mystery, his being "built like those Chinese puzzles which consist of one box inside another," thus defying penetration (D, 27). Samuel Marchbanks knows where and who he is. In *Marchbanks' Almanack* he observes:

> I generally have a pretty shrewd idea of just where I am; I am enclosed in the somewhat vulnerable fortress which is my body, and from that uneasy stronghold I make such sorties as I deem advisable into the realm about me. [People seem] to think that whizzing through space in a car really alter[s] the universe for them, but they [are] wrong; each one remain[s] right in the centre of his private universe, which is the only field of knowledge of which he has any direct experience.[11]

Marchbanks celebrates his centrality in his "private universe," yielding to neither individual pressure nor social force in promoting his position. The diary entries can be seen either as defenses of that personal position against "boobs," "do-gooders," "Puritans," "yahoos," and the threatening doctrine of the Common Man or as articulations of that position—justifications, as it were, of his values and tastes. " 'There is no disputing about tastes,' says the old saw. In my experience," comments Marchbanks, "there is little else" (A, 110). Attacking "the nonsense" practised by interior decorators he proclaims, "Better far the grotesqueries of my own taste than the fashionable foolishness of theirs" (A, 26).

Though certain of Marchbanks's tastes are personal and idiosyncratic, most are carefully established and justified by means of a cultural and traditional context the breadth of which is international, as wide, in fact, as Marchbanks's capacious reading and curiosity.[12] Samuel Johnson is one such guide. Marchbanks's eager discipleship is suggested in the entry, "Went to bed early and read about Dr. Johnson, a man after my own heart, for he loved tea, conversation and pretty women, and had not much patience with fools" (D, 18). Another is Ben Jonson: "The genius of Jonson never fails to astonish and refresh me. What a torrent of golden words! And what a magnificent detestation of cant and folly" (T, 241). Others include Evelyn Waugh, whom he calls "sassy and bright" (T, 245), "that wonderful man Dean Swift"—"I don't care for men who have no silliness in them," asserts Marchbanks in praising Swift (T, 221)—H. L. Mencken whose book of quotations he likes "because it is full of sin and impudence and does not pretend to be familiar" (A, 121), François Rabelais whom Marchbanks declares his favorite humorist despite the fact that "he thought ignobly of women" (A, 202), and Oscar Wilde whose play, *An Ideal Husband,* inspires Marchbanks to proclaim that, "unlike a great many of my hypocritical fellow creatures, I like frankly artificial entertainment" (T, 152).

Such commentary provides a gauge of the kind and quality of Marchbanks's aesthetic values and tastes. Artificiality is for him an important criterion of art. Realism, naturalism, and the Saroyanesque "slice of life" stir him to mockery. "I have never understood why people object to artificiality; almost everything that has raised man above the beasts is artificial in some respect" (T, 152). In another entry he adds, "if the human race had persisted in being natural and unspoiled we should all still be swinging from tree to tree by our tails" (T, 143). Thus, he prefers Wilde's *The Importance of Being Earnest* to a realistic play like Tennessee Williams's *The Glass Menagerie.* The former "wastes no words in foolishly reproducing the emptiness of everyday speech" (T, 242), while the latter forces you to wallow in the miseries of dull, dead-end people who characteristically bring misery upon themselves and with whom one would be loathe to associate in the first place. "I am temperamentally unsympathetic to such pieces," he adds. "When I see them on the stage I do not have to take a humane attitude towards them, and I reflect that it would have been far better if they had all committed suicide before the curtain went up."[13]

Marchbanks admires wit and style. He likes to see language used expansively and gloriously; he laments its degradation to the common man's pedestrian level. Deploring what he calls "the apotheosis of The Squirt" in the modern world, he champions behavioral extravagance and flourish (T, 32). In his world one is either a Drab or a Flamboyant (T, 31), a Hebraic or a Hellenic, a Common or an Uncommon Man, a Puritan or—if only imaginatively and at heart—a free spirit. Trapped in his social role as newspaperman, householder, and citizen, Marchbanks regularly finds release through the diary. Here his much-circumscribed spirit bubbles and soars. A lover of high spirits—"If I tended toward frivolity as a boy, I am incorrigibly settled in it now" (D, 118)—he characteristically seeks occasions to rejoice, be it in celebrating the depravity of bees (T, 74–75), in rhapsodizing about the pleasure of eating grapes (D, 139), or in envying the colorful freedom of gypsies.

Given the cultural dominance of "the Drabs" in the late 1940s and early fifties, given the "Apotheosis of the Yahoo" which Marchbanks deplored as "one of the primary objects of Hollywood" (D, 39), given the sober puritanism of postwar Ontario—a puritanism reflected in its restrictive liquor laws, its occasional bannings of books (Edmund Wilson's *Memoirs of Hecate County* and Boccaccio's *The Decameron* are noted), and its generally joyless culture—Marchbanks has more occasion to defend his position than to articulate it. Consistently he casts himself as a complainer, curmudgeon, and "notionate" man (T, 137). He treasures his grudge-bearing, Welsh disposition. Better by far, he often remarks, to express a dissatisfaction or to judge a folly than to repress the emotion. What is at stake is one's own spiritual health and balance. To accept uncomplainingly the nonsense one is daily subjected to is to risk spiritual impotence.

Marchbanks's bêtes noires range from the trivial to the serious. Seldom, however, is his complaining without point, for he always categorizes cleverly, even with house pets. A cat lover, he enjoys belittling "the jolly doggies," as he despairingly labels the midnight visitors to his garbage cans. Cats are the sleek, only superficially domesticated Flamboyants of Marchbanks's world. They have "luxurious, Bohemian, unpuritanical nature[s]," showing no desire to be "Good Citizen[s]" or to involve themselves in "Service" (D, 80). Dogs, by contrast, are self-abasing, dumb Drabs. Having observed a dog charge the wheels of a car, Marchbanks notes, "My theory is that dogs go mad from the boredom of being dogs and seek to take their lives in consequence" (T, 194).

The drabness, cuteness, and conformism of the "modern" postwar world regularly arouse Marchbanks's suspicions and curmudgeonliness. In the mass-entertainment products of Hollywood he finds much to scorn, from the woodenness of Gregory Peck and the "chubby thrall" of Shirley Temple to the mindless, sentimental scripts of most American movies. He delights in imagining how the contemporary cinema would dress up the story of Karl Marx, who "lived his whole life in the extreme of bourgeois dullness" (D, 140), or how Alfred Hitchcock might democratize and vulgarize Hamlet, turning the Prince of Denmark into "a truckdriver in a small American town" and Ophelia into "Ham's sugarpuss." More penetratingly, he wonders how the Hay's office might respond to a theme "too closely bound up with incest to be tolerable to the pure minds of moviegoers. The movies insist that a good boy must love his dear old Mom, but wisely, and not too well" (D, 137).

But while a vigilant anti-Americanism underlies certain of Marchbanks's views, his most consistent complaints concern the dull, uninspired life he sees in Canada itself and in particular in conservative Toronto. "[T]he Ontario Babylon" (D, 55) is his mocking label for the city he likes to describe as a blancmange. "Personally," he notes, comparing the appeal of "Toronto the Good," as it was then often called, to Montreal's delicious wantonness, "I always think of Toronto as a big fat rich girl who has lots of money, but no idea of how to make herself attractive. . . . [S]he is dowdy and mistakes dowdiness for a guarantee of virtue" (T, 82). Art and culture have little chance to flourish in the fat girl's parlor.

The Marchbanks books are spotted with condemnations of, and bons mots about, Canadian drabness. Canadians are inclined to enshrine work and to praise solemnity, confusing both with respectability. "The true Canadian can be brought back from the grave, lured from his treasurechest or beguiled from his mistress' bower by two things—an argument about religion or an argument about politics" (D, 83–84), notes Marchbanks who, as a Flamboyant, has little time for either. Just as he rails against the strong power of puritan thinking in Canadians ("As a child my gorge rose at the lugubriousness of [Bunyan's] Pilgrim, and I had a wicked hankering for Vanity Fair" [D, 103]), he shows a fundamental antipathy to politics, however fervent or right-minded the cause.

"The presence of a person who has strong political convictions always sends me flying off in a directly contrary direction," he states (D, 111). In an outspoken instance he chastized Morley Callaghan for having written a melodramatic and polemical script for CBC radio about the oppressed "Common Peepul" of Spain: "whichever way you sliced it, it was still baloney, though the author was Morley Callaghan, who ought to have outgrown that sort of thinking by this time."[14]

While politics and institutional religion are subjects that often occasion Marchbanks's mockery, studies of a markedly rational emphasis are entirely beyond him. Like Robertson Davies himself, Marchbanks confesses to a fundamental incapacity to understand mathematics, which he extends to include economics and geography. "I have no desire to learn any geography under any circumstances" (T, 205), he proudly declares. Such incapacity or lack of interest serves two purposes. It makes Marchbanks comical in his ineptness even as he effectively turns it into a matter of choice, pride, and distinctiveness, and it subtly reinforces the concerns that Marchbanks makes synonymous with his specially groomed identity—individuality, taste, extravagant behavior, and capacious knowledge of culture.

Marchbanks is interested in spiritual matters, not conventional religious issues; cultural identity, not party politics; and what is demonstrably good and fine, not what is "cute" or "gracious" as in the *Ladies' Home Journal*'s lexicon of "gracious living" (T, 58). Concerning matters of public fashion and modern values, he thus sees himself as "an embittered reactionary," who is "at anchor in the stream of progress." Happily he adds, "I don't care" (D, 197). Yet, while most things he admires belong to the past, he is unsympathetic to Tory notions per se, which, as he puts it, merely perpetuate "the same old nonsense from generation to generation" (T, 28). Nonetheless, many of his attitudes, to women for instance, are confessedly "romantic" and tradition-bound. An admirer of beauty, poise, elegance, and charm, he will settle for nothing less in women, except perhaps for a fascinating ugliness.

Marchbanks sets himself directly against dourness and repressiveness. Locating these impulses squarely in the Canadian temperament—the effects of puritanism and Calvinism that encourage "the belief that everything which seems fair and delightful is evil, and should be forbidden" (T, 190), the confusion of sobriety with seriousness, and the curse of a cold climate are contributing factors—he sets himself up as the prevailing culture's crusty opposition. Self-denial he condemns as silly. He recommends indulgence, laziness, frivolity, rejoicing, even the luxury of imagining revenge. In his concern for physical and psychological health he advocates the rejection of the conventional wisdom of self-restraint. Even dieting he sees as a crypto-Calvinistic plot against pleasure. "There are," he argues, "more deaths caused by ingrowing, suppurating self-control than the medical profession wots of" (T, 159). Controlling one's temper, he often notes, is a danger to health. "There comes a time in every man's life," he writes, "when he wants to tell somebody who is pestering him to go to hell, and if he does not indulge the whim he is likely to get psychic strabismus, which, in its turn, leads to spiritual impotence. And spiritual impotence is the curse of our country as it is" (D, 136–37).

The Diary of Samuel Marchbanks (1947)

For the first of the Marchbanks books, Davies chose 365 newspaper entries that he arranged seasonally. Like Samuel Pepys, Marchbanks began with "Laus Deo," then set forth his single New Year's resolution: "to keep this Diary faithfully for a year, without cant, and—so far as in me lies (which may not be very far)—without exaggeration." Typical of his hostility toward cant was his dismissal of the idea of self-reform by "resolution." In a remark that anticipates Davies's central concern, Marchbanks comments, "I outgrew such folly long ago. Any betterment in my character will be the outcome of prolonged meditation, and slow metabolic and metaphysical reform—a psychosomatic process, in other words" (D, 3). But if he successfully resists much of the hypocrisy and malarkey of daily life, he had no desire to control his penchant for exaggeration. Indeed, the book's vitality greatly depends on hyperbole and excess, for these are the staples of Marchbanks's idiosyncratic response to life.

Reviews of *The Diary of Samuel Marchbanks* were generally favorable, stressing in particular the book's humor and satire. Simon Paynter in the *Canadian Forum,* for instance, compared Davies to Stephen Leacock, who had died in 1944. "This is great humor," he wrote, confident that the book would join "*Sunshine Sketches {of a Little Town}* on its lonely eminence, and thus double the number of humorous classics in our literature." But Paynter also shrewdly observed the substance behind Marchbanks's values and opinions. Here was a figure who, in his fumblings, reminded one of Walter Mitty, but was "not in the least pathetic" and brought such "enthusiasm" to his complaints that he could not be regarded as diminished or defeated by the misadventures of life.[15] It would be years before the characteristic Davies blend of psychological good sense, satire, and frivolity, inherent in the Marchbanks voice, would be more generally recognized. For the present most observers were content simply to enjoy a humor that recalled influences as wide-ranging as Pepys, Ben Jonson, Samuel Johnson, Swift, Holmes, Twain, Leacock, Thurber, and Mencken, but that seemed without particular definition or design.

In 1966 when *The Diary of Samuel Marchbanks* was revised for paperback distribution, Davies added a preface in which he accounted for numerous textual changes on grounds of loss of pertinency. Thus, the wartime early 1940s flavor of Ontarian and Canadian experience, a quality that gives the 1947 edition a particular historical and nostalgic interest, is diminished. Accordingly, one is often jarred to find alterations—the Beatles replace Frank Sinatra, while movies once seen in the theater become late-night television reruns—side by side with domestic preoccupations that belong clearly to the forties. Gone too are the comic saints and festal days and such effective sequences as the uncomfortable summer holiday at Camp Laffalot in Skeleton, Muskoka (D, 121–23). Despite the alterations, however, Marchbanks himself remains very much of a curmudgeonly piece.

The Table Talk of Samuel Marchbanks (1949)

Following upon the success of *The Diary,* Davies sought a second device for collecting and arranging the best of his Marchbanks items. Perhaps inspired by Logan Pearsall Smith's *Trivia* volumes and Holmes's breakfasting autocrat, he seized upon the idea of offering dollops of polished monologue as a suitable accompaniment to and garnish for a modestly elegant, seven-course dinner party. Choosing some 370 entries written mostly after 1946, he expanded certain of these to include some form of address, usually sardonic, to a dinner guest. Each he captioned—for example, "Of Nature's Malice" or "On the Loneliness of Wisdom"—to emphasize the effect of honed observation and assured performance. For "a good talker,"

Marchbanks observes, "should speak in paragraphs and not in disjointed utterance" (T, v).

The Marchbanksian feast, though not "a great dinner," is Edwardian in scope from the "Soup" through "Fish," "Entree," "The Remove," "Sweet," "Savoury," and "Dessert." The air of the polished conversationalist, at home among the "private houses of our day," is reinforced when at the end of his introductory note, Marchbanks dates the collection not from Marchbanks Towers but from "The Deipnosophists Club."

Overall, *The Table Talk of Samuel Marchbanks* is a more pungent, sharp-edged book than *The Diary*. Marchbanks offers his opinions more firmly and aggressively, revealing an increasingly precise sense of taste and personal identity. Davies also has considerable success in introducing lengthy, sustained narratives—described demurely as "boring stories"—that provide welcome variation from the aphoristic bombardment of the table talk itself. The best of these, Marchbanks's account of his initiation into the Canadian hunting fraternity—"He Ceases to be a Tenderhorn (A Boring Account)"—is a delightful piece of comic writing, poised cleverly on the hunters' habit of "feasting" for a week on salt pork and fried potatoes. The cant of the "Old Hands" becomes self-evidently ridiculous as the narrative unfolds. Structurally, however, *The Table Talk* is less successful than its predecessor. Too many of the entries show no evidence of adaptation to fit the form; on one occasion, for instance, Marchbanks shifts from cider pressing to post-Christmas dullness (T, 166–67), thus undercutting the plausibility of conversational flow. Neither does there appear to be particular effort to fit the conversation to the specific dinner course. The opportunity to develop a discernible table mood by at least identifying and typing certain of the guests, an opportunity Davies takes up with relish in *The Rebel Angels,* is also passed over in the interests of tidbits of polished monologue. One even notices the occasional repeating of entries from *The Diary*.

Appearing in October 1949 in the wake of *The Diary*'s success and the Dominion Drama Festival's recognition of his one-act plays, *The Table Talk* was widely and positively reviewed. Because of his relative youth, Davies's range of talents and sophistication impressed many commentators. Indeed, Hilda Kirkwood observed in the *Canadian Forum,* "His picture has been published so often during the past three years that the plates have worn thin." To this she added, he "is fast becoming a national legend."[16]

Within Canada response ranged from unqualified enthusiasm to, in at least one judgment, disappointment. Reviewers generally praised the wit and humor, labelling Davies "Canada's own Pepys" and "Our Canadian Oliver Wendell Holmes."[17] Several were cheered by renewed evidence of a sophisticated postcolonial talent in Canadian letters, a literary voice to accompany the political achievements of Louis St. Laurent, Lester Pearson, and Mackenzie King.[18] Very perceptively, William Arthur Deacon suggested that the "sheer enjoyment" provided by *The Table Talk* was less iconoclastic, abrasive, and portentous than many had observed.[19] James Scott offered the dissenting view in the *Toronto Telegram,* observing that Davies had done little of interest with the potential that Samuel Marchbanks evinced in *The Diary*. He argued that, as "a very promising playwright," Davies ought to "stick to the drama and give Marchbanks a not too decent burial."[20]

More important, especially for Davies, was the emergence of an audience outside Canada. In June 1951, Chatto and Windus brought out an English edition of *The Table Talk,* its foreword written by the Rt. Hon. Sir Norman Birkett, a prominent lawyer and noted conversationalist. Birkett's enthusiasm was evident:

Who is Robertson Davies? And why have I never heard of him before? This book seems to me to be a sheer delight. Its wit, its humour, its wide humanity, its touch of Rabelais, its whimsical asides, its provoking and stimulating effect upon the mind, its diverting interest in all sorts of conditions of men and circumstances—all serve to make it a book deserving the widest recognition.[21]

English reviewers followed Birkett's lead, finding little difficulty with Davies's Canadianness. While Frederick Laws saw Davies— rather curiously—in the tradition of the obstinate, awkward but sane editors of small-town American papers,[22] most emphasized Marchbanks's interest in "universal experience universally discussed."[23] William Plomer noted that the English reader with romantic notions about Canada as "all gloriously open and free and easy" was likely to be surprised by the images Davies calls up.[24] Virtually all welcomed Davies as a civilized writer well aware of a civilized audience's tastes and priorities.

Marchbanks' Almanack (1967)

With the popularity of Samuel Marchbanks further augmented in Canada by the selection of passages from *The Table Talk* to accompany cartoons in two issues of *Mayfair* magazine, Davies began work on a third collection for Clarke, Irwin. Busy with playwrighting, his commentaries on the Stratford Festival, and his second novel, not to mention his journalistic responsibilities, he did not complete the manuscript until 1954. By then, however, the firm to which he was contracted had undergone managerial changes. Mr. William Clarke, a Davies enthusiast, had passed away. The manuscript was turned down by the new management without explanation. It was not until 1967, over a decade later, that it appeared, considerably revised, under the imprint of McClelland and Stewart, their aim being in part to include a volume of Davies's writing in the expanding New Canadian Library series. Like *The Diary,* it was not published in either England or the United States.

Marchbanks' Almanack is subtitled "An Astrological and Inspirational *Vade Mecum* Containing Character Analyses, Secrets of Charm, Health Hints, How to be a Success at Parties, Fortune-Telling by the Disposition of Moles on the Body and Divers Other Arcane Knowledge Here Revealed for the First Time; as Well as Generous Extracts from the Correspondence, *Pensées,* Musings, *Obiter Dicta* and Ruminations of Wizard Marchbanks." Reflecting Davies's longstanding interest in the literary traditions of magic and how-to-do books, the *Almanack* is, for all its paraphernalia, yet another "miscellany" drawn from the *Examiner*'s columns. Unlike *The Table Talk,* however, there is here more effort to create a structure suitable to the material as well as a further sharpening of outlook, particularly with regard to the theme of selfhood. Notably, the book was illustrated by Davies himself.

Arranged according to the signs of the zodiac, each section begins with what Marchbanks calls an utterly frank horoscope, which, in addition to its parodying of the conventional language of horoscopes, straightforwardly urges acute attention to one's personal powers. Those born under Aries he declares "must be given your own way in everything," adding with a wink, "Your sex-life may cause remark among the jealous: frown them down" (A, 1). The horoscope is followed by "Enchantment-of-the-Month" and "Health Hints" written in a similar tone. Each section then opens up into predictable Marchbanksian subsections like "Meditations at Random," and "From My Notebooks," etc. The most enjoyable of these, entitled "From My Files," contains the ongoing correspondence between Marchbanks and a number of friends and enemies, all of whom are identified as character types by their astrological signs. Originally published in the *Peterborough Examiner* from September 1949 to December 1950, these letters provide narrative continuity for the potpourri of observation and opinion. With his insensitive neighbor Dick Dandiprat, who has put a skunk in his car as a practical joke, Marchbanks engages in a hostile correspondence leading to a lawsuit involving his incompetent lawyers, Mouseman, Mouseman, and Forcemeat. With Mervyn Noseigh, M.A., an aspiring doctoral student, whose thesis topic is "Skunk's Misery to Toronto: a Study of Spiritual Degeneration in the Work of Samuel Marchbanks" (A, 94), Marchbanks fends off impertinent questions about his childhood, "Oedipus Complex," and "sex life," even as he uses each occasion to reveal important facts about his tastes and interests. Questioned, for instance, about being a humorist, he replies that "If I had to name a favourite, I suppose it would have to be Francois Rabelais, but I do not give him my whole heart." In the same letter he interestingly defines a sense of humor: "I would say it lay in the perception of shadows" (A, 202). With the playwright Apollo Fishorn, Esq., he discusses Canadian theater and aspects of the Dominion Drama Festival while with his kindred spirit, Amyas Pilgarlic, Esq., he indulges his curiosity about, and delight in, arcane information. While no brief summary can capture the broad-humored, often slapstick spirit of these numerous correspondences, they provide the *Almanack* with a narrative impetus lacking in the other Marchbanks books as well as a variety of types by means of which one can more fully appreciate the protagonist himself. Interestingly, many of these correspondents, especially Minerva Hawser, Dandiprat, and Noseigh, reappear in variant forms in *Leaven of Malice* (1954), a novel Davies was writing about the same time he was reworking the *Examiner* correspondence into the original *Almanack* manuscript.

Despite the gap in time from *The Table Talk* and the lapsing of the Marchbanks column in 1953 (it had at its height of popularity been syndicated in at least ten papers in Ontario and western Canada), reviewers in Canada responded warmly to the *Almanack*. Louis Dudek, for instance, termed it "really quite extraordinary both as entertainment and humour."[25] Yet there were more dissenting observations this time round. Dudek himself was troubled by the lapses into slapstick irrelevance. J. M. Robson noted a certain tiredness in the "wit and pungency,"[26] while Robert Fulford shrewdly remarked that the book's "charm" was "at best, antique" in that

Marchbanks here seemed to have slowed in "his rate of apprehension of the outside world."[27]

Davies himself likely felt a sense of dissatisfaction in returning to material long since removed from him. As such, Marchbanks apparently died with the *Almanack*. For, as Gordon Roper observed in his introduction, Marchbanks is "fundamentally a Peterborough Everyman," a figure whose agreeable curmudgeonliness was naturally fed by a mistrust of big-city fashion and cant as much as by the conservative habits and blindnesses of small-city folk.[28] The Robertson Davies of 1967 was far removed from Peterborough, and Samuel Marchbanks had outlived his usefulness.

"The Double Life of Robertson Davies" by Samuel Marchbanks

Written originally for *Liberty* magazine (April 1954), this brief essay was included in the revised edition (1966) of *Canadian Anthology,* edited by C. F. Klinck and R. E. Watters. For the anthology Davies made a few textual changes adding footnotes to augment the essay's comic effects.

The essay is, in fact, a delightful piece of Marchbanksian swagger and cantankerousness, predicated on the fact of "a strong physical resemblance between two very different human creatures" (DL, 393)—Davies and himself. Marchbanks claims to be the more colorful and interesting of the pair, slightly older and entirely superior. After brief mention of the double in literature and "The Doppelganger Delusion," Marchbanks shifts into a belittling and comic, biographical (autobiographical) sketch of Davies, reminiscent of the comic self-portrait Stephen Leacock used to set the tone for *Sunshine Sketches of a Little Town*. While Marchbanks mocks Davies's "uneventful childhood" and idiotic incapacity in mathematics, it is clear that Davies employs the cover to reveal a good deal about himself and to place that personal information in a suitably controlled perspective. It allows him, for instance, to comment upon complaints lodged against him by "many Little Theatre people," whose gall, he notes, extends even to cutting and rewriting his plays. Interestingly, it is Marchbanks who claims to be the novelist of the pair, author of *Tempest-Tost*. Aggressively he pronounces, "I do not allow anybody to tamper with my books, and when illiterate hobgoblins suggest changes in them I very quickly let them know that I will write in my own way, or not at all. But I am a creator of jewelled prose. Davies is just a playwright and ought to be glad of helpful advice from anybody who can spell" (DL, 399).

The idea of his own doubleness has clearly delighted Davies from the early stages of his career. Marchbanks became his medium for a particular aggressiveness, outspokenness, and self-certainty with which, in the Canadian microcosm of Peterborough, he found it socially and professionally inappropriate to identify himself directly. That such opinionated forthrightness always had about it the stamp of gentility, orthodoxy, and urbanity must not be overlooked even when Marchbanks champions himself at the expense of his creator's mildness, courtesy, moderation, and "milk-and-water attitude":

> My life has been stormy, for there is nothing I like better than contradicting people and shouting them down. I am rude on principle, for there are too many boobs in the world who trade on the politeness of others in order to air their own ineptitude. I like to go among people and mock and jeer. I am anti-social, but I like society. (DL, 398)

Samuel Marchbanks was, thus, one very conscious side of Robertson Davies, the small-city editor and citizen, his happy means, in Gordon Roper's phrase, of "eas[ing] his own internal pressures."[29] An essay like "The Double Life" illustrates how readily one side of Davies slips into the other. If the author of *Tempest-Tost* is Marchbanks so too is the "somewhat unorthodox" newspaper editor who seeks "a slightly disreputable flavor" to counter "ingrowing respectability" (DL, 397). It is difficult in this sense to accept Patricia Monk's Jungian emphasis that Marchbanks constitutes a kind of "shadow self" in poised relation to Davies's "conscious self," a self that becomes "disturbingly powerful," threatening to usurp its creator.[30] The idea that the dark savage energies within Davies are made manifest in Marchbanks's exuberance is necessarily overemphasized by Monk to provide an early foundation for her study. So much more emerges simultaneously, particularly the lighthearted and frivolous side of Davies, that to emphasize the one at the expense of the other is to disrupt a crucial balance, one to which Davies the stylist is particularly attentive. Whatever "perception of shadows" he may have touched in the creation of Marchbanks, he was in complete control of the energy of his mouthpiece, of what both he and his mouthpiece chose to reveal. Marchbanks's last words on

Davies—"I shall certainly last as long as he does, and it would be the cream of Nature's joke if I were to outlive him" (DL, 400)—nicely emphasize the comic as opposed to the dark perceptions Davies locates in his early alter ego. Marchbanks occasionally hankers for revenge, but he is above all a happy spirit, eager to establish the grounds for his individuality and taste and to celebrate the importance of one's personal sanity and worth.

Chapter Three
The Bewitchments of Simplification: Robertson Davies's Early Plays

"As a playwright, I am old-fashioned," Robertson Davies admitted in 1981; "in the past I filled a place, but that's gone by."[1] Such perspective constitutes a long leap for a man who, upon his return to Canada in 1940, aspired above all to be a successful dramatist. "What I really wanted to do was to write plays. And I did. And most of them have been acted, and some of them have been acted several times."[2] Despite the problems facing the playwright in Canada during the postwar years, Davies, as he suggests, did accomplish a great deal. Eric Nicol recognized that achievement when, in reviewing *A Jig for the Gypsy* in 1954, he called Davies "Canada's most prolific and successful playwright."[3]

Because the theater has played so important a part in Robertson Davies's creative life and ambitions and because his output of plays has been considerable, it is necessary to devote two chapters to the subject. The first considers his short and long plays of the 1940s. The second focuses upon the 1950s, the decade of his greatest ventures and successes as a playwright; it also ranges forward to include his ambitious study of the Canadian psyche, *Question Time* (1975), arguably his last important contribution to Canadian theater. Necessarily, some selection has been practised. Brief mention is made of Davies's two masques, but *Brothers in the Black Art* (written for CBC television in 1974) and the unpublished historical extravaganza, *Pontiac and the Green Man,* which Davies concedes was "vastly overwritten . . . and in consequence . . . not a good play,"[4] are not examined. Overall, both chapters focus upon the kinds of plays Davies chose to write, the persistence of certain themes and preoccupations, and what Richard Plant has called "the spectre of the gap between the complexity of [his] novels and the more open didacticism of his plays."[5]

The King Who Could Not Dream: The Magic of Theater

Though never published, *The King Who Could Not Dream* reveals a good deal about Davies's taste and theatrical inclinations. At home *in* Canada but most alive in his memories of the Old Vic, he did not at first think to write *about* Canada. Rather he tried to write in the spirit of the plays that had most deeply affected him as a young theatergoer and about which he had heard a great deal from his father and certain Old Vic actors. These plays, in the tradition of Henry Irving and his successors, were brimful of spectacle, wonderful effect, and romance. "They enabled us . . . they enabled boys as I was when I saw them—to take a long look back into the nineteenth century. When you saw the *Corsican Brothers* finely played by Martin-Harvey, you were looking back to 1854. You have to be grateful for somebody who enables you to make an imaginative leap like that."[6]

The leap backward has characterized much of Robertson Davies's creative and critical work about the theater. For him the playhouse is "a house of dreams" and a temple,[7] a place of pure feeling and religious intensity quite remote from commonplace cares, events, and language. His often-expressed mistrust of realism, which he typically defines in reductive terms—for instance, as a mere imitation of surfaces—seems in this regard less an aesthetic principle than a function of personal taste. It is taste passionately and obstinately defended, propped up by a multitude of rhetorical flourishes, because it matters intensely to him. When he allowed to Ann Saddlemyer that "my kind of theatre is gone,"[8] he was also acknowledging that he had for decades been seeking to hold back the past in his attempts to wed elements of nineteenth-century melodrama, romance, and comedy to twentieth-century concerns. Magnus Eisengrim's gallant and passionate defense of Sir John and Milady Tresize in *World of Wonders* is his most intense expression of commitment to an imaginative leap backward. Tresize's heroic "fight to maintain a nineteenth-century idea of theatre in the twentieth century" becomes, in a more general sense, Davies's own, as *The King Who Could Not Dream* illustrates.

Though Davies now regards *The King* as an apprentice piece, it is, clearly, a revealing work. He wrote it with John Gielgud in mind and with an eye to the Irving tradition, especially to the use of the double in plays like Boucicault's *The Corsican Brothers* and Scott's *The Master of Ballantrae*. Dramatic entrances, evocative contrasts, heroic confrontations, and internal entertainments enrich the atmosphere of romance and melodrama.

The story depends upon a contrast of ways of life and personalities, thus providing considerable challenge to the lead actor.[9] Act 1 is set in England where Ethelred the Unready, a king without illusions (hence unable to dream), is subjected to the whims and pressures of his family and court. It is 999 A.D., and his wife, Emma, wishes to go on a millennial pilgrimage. Though wanting to keep her with him, Ethelred allows her to go, much to the dissatisfaction of the court. Act 2 takes place in the splendid palace of the Caliph Montasir of Samarkand where Emma is held prisoner. The Caliph is a magnificent Ethelred, freed from restraint, hesitancy, and the thrall of reason. In the transition North has become South, passivity action, dark light, and Christian Pagan. Brave and arrogant, the splendid Caliph recognizes Emma's queenliness. He pursues her with intensity until she admits that he is everything that she once hoped her English king might be. Though tempted to stay in the South and share in the Caliph's promise of love and eternal youth, Emma feels compelled to return home to help Ethelred, having heard of his danger at the hands of invading Danes. The Caliph offers her his magic sword if she will promise to return. In Act 3, once again back in England, Emma gives Ethelred the Caliph's sword whereupon Ethelred undergoes a salutary transformation. The play does not, however, call upon him to perform the ridiculously heroic or historically impossible. There is no military victory. Rather Ethelred does what is best and most plausible under the circumstances. He flees to Normandy, opting for survival and life, and dedicating himself to "the greatest mystery—to learn more about himself." Informed of the Caliph's death, Emma readily accompanies her rejuvenated husband.

The *King* depends upon the double role of "the star" and the uplift provided by Ethelred's inner transformation. Two distinct sides of self, the passive Northern king (who cannot dream) and the ruthless Southern Caliph (who promises Emma a life of endless splendor), are integrated in the final act. Yet, for all its spectacle and romance, *The King Who Could Not Dream* is thinly characterized. Neither Emma's quick emotional shifts nor Ethelred's decision to seek refuge in France are particularly convincing. So too the crucial relationship between king and queen is not effectively developed. On the whole the play talks about depth, attempting to disguise an absence of psychological revelation with a busy plot, sharp contrasts, verbal wit, and theatricality.

What is remarkable about this first play is the evidence it offers both of Davies's affinity for the Irving tradition and his implicit commitment to the theme of self-discovery. Ethelred comes finally to act *for himself,* not simply in response to the pressures exerted by those around him. The buried or unrecognized self is awakened and given its voice; it frees itself from the manipulations of others and from enervating duties. As such, it looks ahead to plays like *Hunting Stuart* and particularly *Question Time.* The latter does for the prime minister of Canada what the Caliph's sword did for Ethelred, applying a good deal of Jungian apparatus in the process.

Hope Deferred: Molière in the Canadian Wilderness

Having written a second long British play, *Benoni* (later rewritten as *A Jig for the Gypsy*), this time with Sybil Thorndike in mind, and having been turned down again, Davies began to revise his goals. Well aware of the lively Little Theatre movement in Kingston and of the postwar revival of the Dominion Drama Festival, he turned from England to Canada, writing one-act plays designed specifically for amateur players. Here, he felt, his efforts might be welcomed.

The first of these, *Hope Deferred,* was begun in 1944, though it was not performed until 1948. It projects Davies's charged feeling—shared by many Canadians at the time—that Canada was indifferent, if not hostile, to the idea of art. To make the point, he borrowed an actual episode in early history of New France, the Catholic Church's banning of a production of Molière's *Tartuffe* planned for Quebec City in 1693.

The action is brief and compact. Count Frontenac, governor of New France and "nobleman, born and bred," is seen observing the stylized dance of his young protégé, the Huron Indian Chimène, just returned from five years of training in France.[10] Frontenac is at seventy-three still handsome and vigorous, very much the accomplished Old World courtier. Convent-educated and schooled in acting by Molière's friend, Michael Baron of the Comèdie Française,

Chimène is intelligent, beautiful, and talented. It is Frontenac's plan that she will distinguish his forthcoming production of *Tartuffe*. Following successful presentations of Corneille and Racine, the play will constitute the high point of his attempt to bring the accomplished art of French theater to the "Rock" in the wilderness.

Their happy reunion is interrupted by the visit of two eminent Roman Catholic bishops, the elderly, amiable Laval and his younger colleague, Saint-Vallier, whom Davies characterizes as "lean, fiery and fanatical" (E, 61). The latter insists that Frontenac not only call off the production—he condemns Molière as the "arch-contriver of evil fictions" (E, 66), echoing church opinion in France several decades earlier—but also cease to present any plays for the time being. Frontenac is incensed. He defends Molière's genius, refusing to accept the argument that drama weakens the piety of humble white men and Indians alike. Haughtily he questions, "Are you asking me to reduce the intellectual tone of this whole country to what is fit for Indians and shopkeepers?" (E, 70).

It is Saint-Vallier's trump card, however, that subdues the governor. The priest argues that a weakening of Church position will mean a loss of vital trade. The English, he asserts, are making great advances with their looser methods based on "religious freedom." While the argument is, as argument, not very convincing, Frontenac yields. Though he suggests cynically that brandy, lacrosse, and presents would be more effective augmenters of trade, he doesn't challenge the authority of his Church. When Chimène jumps into the argument claiming to represent "my land" (E, 72), her role is simply that of devil's advocate. Her questions ("is it also to be a land without art?" [E, 73]) cannot be answered. In the end Davies does grant Frontenac two victories: first, a practical and clever way of avenging Saint-Vallier's insult to Molière and, second, the opportunity to make a declamatory speech in which he simultaneously acknowledges the "dreadful pressure" of "organized virtue" (E, 76) and denounces the baseness and stupidity of placing trade and piety before art. To Chimène who has decided to return to France and acting, he suggests that all they can do for the New World is hope: "*Espérance* be our watchword!"

Stylized and didactic, *Hope Deferred* established the pattern of Davies's persistent focus upon the state of the arts in Canada. As Richard Plant has illustrated, two character types fit the pattern—the natural Canadian who must go abroad to develop his talents and the cultivated, enlightened foreigner who "tries to bring cultural activity to a barren country."[11] *Hope Deferred* is relentless in its treatment of that single theme. Saint-Vallier is too much the straw man to Frontenac's nobility. Debate dominates at the expense of dramatic action. Most disturbingly, the play seems by its very choice of scene cut off from the country it discusses. Frontenac's elegant chamber defines an indoor world in which the wilderness and the North are mere concepts. Relatedly, the play's simple symbol of the land, Chimène, has had her Huron blood and experience, even her appearance it seems, educated out of her in five short years. When she tells the priests that "the future of this land touches me nearly" (E, 72), her passion is not convincing. Like Frontenac, she loves art and theatre above all.

Overlaid: Eros and Thanatos in Rural Canada

Overlaid (1947) is the most satisfying of Davies's one-act plays. Its subject is again the plight of the arts in Canada, but it effectively dramatizes that plight without recourse to overbearing or didactic characters. It captures a vivid instance of grassroots cultural neglect, balancing the enthusiast and the anti-art voice in a way that speaks far more powerfully of the problem than the high-minded debates in Frontenac's chamber.

The setting is Smith County, Ontario. The plot turns on a sudden windfall. In a "cluttered and inconvenient" farm kitchen Pop, aged seventy, listens to the Saturday broadcast of *Lucia di Lammermoor* from New York's Metropolitan Opera House. Attired in overalls, old top hat, and white work gloves, he punctuates his listening with delighted outbursts like "Attaboy!" and "Hot Dog!" (E, 81).

Set against Pop's exuberant enjoyment is his daughter Ethel, a "hard-faced" forty-year old former schoolteacher whose life is consumed by family, farm, and church. To her the "row" on the radio merely worsens her headache and impedes her ironing. As the two bicker and as the sound is turned up, then down, the radio announcer is heard to say, "If our lives lack beauty, we are poor indeed . . ." (E, 84).

With George Bailey's entrance, the conflict intensifies. Bailey announces that Pop is entitled to $1200 immediately, having completed his insurance payments. When G. B. tries to lead him into various company options, Pop resists. A dream has taken hold and he imagines himself in New York at the opera. In one of the play's best speeches, he extravagantly describes his plans, impelled not a little by a desire to outrage his dour daughter and the stuffy G. B.:

> I'll tell you what I'd do, since you're so nosey: I'd get some stylish clothes, and I'd go into one o' these restrunts, and I'd order vittles you never heard of—better'n the burnt truck Ethel calls food—and I'd get a bottle o' wine—cost a dollar, maybe two—and drink it all, and then I'd mosey along to the Metropolitan Opera House and I'd buy me a seat right down beside the trap-drummer, and there I'd sit an' listen, and holler and hoot and raise hell whenever I liked the music, an' throw bookies to the gals, an' wink at the chorus, and when it was over I'd go to one o' these here nightclubs an' eat some more, an' drink whisky, and watch the gals that take off their clothes—every last dud, kinda slow an' devilish till they're bare-naked—an' maybe I'd give one of 'em fifty bucks for her brazeer. (E, 90)

Pop, however, is soon the subject of Ethel's counterattack. She argues concernedly for his reputation, for dutifulness and decency. Despite his resistance—"I've had a bellyful o' duty . . . I want what's warm an'—kind of mysterious; somethin' to make you laugh an' talk big" (E, 95)—deep inside Pop knows he won't really be heard. Just as the local church took the money he donated for a bell and used it to buy a stove, Ethel is unable to understand his inchoate need. *Her* great ambitions are to be remembered as a good woman of the community and to buy a granite tombstone of the best quality to commemorate that respectability. In describing her dreams Ethel reaches her poetic summit, speaking feelingly of what matters most to her. Her conviction is a force Pop wants to, but cannot finally, resist.

It is the quality of balance that most distinguishes *Overlaid*. While there is no doubt that Davies's sympathies are with Pop, whose flamboyance and enthusiasm counter the illiteracy and vulgarity of his rural experience, he succeeds in creating a genuine emotional tension. What makes the play work, as Tyrone Guthrie points out, is Ethel's capacity to evoke a sympathy "which will be all the more moving because the cards seem so heavily stacked against her" (E, xiii). Far more effectively than *Hope Deferred*, *Overlaid* embodies the problem of art and culture in Canada. It matters little that the only opera lover in Smith County confuses opera with burlesque. The play's strength—it has been performed and reprinted many times—

resides in its capacity to move from caricature to character, from comic set piece to genuinely affecting situation, from the black and white of melodrama to an effective juxtaposition of mutually exclusive points of view. "Pop is in love with life, and Ethel is in love with Death,"[12] but *Overlaid* effectively buries the Eros-Thanatos conflict in the characters. It is both Pop and Ethel we remember; the play makes their dreams powerful in themselves.

Eros at Breakfast: Love and the Bodily Functions

Written, like *Overlaid,* for the Ottawa Drama League, *Eros at Breakfast* (1948) is a comic fantasy based on the "health dialogues" Davies recalled from his school days. The idea of a play going on inside somebody delighted him. But rather than have allegorical components of diet debate their virtues, Davies shifted matters to take an internal look at that most typical of stories—boy meets girl.

Everything is presented from within Mr. P. S. (psyche and soma) on the morning when, while breakfasting with his mother, he receives an encouraging reply to his love letter. The scene is a plush office—Mr. P. S.'s Solar Plexus or nerve center—where two civil servants, Chremes and his assistant, routinely monitor his responses. The underlying seriousness of the play is suggested in passing by Chremes who reports that life is a miracle and that "Every playgoer is a psychologist" (E, 4). The opening is followed by bureaucratic visits from Aristophontes, the professorial head of Intelligence; the Byronic Parmeno, who is "quite a power in the Heart now" (E, 15); and finally the beautiful Hepatica from the department of Liver and Lights. Delighting in the chance to speak through the bodily elements, Davies predictably makes the role of Intelligence the most resistant to love. In the end, however, even Intelligence is persuaded to join in numerous toasts with the others, having accepted the argument that love is the intoxication not only of the senses but also of the intellect. It is a very drunk Aristophontes who provides the play's final humor with his indulgent drinking and absurd song.

In its use of bureaucratic parody, overacting, comic costuming, music (Prokoviev's Classical Symphony vies with Strauss's sugary "The Thousand and One Nights"), and conscious play with the audience, *Eros at Breakfast* delighted many audiences in the late 1940s. Recognized as the best Canadian play at the DDF's Eastern

Ontario finals, it was chosen to represent Canada at the Edinburgh Festival in 1949. What is most interesting about the play today is the evidence it offers of Davies's early interest in psychological health. Playfully he puts forward his belief in the importance of feeling and intuition. The action puts overbearing Intelligence in its place. As Chremes forewarns us, when Intelligence is given too much importance, the other bodily elements often react: "Sometimes it means disease, and sometimes madness, but it always means destruction" (E, 25). In a similar spirit Davies uses the occasion to direct criticisms at Canada's unhealthful conformism, dullness, and reliance upon reason. The country's poetry, for instance, is not "written from the Solar Plexus" but is "squeezed out painfully by the Intelligence Department" (E, 10). The snobbish Aristophantes tells Crito that "A Canadian's Intelligence is not an instrument of fun"; rather "it is a curb upon his baser instincts" (E, 25).

The Voice of the People: The Curse of Babbitry

An underlying disgust for the bluster and myopia of "the Common Man" is the distinguishing feature of *The Voice of the People* (1949). Though intended as a comedy, the play is, according to Elspeth Buitenhuis, "a glimpse into the very texture of lower middle-class Canadian life in all its narrow puritanism."[13] Davies, however, has emphasized that his intentions were benign. "The play is intended only to amuse," he wrote; "but it has its roots in truth; when people who do not ordinarily do much thinking or writing suddenly undertake to do both at once, the result may be astounding."[14]

Its plot is simple. Shorty Morton returns from work to find dinner uncooked and Sam North, an electrician, at work on the old stove's wires. After petulantly haranguing his wife, his daughter, Sam, and the newspaper boy, Shorty receives a call from a fellow barber asking him to write a reply to a letter in the evening paper criticizing increased barbershop prices. The letter in "The Voice of the People" column is, Shorty assumes, by a man named Townsend whom he dislikes. He takes the criticism personally, without reading the letter carefully. Puffing up his indignation he composes his reply and reads it to the family. Its silliness of composition, libelous innuendo, and redneck vacuousness are comically self-revealing. Only after his posturing does Sam North disclose that the original letter was a generalized comment having nothing to do with barbers and that *he*, not Townsend, had written it. Sam then departs offering sententious Biblical advice—"He that answereth a matter before he heareth it, it is folly and shame unto him" (E, 54).

While Sam North's proverbial wisdom provides its moral direction, *The Voice of the People* focuses unyieldingly upon the Mortons in all their inadequacies. Shorty is a third-rate Babbitt. Bustling, peevish, and self-centered, he has opinions about everything. Most are negative and ill informed; he reads only the sports and the funny pages, content to blame every problem on the younger generation or a conspiracy of higher-ups—"wheels within wheels" is his favorite phrase.

The Morton women are equally uninspiring. A devoted wife, Aggie finds her strength in "tabernacle" where the wisdom of the stagy Pastor Beamis (who returns in *A Mixture of Frailties*) sustains her. She believes in Beamis and in the conviction that "God wrote the Bible Himself" (E, 45); she defends "sweetness" as a girl's best means to a happy life and suggests that the facts newspapers use as filler—for example, "the piccolo is a small flute"—provide a first-class education. Her daughter Myrtle is a slangy, knowing, "modern" teenager. Her world is measured in candy bars, boys, and movie magazines. Whatever she learns in school, she is unable to apply to her life. Though she studies Latin she can't begin to translate the simple phrase "Pro Bono Publico." To her, art is junk and "Salvador Daley" is an Irishman (E, 40).

Sam North, whose name suggests Canada, prophetic insight, and ordinariness, is a welcome foil to the entire family. Like a chorus, he supplies trenchant comments upon their antics and ignorance. Though Shorty seeks to demean his tradesman's status, Sam's genuine interest in local and world affairs, his detailed knowledge of the Bible, and his personal dignity constitute an inordinate judgment upon the family's vaudevillelike stupidity. They are, in effect, straw men to his superior wisdom. Hence, while *The Voice of the People* provides amusing moments—for example, Sam's revelation of the way Aggie's beloved Pastor Beamis uses a rheostat and coiffed white hair to intensify the emotional effect of his sermons and, more theatrically, Shorty's mute but stagy antics in composing his letter—it is disturbing in its almost total reduction of the Mortons.

Doubtless, as an editor Davies received letters as illiterate, stupid, and mean-spirited as Shorty's. To present "the people" in such negative terms is, however, to overlook the humanity they possess and to reduce them to caricature. Sam's heroic presence, representing the forces of intellectual curiosity and self-honesty, does not counter the imbalance. *The Voice of the People* is too much an indulgent attack upon the kind of people the author dislikes. Unlike *Overlaid,* it fails to take its negative element seriously.

At the Gates of the Righteous: Awash in Satire

The last of Davies's five one-acters, *At the Gates of the Righteous* (1949), is at once the most complex and unusual. Its subject matter grew out of stories he heard from his mother about the once-notorious Balmer gang. Drawing upon this aspect of southwestern Ontario's past and his stock of Victorian lore, Davies was attracted by the Shavian inversions he could practise in characterizing an outlaw band.

The action begins in a "quiet and rather charming living-room" (E, 105) in an Upper Canada country house where the four members of Bill Balmer's gang are pursuing activities typical of a Victorian Sunday. Bill's girl Effie struggles to play "The Maiden's Prayer" on a harmonium. Ronnie Fitzalan, a lisping English remittance man, offers her aesthetic advice and encouragement. The elderly Angus snores and mumbles in his chair, and Bill reads from the *Globe* (Toronto), enthusing over articles that interest him. Phrenology is his great passion. Initially, there is little to suggest that this domesticated group is in fact a band of highwaymen in their hideout.

Their afternoon of "Art" and "Science" is interrupted by a pair of intruders, Fingal McEachern, the rebellious son of a Presbyterian minister, and his girl Jessie McLaren. Contemptuous of society and desiring to be a "free" soul, a part of what he calls "Power in Action" (E, 114), Fingal has come to join the gang. Quoting Keats on Robin Hood, he bursts in at the very moment when, ironically, the outlaws are assuring each other of their desire to retire from crime and to become proper citizens and "social leaders."

Highlighted by the partial stripping of the two intruders, several gunshots, and Angus's death (the result of an earlier wound), subsequent events reveal the romantic excesses of both groups. The Balmer gang is not at all rebellious. Effie considers herself "a lady" and reveres social institutions. Bill, who aspires to social and political position, eulogizes bathetically on "motherhood" and God. Ronnie still feels religion's call despite his disreputable clerical career. Bill in fact credits Fingal with inadvertently initiating "a remarkable reformation today" (E, 125), the suggestion being that the gang will indeed go straight hereafter. By contrast, Jessie reveals herself to be an easily led, frightened girl, while Fingal's inflexible insistence upon society's hypocrisy finds a disconcerting embodiment in the gang he has idealized at a distance. He must swallow several bitter pills: an awareness that, from a thief's point of view, "the best pickings are always inside the law" (E, 125); a recognition of the sentimental cant by which even bandits live; and a painful insight into the folly of his romantic rebellion. To be effective, rebellion must begin at the top, not the bottom of society, Ronnie tells him. Claiming to be a "wealist," he asserts that the romantic Fingal is "poorly versed in ancient wisdom" (E, 128). "If you ever preach a sermon on what you have seen today," he adds, use as your text, "The evil bow before the good, and the wicked at the gates of the righteous." The play ends with the two intruders tied up near Angus's body as the rest of the gang departs.

Years later, Davies tried to explain why *At the Gates of the Righteous* had been seldom performed. It puzzled audiences, he felt, by inverting two truisms—"that roguery flourishes more readily when it co-operates with the law than when it openly defies it and that the youthful notion of revolution as a path to freedom is mistaken. Audiences," he concluded, "do not greatly care for inversions of popular opinions, and when they are combined with mockery of our hallowed, pioneer past the mixture may prove disturbing."[15]

In locating the failure of the play in the limitations of its audience, Davies overlooked its real problems. *At the Gates of the Righteous* is scarcely a play to unsettle or disturb. While it debunks certain myths and satirizes Victorian and Canadian (they are scarcely "pioneer") attitudes, its inversions carry little weight and are seldom striking. Davies's desire to shock conventional tastes, a persistent aspect of his writing, misfires here for he fails to present either his pious outlaws or his impious young rebels with sufficient seriousness or force. His satiric approach effectively discredits the claims of both, leaving the viewer in the end with only Ronnie's rather inept application of "ancient wisdom." The play does provide an interesting, if unremarkable, example of Davies's emphasis upon the tyranny of respectability, but in so thoroughly discounting the rebellious instinct of freedom, it undermines whatever balance the alternatives originally promised. What it finally seems to offer is a suggestive glimpse of the author's particular kind of conservatism and his penchant for didacticism.

Davies's brief experiment with the one-act play reflects his astute assessment of the Canadian scene in the late 1940s. Such plays "were the staple fare of the amateur companies who were the only ones likely to produce them."[16] Eager for any audience, he set out to provide workable, portable comedies on Canadian subjects. His success is evident in the numerous performances several have enjoyed and in the exposure they gave him within the country. They were not, however, plays of the kind he most longed to write—plays that transformed the theater into a house or temple of dreams. Still, in these five comedies, he first began to adapt his "English" ambitions to Canadian subject matter and to accommodate his keenly melodramatic sense of conflict to the conservative and graceless Canada to which he had returned. The roots of much that he would later attempt are readily discernible in them.

Fortune, My Foe: Art's Plight in a Cold Country

Davies's only three-act play to be performed and published in the 1940s was *Fortune, My Foe* (1949). He wrote it hurriedly for Arthur Sutherland, a former Queen's classmate and American-trained actor whose International Players were presenting a summer of Broadway hits in Kingston in 1948. Sutherland wanted a play of local setting and color to cap the season. As author-director, Davies used the rehearsals to revise and hone the script. When, for instance, he discovered that the actor playing Rowlands had a fine voice, he included for him the song with which the play closes and from which, rather forcedly, the play's title is taken.

So successful was the original week-long engagement that *Fortune, My Foe* was extended a week. In 1949 its popularity was further indicated by three amateur productions, a CBC radio broadcast of the play, its appearance in book form (a rare distinction at that time for a single Canadian play), and international interest in translation and possible productions. That same year the Ottawa Little Theatre took it to the Dominion Drama Festival and won the Sir Barry Jackson Trophy for the best presentation of a Canadian play. Davies himself received the Gratien Gélinas Award as author of the best Canadian play. To date it has been produced close to twenty times.[17]

Writing in *Saturday Night,* B. K. Sandwell noted that it is "so much the most important dramatic work yet written in Canada that it is difficult to think of any other as being in the same class."[18] None of its weaknesses (several of which he noted) could diminish its thematic importance or the skill with which Davies handled his range of "lively personages." In the reactionary postwar era when Canada seemed, above all, preoccupied by materialistic goals, it provided both a challenge to cultural apathy and the promise of growth toward an indigenous theater. The focus of *Fortune, My Foe* is the place of art in a country like Canada and the dilemma of the artist and intellectual in a cool, philistine environment that provides little encouragement or recognition. While scarcely the stuff of great drama, the themes preoccupied Davies. He gave them what was, for the time, a stimulating and definitive treatment.

The play is set in a speakeasy on the Cataraqui River near Kingston where, as was the case with the city's notorious Dollar Bill's, its proprietor Chilly Jim keeps his illegal gin cached in the water. Chilly is a self-educated man of "strong individuality,"[19] much like Sam North; his presence, dignity, and assessments of people provide a touchstone for the action and welter of opinion the play expresses. His speakeasy is a place where open-minded men can comfortably meet—men like newspaper editor Edward Weir and Waverly faculty members, Nicholas Hayward, a young and ambitious instructor of English, and Idris Rowlands, an elderly Welsh-born professor and poet. Also included for purposes of low comedy and contrast is a "dissipated and frowsy [bum]" named Buckety Murphy, whom the regulars tolerate (F, 76).

Much of the play involves the curious father-son relationship between Hayward and Rowlands. In the first two acts they argue extensively—too much, Davies now feels[20]—about Hayward's plan to produce a scholarly edition of an old joke book, *Nugae Venalis, or a Complaisant Companion* (London, 1686). Working a favorite Davies theme, that old jokes return in new forms (see *A Voice from the Attic,* chapter 6), Hayward views the project as a means of obtaining a position in an American university and of making enough money to marry an attractive student, Vanessa Medway. Pursuing what he calls "an ideal of civilization" (F, 90), he is ready to abandon the homeland for which he fought in the war.

Rowlands is cast as a wise but embittered older man. Having played safe in the university and thus failed to develop his poetic talents, he blames his condition on Canada—"This raw, frost-bitten country has worn me out, and its raw, frost-bitten people have numbed my heart" (F, 112). While his plight is no more engaging than Nick's, his heart is less numb than his manner suggests. Scorn is something he spreads around in ample measure, demeaning America (the middlemen of civilization) and England (a romantic dream for Canadians). Admiring Hayward but too crusty to admit it, Rowlands browbeats him about leaving Canada, arguing that the superficial Vanessa isn't worth the sacrifice. He sees her as a Medusa figure, the kind of beauty who turned Apuleius's hero into a jackass. Her early scenes confirm his estimate.

Hayward and Rowlands define the problem of the play. To flesh it out and resolve the impasse in their debate, Davies adopted a device he would use often, the play within the play. Chilly's kitchen helper is a Czechoslovakian immigrant, Franz Szabo, who lied about his age to gain entrance into Canada. His aim, if he can avoid deportation, is to establish a Canadian theater for the Szabo marionettes, a proud family enterprise dating back to Shakespeare's time.[21] Unlike Rowlands, Szabo is a practicing artist. Master of his craft, he makes his own figures carefully by hand and has the toughness and sense of purpose never to doubt his efforts, whatever the social conditions. As such, he brings the pure idea of art into the academic controversy, his quiet dignity effectively juxtaposed to the gab of the others.

When Chilly's patrons discover Szabo's plight, they set out to help him. The result is a hasty production of the scene in which Don Quixote charges against the Windmills to impress two influential members of the local recreation committee. Its aim is to obtain some temporary work for Szabo. On a larger scale, it raises the broader cultural question, "what will Canada do to him?"

What Canada does is not encouraging. Vanessa Medway's friend, Ursula Simonds, a parlor communist, tries to persuade Szabo to use his plays as socialist tracts. The recreation committee pair, cast as mindless dogooders and worshippers of respectability, are too blind to see any beauty or art in the performance. As such, they are subjected to Davies's unrelenting scorn. In a melodramatic scene, they are driven from the temple of art, Szabo's makeshift theater, by an inebriated Rowlands who unleashes upon them a catalog of invective in which Ben Jonson might have delighted. "Fools! Fools! Asses! Dolts! Boobies! Muckworms! Dogs-bodies! Maggots! Nameless bastards of dishonoured she-apes! . . . Get out, you sneaking, mealy-mouthed obscenities! You Nice Nellies! Go, you donkeys in the temple of art!" (F, 152).

The ending is sentimental and optimistic. While Szabo remains undaunted by the folly of "the half-educated," Rowlands sings of hope. Hayward decides to stay in Canada, breaking with Vanessa. His final speech dovetails his recognition of the pure value of art, gained through Szabo, with his growth in self-awareness. Twenty years later Davies felt Hayward's words still had pertinence: "Everybody says Canada is a hard country to govern, but nobody mentions that for some people it is also a hard country to live in. Still, if we all run away it will never be any better. So let the geniuses of easy virtue go southward; I know what they feel too well to blame them. But for some of us there is no choice; let Canada do what she will with us, we must stay" (F, 156).

Fortune, My Foe has much to recommend it. Building upon the theme of *Hope Deferred*, Davies devised a larger, more persuasive and contemporary approach to the problems of art and culture in Canada. Like most of the one-acters, its presentation is realistic. Though its setting is off the beaten track, the events and the actions and attitudes of the characters are of a plausible kind. Davies is able to transform stock roles—like Buckety's comic drunk or jester— to provide both comic relief related to the action and a parodic comment upon the art-culture theme. Buckety not only deals in pornography, but he wants to huckster Szabo's talents to Walt Disney in Hollywood. As Judith Skelton Grant has recently argued, *Fortune, My Foe* owes much of its sustained success to Davies's ability to integrate his central theme into "every aspect of the play."[22]

Still, it is difficult today to regard the play as enthusiastically as did Sandwell in 1949. Deeply committed to its subject, it fails to take deep hold on the level of character and feeling. The roles serve primarily to embody and declaim ideas; hence, despite distinctiveness of dress, speech, mannerism, and status, the characters for the most part remain types regardless of which side of the issue they serve. Moreover, in his attempt to cover the subject, Davies wrote a play that lacks a focal character. Clearly, Nicholas Hayward is meant to be the protagonist, but the effect of the talkative and episodic unfolding is that no single character dominates. It is not simply that the question of what Hayward will do with his life is undercut by a certain triviality in his aims. It is also that Davies surrounds him with characters who are more interesting, eccentric, and vivid, notably Rowlands, Chilly, and Szabo.

While Chilly and Szabo have modest roles, Rowlands is a gaudy talker who argues throughout with Nick, browbeating him about his aims and outlook. Another instance of Davies's world-wise, artistic foreigner in Canada, he declaims his ideas out of an enormous sense of personal worth. How, we may wonder, is that worth effectively justified? His arrogance and hectoring often rankle; indeed, his attitudes are on occasion as insensitive and overbearing as those of the recreation committee members. For instance, in mocking Hayward's idea of editing the jokebook, he savagely indicts various studies of popular culture on the grounds that a professor used to be "a man who knew what ordinary people did not know" (F, 79). Those seeking an intelligent view of culture in broader terms are, for Rowlands, buffoons. So too he continually parades his self-importance. "Canadians," he tells Hayward, "do not understand or like good talk. They call me a windbag. It is as though a jury of Ontario housewives condemned Helen of Troy because she was not their equal in bottling pickles" (F, 100). As a portrait of the overbearing, second-rate, English-trained intellectual in Canada, Rowlands makes an interesting study. Davies, however, grants him so much moral and imaginative consequence that one misses a critical perspective in his presentation.

Fortune, My Foe also suffers from its melodramatic excesses. Art is made so central an issue that all other aspects of human aspiration are eclipsed; characters are valued or flattened according to their responses. Theater has spiritual significance for Davies's right-minded characters. Hence, when Chilly comments that Szabo's marionettes give him "a religious feeling," Nicholas adds, "I see exactly what Chilly means. I feel much the same myself. It fills a need in the heart. Why not call the feeling it arouses religious? Look at it: brilliant colour, warmth, and gaiety—qualities men once sought in the churches, and seek in vain, now. Even our theatres are too self-conscious for gilt and crimson; yet many of us crave these things, deep in our hearts" (F, 137). Very close to Davies's own feelings, Nick's speech is one of the play's most powerful and solemn. Those who can see as he does are, accordingly, rewarded. Those who don't are treated melodramatically, though they are given far less power than the villain who holds the deed. The dogooders and to a lesser extent Ursula and Vanessa are placed in this category. While the logic of the play insists that audiences laugh at them, the cartoonish, reductive aspects of their treatment may seem to many at odds with the generosity Davies showers upon the side he favors.

King Phoenix: On Being a Merry Old Soul

Even before Davies began *Fortune, My Foe,* he was at work on another play set in England, written expressly for the capacities of professional London theater. Like his first play, *King Phoenix* was written with John Gielgud in mind; however, neither Gielgud nor Ralph Richardson was willing to take it on. Accordingly, though completed in 1947, it waited until 1950 for its first performance, an amateur production by the North Toronto Theatre Guild under the direction of Toronto drama critic Herbert Whittaker. Its only other production was directed by Davies himself in January 1953 when the Peterborough Little Theatre entered it in the Eastern Regional Drama Festival. While *King Phoenix* won the Kingston Cup for the best Canadian play, the adjudicator confessed to puzzlement about the play's quality; it contained "passages of memorable brilliance," he noted, "made useless . . . by passages of memorable banality."[23] Still strongly attracted to the play's theme, Davies now admits that "It doesn't really work on stage."[24]

In contrast to *Fortune, My Foe, King Phoenix* is an archetypal play, much in the spirit of *The King Who Could Not Dream.* Both draw on distant English history, thus allowing Davies to take aristocracy—or, more importantly, aristocracy of the spirit—as a given, and to use historical detail for his own purposes, his treatment characteristically stressing mythic aspects. When Davies came across brief mention of King Cole in Geoffrey of Monmouth's *The History of the Kings of Britain,* he was inspired to account for and give substance to Cole's legendary merriness. He found his direction less in recorded detail than in what he had learned from *The Golden Bough* about the collective nature of myth and the Druid ritual of vernal sacrifice. To the subject he brought his own commitment to the idea of self-awareness and psychic wholeness, the pursuit of which he regards as the key to spiritual greatness in mankind. It is the goal to which Ethelred finally dedicated himself. Nick Hayward also implies his deep interest in the idea when he complains about being "Despised [in Canada] because I want things from life which nobody else seems to miss" (F, 90). One could argue, in fact, that a richer selfhood is the real concern of both would-be artists, Hayward and Rowlands, of *Fortune, My Foe.*

Sometimes regarded as a transitional figure in England's relations with Rome and usually associated with the negotiation of peace with the Romans, King Cole (Coel) had, according to Geoffrey of Monmouth, a beautiful and intelligent daughter, Helena, who after his sudden death, took the throne and married the Roman envoy Constantius. Davies dropped the Roman connection, shifting Cole's life back to the era of the last of Albion's giants, Gogmagog. Cole, the father of Albion's Golden Age, is set in opposition to the powerful Archdruid Cadno (fox) who stands, implausibly, both for religious tyranny and the idea of scientific change.

Set on the eve of the Druidian festival of spring, *King Phoenix* is melodramatically plotted. It turns on Cadno's ambition to kill the king and implement his new worldview. In act 1 we learn of his efforts to poison Cole and witness his attempt to convince the idealistic Leolin, a Druidian acolyte and Helena's suitor, to do away with the king. Foiled in both efforts, Cadno ruthlessly announces at the evening banquet that the god Mabon has demanded Leolin as a "special sacrifice."[25]

Initially, King Cole is easily Cadno's match. He does not overvalue religious observance, believing there is more value in hearty enjoyment than ceremony. He and Helena share a greatness of spirit that sets them apart from the others, including the honorable but rather stiff Leolin. In act 2, however, Cole's jolly ego and fearlessness before death are unsettled by a sudden sharp recognition of his own mortality. Here, the play's mood darkens. In the sacred oak grove, as an inadvertent result of Cadno's magic, Cole meets Albion's legendary Gogmagog, who, years before, had been tricked and killed by Cadno himself. Gogmagog's fairy-tale-like story chills Cole. In the giant's fall from power he sees his own inevitable death. He is, however, too spirited to shamble as Gogmagog does. Though shaken, he banishes the ghost by asserting, "I am a man of great heart, and I shall prevail!" (K, 154).

Cole's superiority of feeling is further revealed in act 2, scene 2. His merriment, he tells his deaf shepherd, Lug, is not the laughter of the belly but of the heart. "It is more often silent than aloud; it may not bring a smile: it is a glory in the breast, a divine drunkenness, an o'ertopping of the gravity of tight-lipped men" (K, 168). Lug replies epigrammatically, juxtaposing Cole and Cadno:

"For the laughing man the skies stand still; only the dark and glowering man can push them on." The scene closes with a merry song celebrating the life force of John Barleycorn as opposed to the negativeness of Druidian sacrifice.

In act 3 with Leolin still the willing sacrificial victim, Helena succeeds in arousing him to passion and the call of life by biting his lip while they kiss. To bite is her father's advice, and the strategy works. It is at this point that King Cole prevails. Catching Cadno offguard he seizes the sacrificial victim's crown and climbs the Druid altar, thus transfixing his people's attention and taking Leolin's place. On the high altar he dances and seems to become one with the sun; even in death he smiles, fulfilling his desire to be remembered forever as "a merry man, whose death was his best joke" (K, 190). The play ends with Helena taking Cole's place, physically and spiritually, before the people. Together she and Leolin promise a strong check against the Archdruid's schemes. Helena is Cole's phoenix, and the fire from which she rises is the sun he worshipped and the love of life he practiced.

The weaknesses of *King Phoenix* are many. So relentless is its melodramatic scheme that the characters and the values they represent have a tedious predictability. While Davies includes several magical effects and spectacular settings, the play's scenes lack dramatic movement and energy. They do, however, provide ample occasion for declaiming and posturing. As a result, the play seems topheavy in didactic pronouncements. In allowing King Cole to define himself, Davies cannot resist scattered indictments of business ethics, organized religion, mere busyness, change for change's sake, moralistic excesses, and the scientific ideal. That these denunciations are given such didactic prominence is as much a weakness (in terms of dramatic action) as it is a characteristic of Davies's playwriting. That he should draw science into the play through his Archdruid villain reveals yet another characteristic of his work. As improbable as this particular conjunction is, science and official religion are for Davies tyrannies that alike threaten the individual's capacity for feeling and living. As such, he can't seem to resist their wedding.

The importance of *King Phoenix* lies in its forthright declaration of healthy selfhood. Aligning himself closely to Cole, Davies presents him as an ideal of emotional greatness and psychological wholeness. He is the godlike, complete man, alive to the mysteries and wonders of life. He values the natural world, lives heartily into old age, is never busy, deplores halfway measures, and scorns mixed motives. His world is a kind of Eden that Cadno, "the dark and glowering man," will inevitably infect. Cole, however, remains above it all, interested in inner realities rather than outer forms. Years before Davies began to take an interest in Carl Jung's writing, he created in King Cole an image of the individuated being he most admired. To read *King Phoenix* today is, thus, to see in outline a pattern for the more complex expressions of individuation Davies would later celebrate and to consider Davies's first sustained attempt (excepting *The King Who Could Not Dream*) to work with mythology and archetypal pattern.

Chapter Four

The Theater As Temple: Robertson Davies's Later Plays

At My Heart's Core (1950): The Devil in Canada

Robertson Davies's four plays of the 1950s constitute his most sustained achievement as a playwright. *At My Heart's Core, A Jig for the Gypsy, Hunting Stuart,* and *General Confession* are comedies that link romantic and historical or realistic elements. They share the aim of lifting the audience out of the ordinary milieu into an atmosphere of romance where, as Judith Skelton Grant observes, "art, magic, imagination, and love triumph."[1] Taken together with *Question Time,* Davies's major play of the 1970s (which has numerous affinities to *General Confession*), they show Davies at the top of his playwrighting form—confident, witty, often ingenious; melodramatic and eager to link spectacle and joy or spectacle and insight at climactic moments; didactic and moralistic; and attentive, above all, to the glories of selfhood and man's indomitable spirit.

The first of these plays, *At My Heart's Core,* was written for the celebration of the city of Peterborough's centennial. It is not, however, a self-congratulatory pageant play. Drawing upon the lives of three well-known pioneering women who settled in the Peterborough-Lakefield area in the 1820s and 1830s, Davies chose to dramatize the inner regrets—the pain at the heart's core—endured by these British gentlewomen who emigrated with their husbands to the lonely Canadian backwoods. In giving prominence to Frances Stewart over the more famous literary pioneers, Susanna Moodie and Catharine Parr Traill, Davies no doubt delighted in ruffling local feathers. Historically, however, his chosen emphasis had special validity. While Traill's *The Backwoods of Canada* (1836) and Moodie's *Roughing It in the Bush* (1852) brought them recognition, it was Thomas Stewart who had received a large land grant to develop the

Peterborough area in the 1820s and who with his wife, Frances, made the greater contribution to settlement in the vicinity.

To gather material, Davies read widely in the printed records of early Peterborough and environs, studying the responses of British settlers who came to "the backwoods" north of Lake Ontario. *Roughing It in the Bush* and *The Backwoods of Canada* were important sources but so too was the lesser known collection of Frances Stewart's letters published under the title *Our Forest Home* in 1889. In a later epilogue to the play Davies termed Mrs. Stewart's letters "remarkable."[2] He took his title from a simple ballad, "My Hame," printed in the *Cobourg Star,* 27 December 1831, which laments the loss of the poet's native land.

> I canna ca' this forest home,
> And in it live and dee;
> Nor feel regret at my heart's core
> My native land, for thee.

The time of the play was carefully chosen. In the early winter of 1837 a radical journalist, William Lyon Mackenzie, led a loosely organized band of farmers and rebels against the government of Upper Canada and in particular against the politically dominant, class-conscious "Family Compact." With many other British gentlemen, Thomas Traill, Thomas Stewart, and Dunbar Moodie responded patriotically to the government's call for support and set off to help quell the rebellion at York (Toronto), "perfectly ignorant," as Mrs. Moodie would later note, "of the abuses that had led to the present position of things."[3] The rebellion was easily quashed before the Peterborough men could arrive. Still, it was an ominous time for the women, so far from anything but rumor and alone with their young families in the dreadful bush. In setting the play during Canada's only (and minor) rebellion, Davies gave *At My Heart's Core* both a national and a local significance, thus broadening its interest and appeal. As such a recent critic has analysed it as a national history play articulating basic English-Canadian attitudes toward political change.[4]

The play begins with the arrival of Moodie and Traill at Auburn, the Stewart's home. The first act is fast paced and comic. It turns on the presence at Mrs. Stewart's of a young backwoods girl, Honour Brady, who has that very night given birth to a daughter. In pursuit of Honour comes her foster father and would-be husband, the boisterous, drunken Phelim Brady, a local Irish ne'er-do-well. Disgusted that the child is a girl, Brady still wants to take Honour home; however, Mrs. Stewart blocks his attempt, horrified by the impropriety of their relations and the fact that the corpse of Brady's wife lies on his shanty roof, "friz as stiff as a cedar log,"[5] unburied because of the frozen ground and the hesitancy of a fastidious Catholic priest. For her part Honour has sought refuge at Auburn rather than have her baby under such circumstances.

With the arrival of Edmund Cantwell, a "handsome man, in the Byronic-Satanic fashion of the period" (A, 25-26), the serious action begins. Identified in *Our Forest Home* only as a neighbour who is an endless mystery, Cantwell is a cultivated Englishman who has chosen not to fight in the rebellion and is preparing to give up on Canada. He offers to protect the women from the unruly Brady. As act 1 draws to a close Cantwell genially introduces the idea of temptation to the three ladies only to receive assurances from the tough-minded Mrs. Moodie that *he* certainly can't tempt them and from the rather feckless Mrs. Traill that in the backwoods there is "a complete absence of temptation" (A, 35).

Act 2 has a darker cast. After dinner Cantwell takes each of the three women aside to probe her particular "heartsore" and vulnerable point. To Mrs. Stewart, he reveals that during a visit to Ireland, he discovered that Lord Rossmore, who had once been in love with her, still treasures her memory. Finding Mrs. Traill alone, he tells her of a Mr. Sheppard in Quebec who wished to collaborate with her on a study of Canadian flora and who regarded her as a genius capable of doing "for her part of Upper Canada what Gilbert White did for Selborne" (A, 48). Moreover, he chastizes her for wasting her talents and playing "second fiddle" to her second-rate husband. Finally, he bullies Mrs. Moodie into a reawakening of her suppressed dream of literary recognition in England. Claiming friendship with Byron and Maria Edgeworth, Cantwell suggests that her writing talents might blossom under more favorable circumstances, then browbeats her by arguing that it is her "sacred obligation" (A, 57) as an artist to hone her talents. When Thomas Stewart arrives home, he finds a curious situation indeed: the arrogant Cantwell is happily at odds with the three women while the drunken Brady remains outside in the cold, functioning as a loud, irreverent chorus.

Act 3 returns to the high spirits of act 1. It takes the form of an unofficial trial. An amusing conversationalist, Stewart recounts his trip to York and his views of the rebellion, adding that the most disturbing news he heard there was the death of the famous English comedian, Joe Grimaldi. With Cantwell and Phelim, he indulges in one of Grimaldi's best-known songs, a boisterous ditty that mocks genteel standards while reinforcing the theme of temptation.

With the serious business of Cantwell's "trial," however, Stewart makes little headway. Feeling both unsettled and foolish, none of the women will press charges. Cantwell himself is not long in challenging Stewart's authority and in providing the women with his motives. He accuses them of snobbery, lack of charity, and lack of humility, adding that if they had not snubbed his wife or remained so insensitively devoted to the "tight, snug, unapproachable little society" (A, 83) of Upper Canada, he might have been less vindictive. When he takes his leave he is confident that, by means of "the temptation of discontent," he has robbed all three of their "peace of mind" (A, 84).

Despite its serious theme, *At My Heart's Core* is best remembered for its comic elements. The bardic excesses of Phelim Brady and the humorous stereotyping of Moodie and Traill are the marks of an author who strives to entertain. By contrast, Davies has difficulty in making the sources of temptation—his earnest matter—convincing on more than a verbal level. Mrs. Stewart's "victory" over temptation is not a great one. It involves only the recognition that her feeling for Lord Rossmore was "not regret, but discontentment, disguised as regret" (A, 91). Traill and Moodie are more deeply affected, but even in their cases the serious side of things fails to take convincing hold. At first they seem such comic figures, a sort of backwoods Laurel and Hardy in their bickering and their tug-of-war over Honour's baby, that the pain they later experience and the dignity they subsequently muster seem somewhat incongruous. Mrs. Traill shifts from vacuousness to wisdom, Mrs. Moodie from grenadier shrillness to self-honesty.

At My Heart's Core is a woman's play: on the one hand, a glimpse of the hardship and frustration endured by three talented gentlewomen, and, on the other, an answer to B. K. Sandwell's complaint that in *Fortune, My Foe* Davies had created "three of the most objectionable female characters in Canadian imaginative writing."[6] Curiously, however, with the possible exception of Mrs. Stewart, it is the men of the play who are more interesting.

As an elegant backwoods devil figure, Cantwell embodies his name. On the realistic level he is simply the Stewarts' embittered neighbor, eager to avenge their snobbery. On a deeper level—Davies notes in his preface that Cantwell introduces "a judicious dash of exaggeration" into the ordinary (A, vii)—he is an agent of pure malice. His verbal magic is dark and cruel, its aim to inflict a "lasting and serious injury" (A, 84) of a psychological kind.

Cantwell's opposite is Phelim Brady, a low-life, anti-establishment rascal in the mold of Pop in *Overlaid*. Drawn from the stage Irishman, Phelim is not only a source of low comedy, he is also cast as displaced bard, an old-country folk poet whose talents are unappreciated in Canada. Thus, he is literally kept out in the cold, functioning as a choric commentator on Auburn's high-toned events. Cantwell, in fact, credits him with having "the best pair of eyes in these parts" (A, 85). That his name can be pronounced *Failim* or *Feelim* further emphasizes his dual role in the play. A failure from the genteel point of view, he embodies a primitive, unrefined depth of feeling that Davies values very highly as long as it does not threaten rightful order.

Trials of various kinds play a significant part in Davies's writing, notably in *Leaven of Malice* and *The Manticore*. In virtually all his theater and fiction, the values and aspirations of particular characters are put to the test. Pop's dream in *Overlaid,* Dunstan Ramsay's career in *Fifth Business,* and Nick Hayward's academic project in *Fortune, My Foe* are examples. Trials, however, necessitate judges and in *At My Heart's Core* that judge is Stewart, a member of Upper Canada's Legislative Council. Before his court are the problems of Cantwell's temptations and of Phelim's child; the rebellion is rendered inconsequential by contrast.

The operations of Judge Stewart's court are wise and sensible. Though he shows a distinct conventionality in his views, his lightheartedness masks a depth of understanding that keeps him, if not in full control, at least on guard against overreaction and folly. No attitude, the play implies, could be better suited for dealing with the devil. Thus, though he is no match for Cantwell in subtlety, he recognizes that the subject of temptation is "unanswerable" in his court (A, 80). In Phelim's case, by decisive action and direction, Stewart quickly resolves the dilemma in an appropriate manner. The last scene presents a man confident that he "understand[s] women wonderfully well" (A, 88). Concerning his wife's brief temptation, he asks rhetorically, "Is there a man anywhere who is capable of filling the whole of a woman's heart forever?" (A, 90). Such insight, shared with Frances, is the source of their enduring marriage and "victory." Stewart may be guilty of certain blindnesses as when he tells Phelim, "We don't have the Devil in the nineteenth century, and we certainly don't have him in this country" (A, 84), but he has the inner mirth (his affection for Grimaldi) and wisdom to meet the devil effectively even when he is unable to recognize him.

A Jig for the Gypsy (1954): Aristocracy of Soul

Perhaps the most striking feature of Davies's plays is his passionate commitment to his protagonists. In *Stage Voices,* he comments, "I write about a single, dominating character, whose problem shapes the play, and who is surrounded by people who in some way throw light on him and his predicament."[7] What Davies does not say here is even more important; he favors that single, dominating character, identifies closely with him (whatever his venial sins), and conspicuously arranges the secondary characters so as to throw a positive light upon him and his predicament. In plays like *Fortune, My Foe* and *At My Heart's Core* and in novels like *Tempest-Tost* and *Leaven of Malice* that focus is masked by Davies's caution in spreading the narrative focus amongst several characters. Generally, however, he insists upon "a fairly simple and direct line of action"[8] and a conflict of values that, regardless of its intellectual amplification, is essentially melodramatic. The "good guys" either side instinctively with or learn to see the value of the protagonist's view of life. The "bad guys" either can't see that value or by choice refuse to support it. With values so clearly ascribed, too often in their insensitivity or blindness the "bad guys" have the effect of seeming mere straw men to the fine figure in the spotlight. In short, Davies typically dispenses his favors and brickbats with pronounced inequity and deliberateness, despite the complexity of the issues involved. As a result, his best plays are likely to be unabashed, romantic melodramas in which the good and bad sides are both clearly defined yet irrevocably antagonistic. With its sharp distinction between the world of politics and of magic, both as ways of living and modes of perception, *A Jig for the Gypsy* is just such a play.

Perhaps as a result of its long evolution, *A Jig for the Gypsy* was Davies's most accomplished play to date. He had begun it during his student days in 1938. While visiting his father's home in North Wales, a curiosity entitled *Zadkiel's Dream Book* had stimulated his interest in the folklore of magic and dreams and led him to conceive a play based upon "the popular Welsh romance called *The Maid of Cefn Ydfa*."[9] He did not write the first version, which was entitled "Benoni," until 1945. On Tyrone Guthrie's advice he sent the manuscript to Sybil Thorndike who turned it down. It made further rounds without success until in 1954 the Davises, Donald, Murray, and Barbara (Chilcott)—who were of Welsh and gypsy blood themselves—chose it for the Crest Theatre's first season in Toronto. It was presented that September under Herbert Whittaker's "strong and sensitive" direction (J, vii).

Another history play, *A Jig for the Gypsy* is set near Caerhowell, Wales, in 1885. All three acts take place in Benoni Richards's dwelling and concern the far-ranging effects of her involvement in a tea-leaves' prediction of the outcome of a local parliamentary election. The Liberals (Radicals) who have not won in seventy years ask Benoni to tell the fortune of their new candidate, an opportunistic Manchester businessman, Sir John Jebson. She complies, mostly out of fellow feeling for one organizer, Richard Roberts, who respects her abilities and well knows the power of superstition among the rural Welsh. Act 1 dramatizes her actual predictions, which are more vague and tinged with ominousness than the excited Liberals realize, and their immediate effects on the political contingent and local populace.

Act 2 deepens the effects of fortune-telling by means of a series of visits to Benoni's cottage. A local photographer, the Anglican curate, Roberts and his daughter Bronwen, Jenson's aide Edward Vaughan, and a disgruntled Tory delegation all show the unsettling effects of magic's intervention into the realm of politics. In particular, Davies emphasizes the manipulative, self-interested involvement of the Church of England and the aristocracy, as well as the mean spiritedness and cruelty of those adversely affected by the predictions. The Tory delegation, led by the pretentious "Backstair's Earl," Jesse Fewtrell, goes so far as to threaten Benoni with ejection from her rightful property unless she signs a public recantation.

Early in act 3 with the news of the Liberals' remarkable victory, Benoni's fate seems dark indeed. Harassed by vindictive Tories, abandoned by all of the ungrateful Liberals except Roberts, yet too proud and too much a gypsy to confront such unfairness by recourse to the law, she is alone when another local character, Conjuror Jones, suddenly appears. Preceded by thunder and lightning, he proclaims himself Benoni's "fate," identifying himself with the words, "I be life, to speak rightly" (J, 87). Jones is a puckish deus ex machina, bringing the darkness of the play round to a sprightly, unconventional, and joyous finale. Himself a victim of Fewtrell's manipulations, he comes proposing marriage and partnership, both as a practical strategy whereby the two can continue to live in their cherished locale and because "Magic must close its ranks or vanish" in such "bad old days" (J, 93). After some resistance on Benoni's part—"I'd sooner sleep with the goats!" (J, 93), she tells him—she is won over by Jones's joie de vivre, persuasion, and wit. When he reworks a homily she had herself used earlier—"do you think there's no more to marriage than four bare legs in a blanket?" (J, 94)—she recognizes a kindred spirit and the pact is sealed. With her old friend Jack the Skinner as witness, Benoni and Jones marry gypsy-style "over the broom"; the three then drink to the wedding and dance a merry jig amidst lightning and thunder.

It was not until *A Jig for the Gypsy* that Robertson Davies created in a three-act play a convincing conflict between, and effective balancing of, the two worlds and views that constitute the characteristic melodrama of his theater. Like *King Phoenix*, *A Jig for the Gypsy* is excessive in its polarizing of values and use of character types. Like the earlier plays, it also contains a good deal of satire, some of which is hackneyed and formulaic. Such is the case, for example, in the treatment of the relationship between the politically ambitious Edward Vaughan and Bronwen Roberts, a treatment that shows little improvement on the love interest in *King Phoenix*. Like Stephen Leacock and Mark Twain, in his early writing Davies often seems constrained by convention when depicting the relations of young lovers.

But while *A Jig for the Gypsy* has its predictable elements, what makes it powerful is that, on the level of action and image, it provides substantial opposition—the factor of real force in the ordinary world—to make Benoni Richards's fate dramatic. *A Jig for the Gypsy* never loses sight of these forces and Benoni herself, for all her self-certainty and understanding, draws out the audience's empathy precisely because of her vulnerability.

In his preface to the play Davies wrote, "Romance and politics, which many people appear to find mutually exclusive, appear to me to fit together very well, and indeed to be inseparable. The ambitions and actions of politicians, if one does not stand too near to them, are powerfully romantic, especially if they belong to a reform party with strong convictions about the perfectability of mankind through political action" (J, vi). But though Davies could claim in his ancestry a great-grandfather who was the first Radical Nonconformist elected mayor of a Welsh borough, his skepticism about political idealism is one of the play's most persistent elements.

Among the Tory interests there is little place for idealism, Tory strength relying on the old, practical conspiracy of established Church and social system. It is in characterizing the Liberal figures that Davies develops the theme. Edward Vaughan who has been nurtured on Ruskin's sentimental views of the working class is Davies's primary target. An idealist who masks his personal ambitions from himself in a glow of goodness, Vaughan is a failure because he lacks both self-knowledge and sufficient contact with reality or nature. Thus, he quickly proves an inadequate mate for Bronwen who, like Jessie McLaren, is foolish enough not to see on her own her lover's deficiencies. Not surprisingly, the man Vaughan admires, Sir John Jebson, is an egotist. The fool of ambition and success, Jebson is an early prototype of *Fifth Business*'s Boy Staunton. Willing to try anything to be elected, he turns on his aides when the very strategy that facilitates his victory blocks his desire to be a member of Gladstone's cabinet.

Of the Liberals only Richard Roberts is presented in a positive light. A genuine lover of Wales and a man without materialistic ambition, he gains nothing from the victory but the satisfaction of unseating the Tories. Late in act 3 it is not surprising that he should voice one of the play's major insights, a rephrasing of a theme that ranges from *At the Gates of the Righteous* to *Rebel Angels*—genuine revolution and change must begin within man, not without: "We're too much concerned nowadays with helping other people: we don't do enough to help ourselves. If a man wants to be the greatest possible value to his fellow-creatures let him begin the long, solitary task of perfecting himself" (J, 85).

It is not, therefore, the romance of reform—that is clearly a far more complex subject than Davies makes it appear—but romance of a different sort that compels Davies's moral attention in *A Jig for the Gypsy*. It is the romance of personal development, merriment, wise living, and magic. It is the glow of "Merry Old Wales" in contrast to the "Dry Old Wales" of politics that is, according to Jack the Skinner, as dry now as the whole world (J, 96). *A Jig for the Gypsy* dramatizes Davies's commitment to this outlook, a view at odds with the catchpenny realities, worldliness, and sentimentalisms of modern life. Benoni Richards embodies it. She lives close to the earth, glories in her independence, believes in magic, and has no truck with the safe pieties of Victorian society or the holier-than-thou rhetoric of conventional religion. Yet, she is not unreligious. As she tells the Anglican curate, religion is a kind of witchcraft itself: "We're two eggs from the same nest, sir, though you may not like to think so" (J, 42).

To the dry, new world of urban planning and politics, magic is "flummery" or "mumbo-jumbo." The moderns are husks, men "besotted with sobriety" (J, 94). They hide selfishness and self-interest behind cloaks of idealism and cant. Benoni's heroic world is characterized by metaphors of wetness. She is closely linked to Jack the Skinner, like Phelim Brady another of Davies's flamboyant, hard-drinking, antiestablishment bards. For Jack, liquor is a source of "divine afflatulence" (J, 29). With Benoni he delights in the irony of singing temperance songs. Benoni herself is regularly linked to goat's milk, tea ("the very blood of Wales" [J, 13]), rum, and rain. Nowhere is this more evident than in the final scene when Benoni, Jack, and Jones dance in the rain, toasting an event Jack compares to "a wedding o' the ancient gods" (J, 95).

Benoni's threatened world is also associated with insight and vision. Gypsy eyes see differently than ordinary eyes, she asserts (J, 24). Looking deeply into what Dunstan Ramsay calls the "strange world that showed very little of itself on the surface,"[10] she detects the tyranny of conventional values, the hollowness of political rhetoric, the genteel flimflam of the Anglican Church, and the foolishness of certain accepted ideas of marriage. She sees more deeply into people than others can; she predicts Jebson's future more accurately than he realizes and locates in Bronwen Roberts an untapped "aristocracy of soul" (J, 77). Indeed, "aristocracy of soul" might well be the play's real subject—it is what Benoni, Jack, Conjuror Jones, Roberts, and his daughter share. To the Conjuror's statement that "The world shouldn't be a tight-laced corset on a man!" Benoni replies, "every man makes his own cloak and his own world" (J, 96).

Though the special value Davies attributes to magic and gypsies finds its first extended expression in *A Jig for the Gypsy,* it is clear that magic per se is not sufficient to counteract the dry, new world. The play's happy ending is, as in *At My Heart's Core,* a function of good sense in operation. If, then, good sense is a kind of psychological magic, for Davies magic becomes a richly connotative word. It suggests among other things intuition, emotion, independence, and a poetic view of experience. It is, in short, the play's sustaining metaphor for a deeper self-awareness than is possible among those who live by reason and on the surface of events. *A Jig for the Gypsy* is Davies's first play to celebrate this outlook with a dramatic effectiveness to match its melodramatic clarity.

Hunting Stuart: The Malaise of the Ordinary

Magical transformation is the theatrical business of *Hunting Stuart* (1955). Depending on "deft comedy acting" and "an atmosphere of romance," it attempts to make credible certain notions about "the romance of heredity" that intrigued Davies.[11] The play does not, however, effectively reconcile its absurd and extravagant plot with the dull, middle-class situation out of which it springs. Davies's venturesomeness and panache notwithstanding, *Hunting Stuart* totters on its romantic premises, unbalanced by the melodramatic techniques that serve those premises.

The play insists that within certain individuals, who need not *appear* exceptional, there is an inner vitality and potential greatness that is obscured by various self-accepted forms of imprisonment. To know this is to have the scales removed from one's eyes. As one character declares, it is to perceive the world anew: "I always knew there was a lot behind everybody, if we could just get at it. And here we are, see? All of a sudden life stops being gray and messy, and gets bright-coloured and exciting" (H, 81).

To give life a "bright-coloured and exciting" essence is, of course, one of Davies's primary goals. In *Hunting Stuart* various characters are forced to awaken not so much to the fact of heredity but to life's romance. The play may be the first to reflect Davies's awakening to the ideas and language of Carl Jung. As one character states, "every man carries his posterity with him" (H, 44), adding that "not only a racial memory but an ancestral memory resides deep in the consciousness of every one of us" (H, 45). The notion of ancestral memory—what Jung calls "the personal unconsciousness"—is Davies's focus here, and to make the point he devised a curious contrivance, an anesthetic snuff that functions like a time machine, taking the patient or "Guinea Pig" backward in time in proportion to the dosage he sniffs. The result, we are told, is a striking transformation of character, the individual becoming for a brief period one of his own ancestors who treats those about him as if they belonged to that earlier era and situation.

First performed in 1955, the play provided strong roles for Donald Davis as Henry Benedict Stuart, Helene Winston as Stuart's eccentric Aunt Clemmie, and Barbara Chilcott as the cosmopolitan ethnopsychologist, Dr. Maria Sobieska. Stuart is a minor civil servant whose life is radically changed by the revelation that he is, in fact and spirit, "the oldest living direct male descendant of the Royal House of Stuart" (H, 38). The play's three acts are continuous. They take place in the Stuart's fussy apartment, located on the top floor of an old Ottawa house. According to Davies's directions, the set must be designed so that, by means of a change in lighting, it will undergo transformation from "cheap decorations" to "good old quality" and from ladies' magazine littleness to nobility, in order to abet the play's concentration upon the significant change in Stuart himself.

Act 1 is comprised of a series of family confrontations. It begins with an argument between Stuart's wife, Lilian, and his aunt Clemmie. Cast as a worrier devoted to middle-class rituals and proper appearances, Lilian is family-proud, though her pioneer background lacks distinction. By contrast, Clemmie is a vivacious, zany woman whose unpredictable behavior appalls Lilian and her daughter Carol. Because Clemmie has recently posed in laxative advertisements as the Flush-of-Youth lady, Lilian is outraged. Her angry words lead to a tussle with Clemmie just as Stuart returns home. A handsome, good-humored man, he announces his new appointment as "Number One C.I.P."; that is, head of a new bureaucratic department, Correspondence in Pendency. When Carol's boyfriend, Fred Lewis, a "green," would-be psychologist, arrives, Davies has the ingredients for a wide-ranging satire of middle-class values: false ancestral pride, fashion-magazine values, psychological jargon, panaceas, genteel uneasiness about laxatives, bureaucratic waste, and academic dogmatism are among his targets. It is only with the sudden appearance of a New York husband-and-wife team, Drs. Homer Shrubsole and Maria Sobieska, that the action gains direction, and the earlier allusions to family background and theories of heredity become pertinent. With Shrubsole as spokesman, the doctors inform Stuart of his extraordinary ancestry, the curtain falling as Sobieska curtsies dramatically to her majesty.

The second act belongs to the doctors just as, in *At My Heart's Core,* the middle act is dominated by the intruder Cantwell. After explaining the nature of their research, they undertake to prove to the doubtful—Fred especially—that ancestral memory is a major, though often overlooked, factor in personality and behavior. Enter the magic snuff. Using Fred as initial example, they take him back to 1855 where he becomes a tent-show con man practising phrenology—"this supreme psychological system" (H, 50)—upon the awestruck rubes. He also reveals a lustfulness and hypocrisy in his demonstrations that make Carol shudder for her future. With Fred reawakened and somewhat chastened, Stuart, upon Lilian's urging, allows himself to be anesthetized; he awakens as his famous eighteenth-century ancestor, "a confident, aristocratic, charming, wilful and utterly selfish man" (H, 57). Treating his wife like his servile mistress, swearing eloquently, and drinking to excess, he assumes control of the room and ends the act by commanding Dr. Sobieska to attend to his desires in his bedroom.

In Act 3 Davies provides various opportunities for Stuart to justify his superior racial roots. While Stuart shines, Lilian, the proud descendant of the United Empire Loyalists, becomes progressively depressed and the New York doctors—in fact, they are more magicians than doctors—become increasingly eager to carry Stuart off for prolonged research at their New York institute. Undaunted by Dr. Sobieska's resistance to his amorous demands, Stuart continues to dominate the room, be it in conversation, drinking, dancing, or cooking an omelet. His final act is to administer "the Royal Touch," by which he cures Clemmie's gnarled hand and proves, in words that echo Benoni Richards's, that "kingship is not a matter of the crown, but of the spirit" (H, 96). As he enacts this extraordinary expression of his ancestral inheritance, the old house is transformed by congenial candlelight to reveal its previously hidden nobility. The play ends on a romantic and promising note. Reawakened to his Ottawa self, but alert now to his inner nature, Stuart rejects his wife's summons to return to domestic duties and his daughter's desire "to be just ordinary" (H, 100). Instead, he books a flight to Scotland telling the clerk he is involved in urgent "Government business" on "the highest level" (H, 101).

Taken simply in the spirit Davies suggests—that is, as "romance" and pure theater—*Hunting Stuart* was an unusual play for conservative Toronto audiences in 1955. To the serious theme of ancestral inheritance he brought his customary air of intellectual and aesthetic assurance, his lively satiric bent, and some adventurous touches of sexuality. The play gave its audience much to ponder upon and to laugh about, both in inviting identification with Stuart, the likeable "ordinary" man of unsuspected greatness, and in pointing out the ways that bourgeois values repress a full expression of self.

Hunting Stuart is not, however, a play carefully enough devised to withstand an examination of the ideas upon which it is based. The notion of the personal unconscious, which Davies would develop to greater effect in the ancestry that Boy Staunton unexpectedly discovers, is here too simplistically, rhetorically, and glibly presented. The gimmick of the snuff (the age of Freud and Huxley demanding other than time machines) and the device of reawakening the spirit of a single ancestor to reveal the essence of Fred and Stuart, are not sufficient to make a convincing case. The personal unconscious must surely have its collective dimension as well and can scarcely be defined by pressing a metaphorical button marked simply 1855. Given such flummery—the kind of thing Davies often condemns on other fronts as "higher hokem"—the play depends tremendously on the rhetorical and theatrical wand waved by the intellectually superior doctors. Indeed, the authority vested in them is excessive, though by way of balancing Davies does inject satiric thrusts at certain of their personal traits and at scientific pretentions and methodology. Combining the influence of biology, ethnopsychology, and cosmopolitan experience, they present themselves unabashedly as "two highly-respected people in the world of science" (H, 47) whose wisdom leads them to take seriously the nature of mysterious powers.

Davies clearly enjoyed identifying himself with the learned doctors. They not only voice many of his views, but they throw their weight around in ways that leave no doubt about the third-class status of Fred as thinker or of Lilian as wife and woman. Dr. Sobieska, for instance, denounces her as a woman "with the hectoring, possessive, self-assertive airs of a North American *bourgeoise*" (H, 91). So great is their superiority that the audience may mistrust it, reacting against the way in which Lilian is made to bear the weight of what is, after all, an insensitive intrusion into *her* home and peace of mind, as well as Stuart's. Here again, as in so many of his plays, Davies discriminates against certain lesser characters, using them as unredeemed objects of satire, straw men to the values he advocates without giving serious consideration to their humanity. The feeling he breathed into Ethel in *Overlaid* is lacking in his presentation of the pathetic Lilian. Indeed, the entire ordinary world is so undercut by his satiric strokes that, late in act 1, it is difficult to take anyone on stage very seriously.

But if Lilian sinks in *Hunting Stuart,* it is because Stuart must rise. The play celebrates willful, unrestrained egoism as the greatness of spirit that is hidden in some men. Stuart is in this sense never ordinary; he has only needed to shed his complacency in order to see the full color of the world. To his conservative daughter he declares, "in spite of environment and heredity and all that, I suppose what one is always remains very much a matter of choice. If you really want to be ordinary, I don't suppose anything can stop you" (H, 100). In opting to be extraordinary, Stuart rejects the outward world and its forms of imprisonment. His gesture at the play's conclusion is a declaration, albeit an unconvincing one, of heroic, independent selfhood.

Having studied Ben Stuart's two sides—the contented mouse and the passionate lion—Davies faced the problem he created in *The King Who Could Not Dream.* Quo vadis? It was not one for which he had an effective solution. The climactic phone call tells us little. It is not clear whether his wife has any place in his extraordinariness or whether Scotland has anything to offer him. If he is to reject Lilian, we must remember Dunstan Ramsay's caution to Boy Staunton that you reject those closest to you at your peril. The ending is, thus, though flamboyant, a disappointment. Like the romance of heredity, it has too much of mere gimmickry about it. The final spectacle of dance, song, and swashbuckle fail to counter the play's essential weaknesses.

General Confession (1956): Shaping "The Obstinate Granite of Experience"

Early in 1956, Robertson and Brenda Davies hosted a dinner in Toronto for the visiting J. B. Priestley. Other guests included the Davises of the Crest Theatre. Struck by their remarkable family resemblance, Priestley wrote *The Glass Cage,* his only play to use a Canadian setting, specifically for them. So appreciative were the Davises that they chose it for their 1956-57 season, turning down

Davies's *General Confession,* which also had been written with the three actors in mind. Davies's disappointment—one might even say his sense of betrayal—was still apparent fifteen years later:

> I did . . . write *General Confession* for the Davises. Donald Davis wanted to act a romantic lover before he was too old for the role and asked me to write a play for the Crest Theatre. Michael Langham wanted to direct the play and it was actually in the works. But J. B. Priestley visited Canada, fell in love with the Davises, and wrote them *The Glass Cage,* which they produced instead. It was a flop. But *General Confession* is my best play and my favorite; in it is my attempt to explain what an artist is. It has never been produced.[12]

It is difficult to disagree with Davies's high estimate of *General Confession.* Like *Question Time,* it experiments interestingly with Jungian ideas, though its subject matter is historical and non-Canadian. Focussing precisely on the loves and the "philosophy" of Casanova, *General Confession* is less given over to scatter-gun satire and is more surely handled than the later play. At the same time, as in *King Phoenix,* Davies is exuberantly supportive of his protagonist. Casanova he has called "one of my favourite characters in history"; he was "a high-hearted" philosopher whose *Memoirs* reveal an individual who "knew precisely what he was doing and watched himself with a gently amused eye." [13]

General Confession is a cleverly constructed play. An old-fashioned costume piece that features plays within the play (charades) and "calls for acting in the classic-romantic style,"[14] it makes a virtue of artifice. The time is 1797 and the setting Count Waldstein's splendid eighteenth-century library where Casanova is living out his retirement as librarian. Moonlight partially illuminates a cabinet comprised of three panels of forbidden books, a cabinet reputed by the Count to be haunted.

The play begins with Casanova overhearing the impassioned wooing of Countess Amalie, Waldstein's daughter, by a young Napoleonic officer, Hugo de Grimes. He is about to leave her in frustration when Casanova emerges from the shadows. Recognizing Casanova's name, Hugo moralistically accuses him of being "a notorious amorist—a wholesale seducer" (G, 205). The aristocratic officer is thus caught in the position Davies typically ascribes to young men. Insensitive to irony, he is pigheaded, proud, and humorless before an older, wiser, and more complex individual.

Roused by Hugo's hostility and encouraged by Amalie's interest, Casanova offers to recount his life. "Every man," he remarks, "wants to tell his story" (G, 208). He has in fact been struggling to write his *Memoirs,* trying to impose some order on what he calls "A long story with little form and no moral" (G, 208). Using his magical powers, he raises spirits from the three forbidden panels: Voltaire emerges from "the cynical, un-Christian philosophers," the Ideal Beloved from "the erotic books, the tales of love," and the menacing Cagliostro from the panel of "the magicians, the alchemists, the men who sinned against the light" (G, 210). Casanova has known Voltaire and Cagliostro in life; indeed, it is clear from their first appearances that each has powerful connections to his inner life.

Act 2, is brilliantly magical. As Amalie says, it is "like being in those Arabian tales where animals suddenly speak" (G, 219). Rejuvenated by the presence of the spirits, Casanova appeals to Voltaire to help him to justify his life, to "help me to make myself understood!" (G, 220). Voltaire obliges by becoming stage manager of three "charades" that reveal aspects and stages of Casanova's search for his ideal in love. Each is colorful and exotic, and carries with it a nugget of truth—first, that "Except in trivial things, life has no rules" (G, 225) and second, that "Nothing is so delusive as the notion of freedom" (G, 235). The third, deeply humiliating charade does not resolve itself into an epigram. Rather it takes the third act to explicate it.

General Confession's final act is both thematically rich and dramatically heavy-handed. It turns upon the problem of justifying and evaluating Casanova's life. Various charges are rehearsed by Cagliostro, who functions as prosecutor. Casanova is accused at length of having indulged in the seven deadly sins, especially lechery. He makes his final defense as a conscious artist:

God will know that in all the makeshifts of my life I have loved some things truly, held some things sacred, and that I have striven to give some pattern of the muddle of experience which the moving years have brought me. Where I could, I put a shape on the obstinate granite of circumstance; when it was possible I gave some grace to the insubstantial and often shoddy stuff of my character. The result is no saint, nor yet a vulgar whimpering sinner, but an artist whose work was sometimes good and sometimes bad. God gave me life, and I have lived it, with the gifts and the blemishes he gave me, with as much . . . style, as I could. (G, 268)

Having attained such a perspective, Casanova is able to put his spirits to rest, thus resolving the action. He is last seen eating breakfast with gusto, a man at peace with himself, now ready to complete his *Memoirs*.

The final act also bears the large burden of unfolding the Jungian configurations built into the play. On one level a flamboyant, racy piece of historical melodrama, *General Confession* offers up a configuration of archetypal images: the Hero (Casanova), Wise Man (Voltaire), Heroine (Ideal Beloved), and Enemy or Villain (Cagliostro). On another it is a psychodrama that embodies the four archetypes of Casanova's psyche—the persona (Casanova prior to the play's "unique experience in self-recognition" [G, 247]); the self (Voltaire who is Casanova's "Magus" and "better judgement" [G, 246]); the anima (the Ideal Beloved in her many guises, notably as Sophia and Marina); and the shadow (Cagliostro who is Casanova's "Evil Genius" [G, 269] and "Contrary Destiny" [G, 247]).[15] Casanova's necromacy has called up spirits from the past who are also fundamental aspects of his personality. It is as if, in an image Davies uses more spectacularly in *Question Time,* a prism has refracted the light of personality into its component parts as a result of the pressure Casanova is undergoing in writing his memoirs (G, 260).

It is one of the anomalies of English-Canadian theater history that a play as interesting—both in itself and in relation to its author—should have remained unproduced for so long. Few of Davies's plays take us as close to the author's romantic outlook and aesthetic credo as does *General Confession*. In an atmosphere at once baroque, aristocratic, and melodramatic, Davies traffics effectively between the everyday world and the magical realm where the animals suddenly speak. Freed of the need to make cultural criticisms and national pronouncements, he presents a kind of human experience about which he can smack his lips. Casanova's *Memoirs* provided him with an egoism he could deeply admire, a high temperament that did not hesitate to avenge itself by duping a fool or by condemning "the stupid or the unworthy" (G, 262). In the larger moral realm of Jungian individuation upon which the play draws it matters little that Casanova is "a thoroughgoing crook" or, for that matter, a self-justifying sensualist who masks an ethic of quantity in aesthetic rhetoric. For Davies he is a hero, extraordinary for his bravery, daring, "unique cleverness," and "intellectual quality."[16] As an artist, Casanova bears important similarities to the central figures of *A Mixture of Frailties,* a novel written during the same period. He also looks ahead to Magnus Eisengrim and to the wisdom of Paracelsus in *The Rebel Angels*—"Be not another if thou canst be thyself."

Two Masques: The Masque as Morality Play

In its integration of the techniques of the masque, *General Confession* compares with Davies's two schoolboy entertainments, *A Masque of Aesop* (1952) and *A Masque of Mr. Punch* (1963).[17] The former uses three plays (Aesop's favorite fables) within the play as the storyteller's defense against charges brought against him by various of Delphi's citizenry. The judge is Apollo, the god of music, arts, and order. He finds in favor of Aesop the artist whose fables, he judges, will delight future children and provide wisdom for older people perceptive enough to grasp it. That wisdom is a gentle variation on what Casanova learns. Aesop's truth—that "peace of mind is an agreeable possession"[18]—is, for instance, achieved by Casanova, who, with the help of his better judgment (Voltaire), is able to accept his personal demons and judge himself positively.

A Masque of Mr. Punch uses similar patterns—internal plays and variations on the trial—to celebrate one of Davies's favorite characters. Mr. Punch is, for him, "the Spirit of Unregenerate Man,"[19] always in control, always unmanageable. As Punch complains to a character who rewrites one of his playlets, "The whole point of Punch's Show is that nobody beats Punch" (P, 53). The masque, in fact, makes the irrepressible Punch a match even for the devil. In his introduction to the play Davies remarks tellingly, "I have admired and coveted his gaiety, his masterful way with physical and metaphysical enemies, and his freedom from remorse" (P, xi).

As a slapstick puppet figure Punch enjoys a liberty unusual in life. Davies would later create a series of characters exploring aspects of the Punch temperament he "covet[s]"—Blazon of *Fifth Business,* Eisengrim of *World of Wonders,* and Parlabane of *The Rebel Angels* stand out respectively as images of gaiety, masterful vengeance, and remorselessness. By contrast, Casanova's seriousness and his advanced age muffle much of his high spirit. Still, he shares with Punch the "exuberance and passion of a man fully alive" (G, 267), a spirit not cowed by assaults or harsh judgments. He also shares with Punch a commitment to the art form he serves and the capacity to meet his personal devil unflinchingly.

As *A Masque of Aesop* anticipates *General Confession*, so *A Masque of Mr. Punch* anticipates *Question Time*. One of the latter masque's distinguishing features is its exuberant satire of Canadian attitudes to theater. Set in a drab mid-Victorian drawing room, it burlesques the Canadian media, academics, and festival adjudicators even as it parodies contemporary trends in theater (Brecht, Beckett, and Williams). Punch is criticized for being "terribly out of touch with the theatre as we know it in Canada" (P, 35). What Canada does and doesn't know is very much at issue in *A Masque of Mr. Punch*. In *Question Time*, as in *General Confession*, Davies deepens matters by turning to serious psychological inquiry. What Canada does and doesn't know about itself becomes the issue in Davies's most ambitious play.

Question Time (1975): "Democracy Be Damned!"

Question Time weds two of Davies's deepest interests—the study of the inner self and the desire to interpret Canadian culture. Highly ambitious in its scope, it harkens back to virtually every play he had written. It most closely resembles *General Confession* but declares its primary difference in its title. The earlier play takes it name from the private sphere; Casanova describes his *Memoirs* not as "impudent boasting" but as "a general confession" (G, 197). *Question Time* declares its publicness in its title, for "Question Time" is, in parliamentary debate, that period given over to free or unprescribed questions from the opposition party. The title is, thus, a clever metaphor for the unexplored inner life and emotional "opposition" of a representative political figure, the Prime Minister of Canada.

The play begins with the recovery of the Prime Minister after a plane crash in the remote Arctic. Physically unhurt but in a deep coma, he is taken to a shelter. There he is attended by Dr. Angatkok, an Eskimo trained in Edinburgh who, opting for "the primitive" over "the modern" world, has become a shaman. Radio contact is established with Ottawa, but because of remoteness and bad weather, little can be done but to wait and see about Peter Macadam's condition.

Realistic details play only a small part in what is a romantic and generalized concept. The Arctic into which Macadam plummets is his own terra incognita, the icy reaches of his inner life, which as public figure, he has long neglected. The Shaman serves as his spiritual guide, clarifying for him that his primary choice is whether to live or die. He leads Macadam through various confrontations with figures from his public life emphasizing that, "In important things there is no public or private."[20] Resistant at first, Macadam encounters brutal truths about his life in the form of "fantasies . . . as rough as nightmares" (Q, 36). The Shaman allows him to see the way his imminent death is treated in Ottawa by political colleagues, his wife, civil servants, and the public. Inclined to self-pity, Macadam is slow to focus the fighting spirit of his personality. As act 1 ends, however, he rallies somewhat and chooses the form in which to find his answer to the overwhelming question before him.

The form of self-trial Macadam chooses is, as in *The Manticore*, one in which the protagonist professionally excels. In the "Parliament of the Terra Incognita" (Q, 44), the Shaman becomes the Speaker while Macadam assumes the dual role of Prime Minister and Leader of the Opposition, switching places with his double at opportune moments in the dialogue. "The queen" to which this "Parliament of Irrationalities" (Q, 67) is responsible is not Elizabeth II but La Sorcière des Montagnes de Glace, an eerie and regal embodiment of God or, perhaps better, that aspect of experience that arouses man's religious feeling, filling him with terror and awe. During the trial the other characters align themselves either with the party in power or the opposition.

What surprises—and finally disappoints—about the shorter second act is its conspicuously public emphasis. Invited by the action to follow Macadam to his inner depths, the audience finds itself forced to linger over "the supplementary question: What kind of country is Canada?" (Q, 52). As answer Davies marshalls a symbolic Herald ("I am the continuance of history" [Q, 54]) and a comic Beaver whose "policy of appeasement," when confronted, is to bite off his own testicles and offer them to his enemy (Q, 60). Such shows are, however, flashy diversions, delaying Davies's revelations from the Queen. She is "the final reality; she is ourselves, our forebears, and our children; she is this land—so old it makes all monarchies seem like passing shadows on her face, and all forms of power like games children tire of" (Q, 67). Dissolving his inner parliament, Macadam meets the Queen and, in an echo scene, he humbles himself as "child and lover." This "act of homage and submission" is his recognition of what matters in life (Q, 70). Having done so, he can opt to live and to leave his personal Arctic with "More than I brought" (Q, 70).

Question Time is not only Robertson Davies's most ambitious play, it is in several ways his most inventive. It makes effective use of music to suggest the mysterious sound of the Arctic and of television to provide an ongoing sense of national concern about the Prime Minister's situation. It brings certain dramatic techniques of the theater of Sir Henry Irving, for example, the echo scene and the double, onto the contemporary stage. Its setting, Les Montagnes de Glace, provides a vivid and dominant image for the refracting of personality into its Jungian components. And in Sarah Macadam, the P.M.'s wife, it presents one of Davies's more effective characterizations of a woman.

Not surprisingly, *Question Time* has received considerable praise. In stressing its debt to the medieval morality play, Patricia Monk prefers it to *General Confession*.[21] Frederick Radford agrees, noting it "is probably the most successful of Davies' Jungian plays, suffering less than the others from the weakness of telling rather than showing."[22] Despite such praise it is difficult to be overly enthusiastic about the play. While it apparently focuses upon the realization of the inner self, it does so in a way uncongenial to Davies's strengths as playwright. The romantic celebration of selfhood that makes *A Jig for the Gypsy, General Confession,* and, to a lesser extent, *Hunting Stuart* engaging plays is missing here. *Question Time* poises itself on the familiar premise that the great danger a public figure faces is the loss of his private self. It makes Macadam, as his name so evidently indicates, a Canadian everyman of the most conspicuous sort. Macadam's selfhood thus turns on another uncertain premise, that a Prime Minister must in some way embody and represent not only the political views but also the inner reality of his constituents. Having often used Mackenzie King's secretive mystical habits as cultural metaphor, Davies did not hesitate in *Question Time* to wed the medieval morality play and Jungian interpretation of personality as a means of diagnosing Canada.

What *Question Time* misses is precisely that sense of inner self, both in the Prime Minister and in the nation he typifies. As Urjo Kareda noted, the play on stage was "a very grand, ambitious and idiosyncratic disaster," in part because it lacked "a central figure of any depth." To Kareda, Macadam seemed "a nullity."[23] *Question Time* appears to concentrate upon the inner journeying of Peter Macadam, but the result is insubstantial and disappointing. What one gets is not Macadam's character but a review of certain wittily poised cultural observations about Davies's cold countrymen. *Ques-*

tion Time embodies in Macadam Canada's protectionist policies, devotion to reason, and emotional repressiveness. It looks into popular myths—Canada as world peacekeeper, Canada as a new country, Canada as a fresh start, Canada as a democracy. It delights in undercutting political clichés.

With such material Davies the teacher is clearly in the saddle. He uses Macadam's inner "wandering" to satirize prevailing attitudes and to express his own views. Most offensive is his presentation of Tim and Marge as the play's representative Common Men. They emerge as illiterate cretins. Slobbish, opinionated, and irreligious, they get their wisdom from bowling alleys and union meetings. So extravagant is their caricature that they are an embarrassment within the play. They constitute yet another instance of Davies's contempt for and condescension to ordinary people, even as they image his mistrust of democracy as political ideal and system. "Democracy be damned!" shouts Arnak, a character representing Macadam's intelligence (Q, 47). The price paid for democratic life, the play further proclaims, is both loss of individuality and "the gelding of the Hero" (Q, 47). In mixing political satire with Jungian thinking, Davies offers many striking insights. However, if one stands outside the mere rhetoric and the novelty of the play, certain of the views expressed seem myopic and politically, if not socially, frivolous. In *Question Time,* psychological investigation becomes a license for cultural satire and opinion.

Among Davies's jokes the Beaver is his tour de force, an instance of self-gelding connected to Canada's national image. Drawing upon medieval bestiaries, Davies concocted a biological lie about the beaver to suit his serious cultural criticism. So eager, in fact, was Davies to underline the point that he makes his attitude to the beaver one of the questions he addresses to himself in the play's didactic preface. His explanation of the beaver's appropriateness as symbol cannot, however, disguise the fact that as playwright he could not resist the joke;[24] in this case a joke that superficially masks an absence of substance in the play's final act. *Question Time* needs such devices to reach its conclusion, for Macadam as character arouses insufficient interest. As Patricia Morley has argued, *Question Time* fails because it is unable "to present in real terms any genuine advance towards integration and maturity, either in Peter Macadam or in the nation which he represents."[25] The play does not satisfy the expectations it creates.

The Theater As Temple: Robertson Davies's Later Plays

In the light of Robertson Davies's contributions to the novel (a contribution that begins with a play about theater and in frustration with the difficulties of staging plays in Canada), it would be inappropriate to attempt too great a case for his playwrighting. Certainly, his plays have value as entertainments and as social commentary. Both his one-act plays for Canadian amateur companies and his corpus of full-length pieces have an historical and cultural importance it would be folly to overlook. It was not, however, as a dramatist that Robertson Davies found his most effective and flexible voice. Having committed himself to a limited view of theater, he left himself little leeway to experiment and develop. What new and attractive ideas he brought to his playwrighting had to be accommodated to the structure of nineteenth-century melodrama he admired so much.

Typically, his plays lack strongly developed and dramatically moving conflicts. The temptations of imbalance inherent in melodrama often proved too much for the romantic in Davies. Even in the Jungian plays with their interest in psychological complexity, the reader is often struck by an absence of significant characterization or character development. Indicative of the influence of Ben Jonson, typing has remained an inescapable dimension of his theater, a function of his melodramatic vision on the one hand and his view that the playwright should leave the creation of depth of character to the actors themselves. The weight of allegory and didacticism is, moreover, often a problem in plays that pile issue after issue upon the melodramatic poles.

What most counts in Davies's plays is to be found in their very insistence upon simplification and polarization. In them the emphasis upon man as self-celebrating, self-justifying egoist is clear. Davies's fervent commitment to a merry, energetic, and serious selfhood lies at the heart of his plays. What Ralph Waldo Emerson wrote in his essay "Self-Reliance" applies surprisingly well to the kind of heroic selfhood Davies has made the center of his theater. One must be able to "live wholly from within": "Who would be a man, must be a nonconformist. He who would gather immortal palms must not be hindered by the name of goodness, but must explore if it be goodness. Nothing is at last sacred but the integrity of your own mind. Absolve you to yourself, and you shall have the suffrage of the world."[26]

If Robertson Davies grants his heroes "immortal palms" rather too readily and too easily in many of his plays, it is, nevertheless, the very celebration of egoism that makes them particularly fascinating.

Chapter Five
The Salterton Novels
The Emergence of a Trilogy

In 1950 Robertson Davies began to sketch out a new play about the struggle of an amateur theater group to stage and perform a Shakespeare play outdoors. *Fortune, My Foe* had stirred his memories of Kingston's many amateur theater groups and its distinctive cultural attitudes. Moreover, given his own experiences directing Shakespeare in Peterborough, he was well aware of the comic potential in the subject. The idea, however, led Davies in a different direction, one he had contemplated for several years.

Despite his love of the theater, he had increasingly been feeling a dissatisfaction with the play as vehicle. He had come especially to lament the vulnerability of the playwright whose work, once released, became the plaything of others. At the same time, his frustration with the condition of theater in Canada was becoming more and more evident as the 1940s drew to a close. Plays could be performed only where theaters existed—often only "a school hall, smelling of chalk and kids, and decorated in the Early Concrete style," as Samuel Marchbanks sardonically observed[1]—and then only to the house's limited capacity, and for limited runs. With few outlets for serious performances, indigenous plays at best were likely to arouse a local interest before being set aside.

By contrast, the novel offered the possibility of wider exposure and a larger audience. It also provided certain advantages in control. As Davies recalled,

> I came very strongly to realize that if you wanted to produce particular strong effects you had to do it yourself, because you have to rely in theatre on the big combination of people who are working together. It may come out as you wanted or it may not. I think the real dyed-in-the-wool playwright likes the surprise of things taking on quite a different aspect in rehearsal. But I wanted *Tempest-Tost* to come out as I saw it. Therefore I thought it would go better in novel form than as a play.[2]

Strong dramatic effects and firm authorial control are characteristics of *Tempest-Tost* and its successors, *Leaven of Malice* and *A Mixture of Frailties*. Davies's treatments of seduction scenes, tête-à-têtes, child-parent showdowns, confrontations between strong-willed characters, and attempted suicides stand out as vividly as do his party and trial scenes. The Salterton novels depend for their flavor upon his control of omniscient narration, the omniscience freeing him to offer a wide range of satiric commentary on the social scene and psychological insight into patterns of human behavior, just as it enabled him, upon a suitable pretext, to digress at length, especially for comic effect. The play form allowed him no such opportunity for leisurely observation or amplification. The theatrical and Marchbanksian sides of his sensibility and temperament found their places comfortably within the new dispensation of fictional narrative.

The Salterton novels are comedies of manners in which the social forms, conventions, and values of a typical Canadian city of the 1930s and 1940s, a city marked by the "fossil relics of colonial days and the British ascendancy in Canada,"[3] are made to clash with individual needs, appetites, and expectations. Modelled clearly on Kingston, Salterton is a powerful force in the novels, its "real character" lying below the surface of ordinary behavior and local pride. That exact character is never precisely defined for it contains many elements, among them a tenacious but waning establishment characterized by class consciousness and snobbery, a large measure of gloomy, debilitating Presbyterianism, and a tendency on all social levels to worship the mediocre and second-rate. Only in the third novel, *A Mixture of Frailties,* does Davies provide a glimpse of Salterton's working class and then mostly to satirize and burlesque the limitations of unmitigated materialism, empty-headed fundamentalism, and the union mentality. As *The Voice of the People* had indicated, this is the class with which he is least at ease and upon which he almost reflexively heaps scorn.

The satirist in Davies finds much to criticize in Salterton. His overall perspective is, however, kindlier. In Salterton there is some space for living—room for self-sustaining individuality and willful eccentricity, occasion for communion with kindred spirits, and some opportunity for awakening to one's inner potential. Though the city is socially at the mercy of the Mrs. Caesar Augustus Conquergoods, Mrs. Louisa Bridgetowers, and Nellie Forresters, though its artistic people have to leave to develop their talents and are, typically, misunderstood when at home, Salterton nevertheless provides room for individualists like Humphery Cobbler, Tom Gwalchmai, and Gloster Ridley. Their presence serves to leaven the lump of snobbishness, conformity, vulgarity, and mediocrity that would otherwise dominate. It is a fundamental premise of Davies's comic vision that such individuality is able to sustain itself with gusto, no matter the frictions or pressures that society brings to bear on daily existence. The individual's struggle and eventual victory, however realistically circumscribed that victory, is the matter Davies celebrates in his fiction. The forces that would defeat or limit that individuality are the subject of both his social analysis and his satire.

The similarity in structure of the Salterton novels attests to the importance Davies places upon the triumph of individuality *within* a social context. They are at once comedies and romances. Davies's commitment to and optimism about the individual spirit necessitate a comic form. He has to see his protagonist(s) through, if not to a happy ending, then to a more enlightened, sustaining state of psychological, emotional, and imaginative development than seemed possible at the outset. The dramatization of that growth within the realistic context of the comedy of manners (that context is a given for Davies) demands a very careful usage of romantic elements. While in many of his plays of this period Davies used explicit magical devices to effect salutary and extraordinary transformations in character, in the Salterton novels he employs more muted means to effect more modest, though equally salutary, changes. Very much "a serious writer of romance" both as novelist and as playwright,[4] Davies makes his magic engagingly out of the ordinary and probable. The subtle and inventive ways in which he introduces romance into realistic events account at least in part for his success in appealing to a larger, more appreciative audience.

In *Tempest-Tost* romance and magic enter the lives of the Little Theater group through their involvement with *The Tempest,* a play celebrating the imagination. Metaphorically, Davies frames the adventures in heightened feeling undergone by his protagonist Hector Mackilwraith by references to a hidden cache of cider on the site of the performance, a cache "bottled just at the psychological moment."[5] As the cider ferments so the magic slowly but surely affects Hector. In *Leaven of Malice,* the unexpected takes the form of a false engagement announcement. The hoax disturbs the equilibrium of the major characters, leading some to embarrassing overreaction and self-exposure, and others, over the course of the novel, to deeper personal awareness and improvement in their fortunes. The malice behind the announcement proves a powerful leavening agent. In *A Mixture of Frailties,* the most complex novel of the trilogy, it is Louisa Bridgetower's will that operates like slow magic in two distinct narrative directions. It places inordinate pressure on her son and his wife to break free of her "Dead Hand" while its eccentric bequest allows a Salterton singer of raw talents, Monica Gall, to be transformed in England into a capable artist and deep-feeling individual.

As novelist, Robertson Davies is master magician and trickster, bottling and fermenting events so as to generate narrative confrontations, humorous presentations of manners in action and, most important, psychological pressure. He operates mischievously, delighting in ticklish situations. One of his early signals to the reader of *Tempest-Tost* is "a wall-painting of a goggle-eyed gnome, just identifiable as Shakespeare's Puck," overlooking Hector Mackilwraith as he takes his meals and weighs his personal decisions (T, 47). Humphery Cobbler, a dominant figure in *Leaven of Malice* and the discoverer of Monica Gall, most closely approximates the magician-trickster spirit of Davies within the novels themselves. Described as a man who likes "sheer mischief-making," he tells Hector, "The unthinkable has always been rather in my line" (T, 231, 240).

Tempest-Tost: "Shakespeare Will Test All of Us to the Uttermost"

Though it may seem excessive to call *Tempest-Tost* a "ridiculously good first novel,"[6] it was a surprisingly successful book as its generally positive reception in Canada and the United States indicated. "Let me say at once that *Tempest-Tost* is fun to read," remarked Margaret Stobie.[7] The delight occasioned by the novel's appearance, especially in Canada, is too easily overlooked in the 1980s. Not only was it an entertaining and sophisticated story but it revealed a promising new dimension of a promising writer. It seemed to many a serious and important step forward. Comparing Davies with la Rochefoucauld and Shaw in his ability to be serious but not solemn, Glen Shortliffe argued that it marked "en quelque sorte une date dans le développement de la littérature canadienne."[8]

B. K. Sandwell was struck by the novel's civilized ebullience. Like Smollett Davies evinced "that gift for rapid characterization which inevitably tends towards caricature, that breeziness of style, and that frank recognition of the animal aspects of human nature which distinguish the author of *Humphrey Clinker.*"[9]

To such enthusiasm William Arthur Deacon offered a rare dissenting view. Sandwell had praised Davies as "the best propagandist we have had for the social value of art," showing Canada's different social classes "rubbing shoulders together with scarcely any consciousness of their economic status."[10] Deacon reacted very differently. Here was an author who lacked the sincerity or social seriousness of Shaw, one who in his "waggish" superiority was "cruel or malicious" to his characters, showing them up as "various kinds of fools." Always a champion of realism and the social purposefulness of fiction, Deacon saw *Tempest-Tost* as a novel that led "nowhere" as narrative and statement. Hostility to the implicit elitism of Davies's writing, an elitism praised and shared by Sandwell, characterized Deacon's review.[11]

Tempest-Tost is an April comedy that takes its mood from the season, the pastoral setting of the outdoor production, and the play, which in many ways it parallels. The action covers a period of six weeks from the Salterton Little Theatre's first foray onto the grounds of St. Agnes, the estate of a wealthy Saltertonian George Webster, to the aftermath of the hectic opening night performance of *The Tempest*. The early chapters are devoted to matters of organization and production, the heavy-handed manipulations of the Little Theatre's leaders, Nellie Forrester and Professor Vambrace, the jockeying for roles, the actual auditions and casting, and the professional insights and strategies of the play's guest director, Valentine Rich. Quickly establishing Rich's authority, Davies develops various tensions and rivalries among the cast members and supporting crew. A book auction, several parties, and the local military college's annual ball provide occasions for amplification. Personal matters are thus heightened while the dull dog work of rehearsals is minimized in the narrative. Davies returns attention to the actual production only after the dress rehearsal, thereupon completing the stories of his characters in the anxiety and excitement of the first performance.

St. Agnes is the novel's enchanted isle and "fearful country." The privacy of its beautiful gardens are the setting for a magical "seachange" in a contemporary Canadian setting. Significantly, St. Agnes is an English legacy, one of "four houses of real beauty . . . built in Salterton by the eccentric Prebendary Bedlam, one of those Englishmen who sought to build a bigger and better England in the colonies" (T, 14). It maintains its image of wealth, taste, and tradition, providing a charged atmosphere appropriate to *The Tempest* itself.

Casting for the play generates, as Hugo McPherson noted, "a series of chilling ironies."[12] Prospero is Waverley University Classics Professor and the Little Theatre's "saturnine hatchet-man" (T, 19), Walter Vambrace. Baleful and histrionic, he is characterized by an unyieldingly "passionate egotism" (T, 146) by which he reduces those about him either to acolytes or nonentities. He works no magic in his role; in fact, he often makes a fool of himself. More significantly, his oppressive vanity leaves little room for his daughter Pearl to develop her sense of self. Protectively nurtured, she is a shrinking, vulnerable Miranda. In casting her, Val Rich is alone in recognizing "a quality which was close to beauty" (T, 283). Rich's instincts prove correct. Shyly sensitive to the brave new world of *The Tempest,* Pearl tentatively begins to show signs of her inner potential. For most of the novel, she is, however, overlooked and disparaged because of the cowed and dowdy wallflower image she projects. Thus, the Prospero-Miranda relationship reflects ironically upon one of the major underlying themes of *Tempest-Tost,* the power of the parent to inhibit rather than to encourage the development of his child's individuality and capacities. Sigmund Freud is very much "the old fantastical duke of dark corners" of Davies's first two novels.[13]

Another much-repressed offspring is Solly Bridgetower, Pearl's real-life Ferdinand. A Cambridge student, Solly has been forced to return home to attend to his widowed mother, a strong-willed and resourceful woman "determined that she should not be [alone in the world] so long as there was a man from whom she could draw vitality" (T, 166). Mrs. Bridgetower is an emotional vampire. She holds Solly in her maternal thrall, allowing him to amuse himself with local theater activities and suitable infatuations. Slated at first to be the play's director, Solly cheerfully accepts the role of assistant when Val Rich becomes available. Emotionally, he fixes his attentions first on Griselda Webster (Ariel), then on Rich, scarcely realizing that Pearl, the young woman he unwillingly escorts to the military ball, is his kindred spirit in parental victimization and unrealized individuality. The careful ways in which Davies parallels their situations suggest that, even in writing *Tempest-Tost,* he had the plan of *Leaven of Malice* in mind.

The wealthy and attractive Griselda Webster gets her role, as she well knows, less from ability than from her part in arranging that the Little Theatre have the use of St. Agnes. Nevertheless, as a young girl recently "freed" from boarding school and becalmed in Salterton, she is eager for the adventure and conviviality of the theater group. Her beauty, manner, and wealth all contribute to her role as Ariel. "You have the air of one who wants rather special things, and special people" (T, 89), Solly tells her. Griselda enchants not only Solly, but Roger Tasset (the play's Ferdinand), and finally Hector Mackilwraith. Throughout the novel, Davies cleverly connects his impatient Griselda's worldliness and charm to her dramatic role as Fate. He keeps development of her character to a minimum. Like Ariel, she remains for the most part impervious and aloof, preserving her chastity (T, 316) and helping to bring about modest "transformations" in Solly and Hector.

The serious threat to Griselda's chastity is Roger Tasset. Superficially, the handsome military officer makes a vivid Ferdinand. But as his name implies he is what Davies in *The Manticore* calls "a swordsman,"[14] an egotist to whom "women were all alike" (T, 125). He nurses an "ideal portrait" of himself as "a devil with women":

He was not of a reflective temperament, and thus it could not be said of him that he embraced libertinage as a philosophy or a way of life, as did Don Juan. But he had convinced himself that sex meant more to him than it did to most men, and that by attracting and seducing women he was being true to his nature and fulfilling a rather fine destiny. (T, 124-25).

Like Boy Staunton he is incapable of inner growth. Hence, though he seems godlike to the inexperienced Pearl, he is, to others, second rate, a yahoo or simply "a smooth, good-looking heel" (T, 231, 235, 312), the very kind of man Prospero would have shunned as his daughter's suitor.

The moralist in Davies, sensitive particularly to the overvaluing of sex in contemporary society, is evident in the depiction of Tasset. At the same time, he probes, as novelist, the psychological essence of the seducer. The result is a reflective balance often lacking in the melodramatic characterization in his plays. "If anyone should think that Roger's attitude was somewhat calculating and joyless," Davies's narrator comments, "it must be said in his defence that he approached seduction professionally, or as a business; he believed success in that field to be a necessity, without which he would lose faith in his own reality and importance in the world. One does not take risks with the source of one's self-respect" (T, 125). Humphrey Cobbler later scorns Mackilwraith for his moralistic condemnation of Roger, asking "if it's his nature to chase women, should we judge him?" (T, 240).

Set against Tasset are Griselda's chivalric defenders. The romantic Solly, whom Tasset mocks as a Peter Pan figure, gets his nose bloodied when he strikes a "Heine-like" posture of scorn (T, 236) after insulting the soldier. It is Hector Mackilwraith, however, the type of the rational, emotionally undernourished man, who suffers most and who seems most to interest Davies. Seeking to live out an ideal of self-control, he has never learned to express himself. He is as inarticulate before Tasset's callousness as he is in his worship of Griselda.

Hector is made to carry a great weight in *Tempest-Tost,* a weight that is more than he can, as character, bear. Cast as Gonzalo, the "wise old counsellor" (T, 77), he is lacking both in wide experience and personal insight. Indeed, he is an underdeveloped middle-aged man caught in what one character pointedly calls his "male climacteric" (T, 370). As such, he is impelled for the first time to try acting, and he falls in love though he "had never, in all his forty years, kissed any woman but his mother" (T, 205). With Hector, as with Ethel in *Overlaid,* Davies's problem was to temper animus with sympathy:

My feeling about Hector was very strong, because I know the man who was the inspiration of Hector. He was a man who taught me mathematics, and I think he was like that. . . . He humiliated me repeatedly. The tendency to make a clown of him was tempting, I can tell you. Believe me, he and I were in a kind of struggle for a long time. I got to know him, I think, and I don't think he got to know me. But I was a kind of challenge to him, and he never failed to meet a challenge. It was rough.[15]

A mathematics teacher whose pedagogy consists of reason and ridicule, Hector was for Davies the kind of monster who would "geld" (T, 63) his students by deducting marks for "stupid" errors. For years he has allowed his one-cylinder mind dominion, governing his life by "Plans of Conduct" and living according to joyless, self-disciplinary rituals. "He very rarely read a book which was not about mathematics, or about how to teach mathematics" (T, 65).

But as pathetic as Hector is—and the men in the novel have little sympathy for him—Davies does try to make his dullness understandable and his transformation remarkable. The son of a dispirited Presbyterian minister nicknamed Misery, Hector had to fight for his life to escape the humiliations and bleakness of his rural Ontario upbringing. Drawing upon his own experiences, Davies makes Hector's struggle a painful victory over schoolyard bullies, the humiliation of cathartics and of privies, and a bleak, rural horizon. Making common sense and planning "his gods in this world" (T, 114), Hector so devotes himself to his profession that he has no time "to be young, or to invite his soul" (T, 121). To him literature is only "ambiguous and unsupported assertions by men of lax mind" (T, 64). The experience of acting, however, suddenly opens him up to the possibility of "chang[ing] his role in the world" (T, 93); thus, unwittingly he draws repressed energy from "the cellerage of his mind" (T, 123). Hector is not one of fortune's children. What professional success he has is the result of his own carefulness and determination. But that alone, *Tempest-Tost* implies, is not enough.

It is by means of Hector's curious "fate" that Davies pulls the many threads of *Tempest-Tost* together. Hector's "psychological moment," a conspicuous mark of his inadequacy, is his failed suicide attempt during the play's opening night. The situation is, however, remedied by the actions and succor of Valentine Rich, the novel's true Prospero. It is her superiority as theater professional and woman that makes possible what Ferdinand in *The Tempest* calls "a second life." Under her control, though Hector is "tempest-tost," "his bark cannot be lost" (T, 2). She is not only compassionate to him but effectively takes over his role in mid-performance. Val Rich is, in fact, a study in unmitigated hero worship. In a book rife with comically flawed characters, she is gracefully superior. While Solly and Pearl are victims of "the mordant old comedy" of parental power (T, 237), she has put her dead grandfather, Dr. Adam Savage, in intelligent perspective. "She had loved and honoured him, and although she did not wish him alive again, she missed him sorely"

(T, 61). She fully understands the theater, defining it as "utterly undemocratic" (T, 38), yet she rules the production with sensitivity for all concerned. She is a worker, not a theorizer or talker. In short, she would seem to be everything Davies admires in a professional, a collage of the best he had known from Esmé Church to Tyrone Guthrie. Nevertheless, some years later Davies acknowledged reservations about his presentation of her:

One of the characters who appears a lot in the book, who meant a lot to me, and who I don't think has emerged attractively enough is Valentine Rich, the Canadian woman who comes back from New York. She is a person I am so much concerned with—the Canadian artist—and she has had to go abroad to do her work, and she has come back, and she knows why she has to go abroad all over again.[16]

The problem is that she emerges *too* attractively. Her many fine moments, all appropriately subdued and unsought, make her seem to belong to a race apart. Yet, to see her as Prospero—to see the director or conductor in Davies's personal mythology as Prospero—is a fruitful approach. The first of Davies's fictional portraits of the Canadian-born artist, she is given a wide dominion of powers. In the realistic context of the novel, however, such adulatory treatment seems excessive, her fine moments too easy victories at the expense of straw men and women.

Abetting Val Rich as Prospero is another nonactor, Humphrey Cobbler, the organist of the Anglican cathedral, whose responsibility is the play's music. Eccentric and high-spirited, Cobbler seems to be Salterton's only genuine resident professional in the arts. Though he does not enter the action until midway in the novel, his presence serves as a catalyst. He becomes a sort of ubiquitous psychologist and clown, stirring up rivalries, antagonizing brittle egos, and pronouncing succinctly upon the states of mind he encounters. During a late-evening conversation, for instance, he ignites the susceptible antagonisms among Tasset, Solly, and Hector in order "to find out what Tasset was up to " with Griselda (T, 239). He has "fun" both provoking the quarrel and mocking the participants: Tasset for his "second-rate man-of-the-world manner," Solly for his "devitalized charm," and Hector for living in "the granite fortress of [his] obtuse self-righteousness" (T, 231–41). He specializes in outraging self-images and narrow views, and in suddenly injecting the candid into the decorous, as when he suggests to Tasset that he has "already bruised the teats of [Griselda's] virginity" (T, 233). When the occasion is right "Cobbler like[s] mischief" (T, 231).

What Cobbler makes clear is that one must distinguish between positive and negative mischief. In a way that anticipates *Leaven of Malice,* malice and malignity are mentioned often in *Tempest-Tost* as negative motivations. By contrast, Cobbler's "mischief" is implicitly commended. His actions stem from high spirits and psychological interest, and are supported by a superior moral outlook. When he cites Galen as "a first-rate psychologist" (T, 241), it is to suggest to the obtuse Hector the essence of the latter's problem— "If natural seed by overlong kept, it turns to poison" (T, 240)— a problem that, in time, affects all aspects of his life.

At the same time, Cobbler is an authority on taste in a novel in which taste is everywhere a matter of concern. "Taste is at the bottom of everything," he declares (T, 248). A man joyously committed to his music, he champions Purcell and Beddoes as artists "still unmauled by the mob" (T, 245) and trumpets his own love of "Ornamental Knowledge" over Hector's faith in "Useful Knowledge" (T, 242). All the while he epitomizes zest. To Solly he is "a man so alive, and so apparently happy, that the air for two or three feet around him seemed charged with his delight in life" (T, 224–25).

Little wonder, then, that the collective authority of Val Rich and Humphrey Cobbler holds dominion at St. Agnes. Rich and Cobbler know who they are; they know what matters and what has genuine value. They have taste of a quality readily distinguishable from Nellie Forrester's heavily debunked "Taste" in interior decorating (T, 34–35); their outlooks are superior to her "insufferably cosy mind" (T, 230). They are Davies's true professionals, artists who have made their individual way in the world. The novel makes tentative attempts to define their specialness in psychological terms. Solly notes that "[t]he only people who make any sense in the world are those who know that whatever happens to them has its roots in what they are" (T, 370). In defining wisdom, Cobbler says of Galen, "That's what makes a man great; his flashes of insight, when he pierces through the nonsense of his time, and gets at something that really matters" (T, 241). Cobbler enacts his definition whenever he has opportunity and audience. Measured against the general lack of distinction of the others, Cobbler and Rich are *Tempest-Tost's* aristocrats of the spirit. It is as if to be superior in art is to be a better and wiser human being.

As a piece of satire *Tempest-Tost* is most effective in its public scenes. It is in many ways the most humorous of the Salterton novels. Davies's treatment of the greedy behavior of various clergymen at the distribution of the library of Val Rich's grandfather is a fine piece of comic writing, fitted effectively to several themes in the novel. Preparations for and the activities of the military college's annual ball are also amusingly handled. Though these events are to some extent tangential to the plot they show a writer keenly sensitive to both the ludicrous and serious aspects of representative social behavior.

By contrast, in satirizing individual characters, Davies is occasionally so overpowering as to be more reductive than amusing. When taste and values are at issue his judgments are unyielding. This is one reason that his attempt to put Hector Mackilwraith at the center of the narrative does not suffice as a dramatic strategy. It is not just that Hector's attempted suicide seems "completely unbelievable and out of place in the novel."[17] It is, more precisely, that despite modest attempts to involve the reader in Hector's life, Davies cannot treat him with sufficient seriousness. When Cobbler tells Hector that he has "amazing personal impact" (T, 243), the reader is simply confounded. Hector is too much a second-rate figure among the play's participants to merit such commendation. Val and Griselda come forward to offer him the sweetness of feminine compassion, but there is little sense that he has learned very much about himself. He remains "a pinhead" and "a crass soul" in the opinions of Cobbler and Solly. According to another character, his problem is more representative. Too many modern people, like Hector, "don't believe, and they haven't got the strength of mind to disbelieve. They won't get rid of religion, and they won't go after a religion that means anything" (T, 373).

It is Cobbler who reads Hector's uncharacteristic action correctly. In a way that anticipates Davies's later interest in Jung, he argues that Hector "probably imagined he was wrapped up in his sorrows, but we all have keener perception than we know. The superficial Mackilwraith, the despairing lover, thought the rope would do, but the true, essential, deep-down Mackilwraith knew damn well that it wouldn't. You don't play safe for forty years and then cut loose. Our Hector was looking for pity, not death" (T, 369). It is Hector's good fortune that he finds compassion instead.

Leaven of Malice: Living on Good Terms with Oneself

Reviewing *Leaven of Malice,* Eric Nicol remarked that while it contained "a good number of funny moments, yet somehow the author never gets the chill off his humor."[18] To Hugo McPherson it was a "hopeful" but "not a warm book."[19] Malcolm Ross was struck by the author's "tonal control." "Here surely the dominant note is that of compassion—not the drivelling tear-jerking sympathy of the more vulgar romantics, but the iron and enduring compassion of the Anglican Prayer Book from which Mr. Davies has derived not only his title but also, I think, his temper."[20] Such observations point to a significant change from *Tempest-Tost* to *Leaven of Malice*— a toughening, and to some extent, a darkening of Robertson Davies's vision. The emphasis in the first was upon comedy as Davies sought to woo a new audience. Its successor, however, probes deeper, looking more closely at the mainstrings of motive and behavior in a community that, from a distance, appears to be quaint, well bred, and imperturbable.

Leaven of Malice was greeted enthusiastically in Canada, England, and the United States. Kingsley Amis praised its "series of very sharply-drawn and very amusing satirical portraits," calling Davies "a most attractive talent."[21] Edmund Fuller termed it "One of the funniest, shrewdest, wittiest, and withall wisest novels to come along in recent seasons."[22] Stuart Keate commended Davies's urbane presentation of "as choice a dossier of cranks as ever harassed a small-town editor."[23] Claude Bissell linked Davies to the Victorian novelists. He also noted astutely that "this novel could not have been written outside of Canada." Lacking a focal protagonist, he added, its real hero is "the gay, disinterested mind" of the author himself.[24]

On one level, *Leaven of Malice* is a whodunit. It turns upon a practical joke, the appearance of a false engagement announcement on Halloween in the Salterton *Bellman.* Solly Bridgetower is to marry Pearl Vambrace on 31 November. The joke cuts to the quick of Pearl's father, Walter Vambrace, who has long nursed an academic grudge against Solly's deceased father. Vambrace takes the announcement as a personal affront. Demanding apology on his own terms and threatening a lawsuit, he storms the office of *Bellman* editor, Gloster Ridley. He will not be mollified. Thus is set in motion a process whereby a small act of malice works its dark magic upon many people. Underlying the darkness, however, is a leavening force, for, like yeast, the malice promotes a lightening and rising in ways that most of the characters cannot perceive. Again Davies's Puckish agent and spokesman, Humphrey Cobbler, is one of the gifted who is able to see beneath the surface of events. "Now the scales have fallen from my eyes," he tells Solly. "Not only is the hand of Fate discernible in this affair [the inadvertent development of Pearl and Solly's romance]; Fate has been leaving finger-prints all around the place ever since [the announcement was placed]."[25]

As *Tempest-Tost* takes its mood from the magic of *The Tempest*, *Leaven of Malice* takes its spirit from Halloween. That spirit is associated particularly with Cobbler who the same evening of the false announcement is discovered raising a "dreadful, unholy sound" (L, 59), revelling with some of his students in the cathedral. Dressed like a gypsy and sporting "an air of invincible cheerfulness" (L, 63), he exposes himself to a different kind of malice. His actions give impetus to the efforts of the elderly Puss Pottinger (a myopic make-up lady in *Tempest-Tost*) and cathedral chancellor, Matthew Snelgrove, who wish to rid the church of its irreverent organist. Snelgrove is also the lawyer Vambrace hires to sue Ridley and the *Bellman*.

Ridley, Solly, Pearl, and Cobbler all find themselves hard pressed by the events with which the novel begins. While their separate stories unfold—Cobbler stands in sharp contrast to the others in his self-certainty and freedom from worry—Davies sustains the mystery of the wedding announcement and broadens his canvas to include a range of characters representing Salterton's mixed society. As in *Tempest-Tost,* party scenes and other social gatherings are used to promote the plot and to provide targets for Davies's satire. Folly-prone characters like Professor Vambrace and Norm Yarrow are thoroughly embarrassed when given their own head. In *Tempest-Tost* Vambrace almost chokes on stage trying to eat grapes during a speech; in *Leaven of Malice* he plays the fool in attempting to trail Gloster Ridley like an amateur detective. Wounding comeuppance follows quickly upon acts of stupidity in these novels.

The action concludes with a kind of improvisatory trial in Snelgrove's legal offices. The domineering Snelgrove seizes the opportunity to play "the stage lawyer to the life" (L, 289). Ridley, however, is prepared for him. He reveals that the perpetrator of the malicious announcement was not Cobbler, as Snelgrove argues, but Bevill Higgin, a second-rate Irishman and heretofore secondary character who sought to revenge himself upon several Saltertonians who he believed had slighted him. At this point the effects of Higgin's act are judiciously measured. As in many realist novels, a minister steps forward to offer a wise, moral perspective. Jevon Knapp, Dean of the Anglican Cathedral, serves this purpose, telling the assembled that "quite unforeseen good results" can follow from an act of malice. "It works like a leaven; it stirs, and swells, and changes all that surrounds it. If you seek to pin it down in law, it may well elude you. . . . But those things which it invades will never be quite the same again" (L, 301).

The comic patterns of *Tempest-Tost* and *Leaven of Malice* are similar. Subjected to an unanticipated kind of testing, certain characters experience troubling, potentially damaging pressures. Through personal resources and the help of others, they must struggle to regain their peace of mind; in the process they find they are the richer for their troubled passage. Of the two novels, *Leaven of Malice* approaches both the matter of human shortcomings (which promotes the testing) and the achievement of self-knowledge (by which a character gains his perspective) with increased curiosity and intensity. The satire Davies directs at the maliciousness, aggressiveness, silliness, and shabbiness he finds in Salterton is better balanced by the psychological gains he spreads among Ridley, Solly, and Pearl.

Among Davies's satiric targets are Puss Pottinger, Snelgrove, Swithin Shillito, Norm and Dutchy Yarrow, and George and Kitten Morphew. All are decidedly comic types and make most sense when seen as such. As indices of society, they reveal as much about Davies's politics and values as they do about the social reality under investigation.

Puss, Snelgrove, and Shillito belong to the faded Anglo-hierarchy of Canada. A soldier's daughter who takes a proprietary view of the cathedral, Puss is a devotee of military honor, of "good breeding and of Victorian Anglicanism"—"what she believed to be the public good" (L, 65–66). She is also a busybody who brings "a martial spirit" (L, 66) to her efforts, in this case, the sacking of Cobbler whose bohemian deportment violates her notion of propriety. Moreover, she is a snob who cherishes the favor of Louisa Bridgetower and other socially prominent types. Abetting her justification of "useless mischief" (L, 173) is Matthew Snelgrove, a snob and Tory whose ideal self-image is that of "the lawyer-squire of the eighteenth [century] . . . ready to play the dignified toady to anyone whom he considered his superior, and heavily patronizing to those beneath him" (L, 82). Grasping for a solid reason to encourage Vambrace's libel suit, Snelgrove argues that "Fine old families should not suffer affront in silence" (L, 86). With an enthusiasm that is folly, he welcomes any occasion for personal histrionics or a heroic stand on behalf of "the old squirearchy" against the forces of "rampant democracy" (L, 93). Sillier still, as his name suggests, is Swithin Shillito who defines himself as "an Englishman of the Old School" (L, 14). He is a fussy, superannuated journalist who specializes in trivial essays about walking sticks, toothpicks, and snuff. His aggressiveness in resisting his retirement is sufficient to cow Ridley who realizes that he should have fired him long ago. It is Shillito's British sentimentality that provides Higgin with the opportunity to place the malicious announcement upon which the novel depends.

Davies is more cutting still in his satire of that "rampant democracy" Snelgrove fears. The damning diagnosis takes place on two fronts. Representing modern education and marriage are the Yarrows. Of a piece with the pathetic social workers in *Fortune, My Foe* and Fred Lewis in *Hunting Stuart,* Norm and Dutchy are relentlessly and unfeelingly debunked. Norm is a Ph.D. specializing in psychology and social service, hired as assistant to Waverley University's chaplain. His wife is a recreation director whose success lies in overwhelming "people who were poor, without being in poverty" (L, 133) by means of her energy and enthusiasm.

The two are virtually without redeeming features. Their states of mind, values, language, and particularly their idea of fun, are the subject of a crude humor that reflects at once Davies's scorn for illiteracy, tastelessness, and pedestrian notions of group activity even as it reveals a complete unwillingness on his part to identify with or to try to understand certain kinds of characters. The ghastly party given by the Yarrows is of a piece with their naive credo of normality. That the childless Dutchy could have written at age nineteen a thesis called "Preparing the Parent for the Profession of Parenthood" is matched by Norm's folly in seeking to counsel Walter Vambrace, a Classics professor, about "a kind of an Oedipus thing between [him] and Pearlie" (L, 235). Having read only a chapter on Freud in a "general textbook," Norm is entirely out of his element. Vambrace's angry putdown bristles with authority: "But you are, like many another Sphinx of our modern world, an undereducated, brassy young pup, who thinks that gall can take the place of the authority of wisdom, and that a professional lingo can disguise his lack of thought" (L, 238). Notwithstanding Vambrace's righteous indignation, it is difficult to take seriously characters whose conversation and actions are so relentlessly burlesqued. When Dutchy asks Norm about his plans to help Solly and Pearl—"You mean you think we could do some social engineering, and make everything jake for those two poor kids?" (L, 205)—Davies shows a crudity of ear that is best described as indulgent.

The Morphews represent lower middle-class life, the realm of travelling salesmen, painted toenails and club "smokers." Connected tenuously to the plot (Ridley's housekeeper, Edith Little, is Kitten Morphew's sister, while Higgin, who boards with them, tries to seduce the widowed Edith), the Morphews are a study in grossness and vulgarity. Pawing sexuality and bawdy songs keep the husband amused and provide Davies with ample opportunity to revel in their tastelessness and insensitivity.

In the Salterton context of fading gentility and rising vulgarity, malice, or mischief in negative form, abounds. *Leaven of Malice* is a highly perceptive study of an era in Canadian manners when the post-Victorian staidness that had held sway for decades was, in the wake of World War II, beginning to yield to new pressures. So much of the malice that abounds in the novel is directly or indirectly a response to these new pressures. Members of the old guard, whatever their station, resist change and dislike anything unusual. Suspecting a plot linking the engagement announcement and the hubbub in the cathedral, Puss Pottinger "wants to hang Mr. Cobbler's hide on the fence" (L, 174). Snelgrove, who is described as "one of those men who gravitate to the law because they delight in mischief" (L, 124), sees himself as the defender not only of the cathedral and good families but of a vague eighteenth-century cultural legacy.

Outmoded emphasis upon family is particularly embodied in the domineering parents, Walter Vambrace and Louisa Bridgetower, whose surnames denote defense. Both are aggressive and dirty fighters. They use their commanding personalities and familial positions to dominate and constrain those closest to them.

Vambrace relies upon his academic eminence and his claims of aristocratic (Irish) kinship to bolster his self-esteem. He thinks always in terms of enemies and plots. To his browbeaten wife he proclaims, "There is what I suppose may be called the aristocratic tradition, which is chiefly a tradition of not allowing oneself to be trampled over by a pack of louts and cheapjacks. So far as family gives one courage to resist what is vulgar and intrusive and impertinent, family is a very good thing" (L, 123–24). Casting himself as defender of the faith, he is against everything that reflects "the spirit of the age, and of the New World" (L, 130). He mounts campaigns, quarrels whenever possible, skulks about like a detective, and relentlessly pursues an apology for what he regards as *his* degraded honor. Yet for all his aggressiveness, he uses sentimental postures to control his wife and daughter. When he tells Pearl, "I had hoped that as a family we would see one another through this" (L, 130), he makes her feel "thoroughly ashamed of herself." Never, however, has he considered his daughter's feelings about the matter.

Louisa Bridgetower is also a defender of the past. Her "At Home" afternoons, begun just before World War I, are an unusual phenomenon in the Salterton of the present; as a tradition they made her "a captain among those forces in Salterton which sought to resist social change" (L, 171). She commands regular participation even as she somewhat nastily wields her power. "Pouring salt into wounds was a speciality of Mrs. Bridgetower's, and the older the wound was the better she liked it" (L, 174). As Davies's treatment makes clear, the old guard is very much torn by hostilities and disagreements, however much it might appear to the young as a unified front.

It is in her resourceful control of her son, Solly, that Mrs. Bridgetower is at her most formidable. She plays the lonely, aggrieved widow with consummate control, not out of hypocrisy but out of need. Loath to give up her son, she refuses to let him live his own life. On the one hand, she sucks Solly's vitality from him; on the other, she is, as a mother, a woman desperate for the only familial love left to her. As Solly compassionately realizes, "filial piety isn't simply a foolish phrase. It's a hard reality. Some people never seem to feel it. In happy families it is never put to any real test. But duty to parents is an obligation that some of us must recognize. However hellish parents may be, the duty is as real as the duty that exists in marriage" (L, 256).

It is in presenting the struggle for psychological freedom of the offspring of such "hellish" parents that *Leaven of Malice* balances the aggressive forces of the old guard. As in *Tempest-Tost*, Pearl is the overlooked gem. Four years after *Tempest-Tost*, a graduate of Waverley now working in the university library, she still lacks the ability to present herself in an attractive way. She has not in fact had a date in those four intervening years, and it does not seem to her cause for complaint.

Finding outlet in modest pleasures, she does not seek to resist her father's tyranny until he reacts excessively against her. Matters come to a head when, in the novel's most harrowing scene, he spots Pearl getting out of Solly's car. Acting "quite beyond reason," he pulls Pearl to the pavement, then "cuff[s] her shrewdly on the ear," calling her a "dirty little scut!" (L, 165–66). In a novel where martial imagery and aggressiveness abound, this brief outburst of actual violence has a powerful effect. It is the scene the reader is most likely to remember.

Like Catherine Sloper in James's *Washington Square*, Pearl is neither rebellious nor antifamilial in her response to parental dominance. Feeling "utterly alone and forsaken" (L, 167), her instinct is to take herself more seriously as an independent being and to consider her parents in a more critical perspective. Pearl knows that "she had lost her father, more certainly than if he had died that night" (L, 167). To lose him is, however, to gain herself. A stronger Pearl emerges from her test, a kind of Sleeping Beauty awakened from her thrall. Solly becomes her ordinary Prince Charming (L, 129). In choosing a new name for herself (a saint's name, Veronica) and in capably meeting her father on his own ground, she so reveals her inner nature that it is Solly who awakens to her. In the end, she publicly kisses her father and privately offers Solly the compassion he needs, her healthful emergence being of a sweetly conservative kind.

While Pearl struggles against her egotistical, overbearing father, Solly's problem is that of a son manipulated by a clever, powerful mother. In neither case is there much trace of sexual undercurrent, a point Davies emphasizes in Vambrace's authoritative put-down of Yarrow's Oedipus-complex nonsense. Now a junior faculty member at Waverley and tied to an academic career that compromises his desire to write creatively, Solly is more introspective and less firm than Pearl. He needs guides like Cobbler and compassion such as he receives from Molly Cobbler and Pearl to break his mother's emotional hold.

The first of Davies's three-in-a-bed scenes (see also *World of Wonders*) triggers Solly's personal emergence. Invited to share the warmth of the Cobblers' bed, he partakes of Humphrey's mockery and advice, the best part of which comes last—"You think life has trapped you, do you? Well, my friend, everybody is trapped, more or less. The best thing you can hope for is to understand your trap and make terms with it, tooth by tooth" (L, 219). Molly, by contrast, gently assures Solly that he'll find a way out even though no full escape from his mother is possible. Mrs. Bridgetower's powerful needs and Solly's "filial piety" constitute his trap. All he can do is battle her. Thus, torn between his love for Pearl and his mother, he goes to bed that night with "life and death warr[ing] in [his] bosom," while "in her bedroom his mother lay, yearning for him, willing him to come to her" (L, 259). Davies's concluding paragraph is particularly haunting, notwithstanding its typical swipe at modernity:

Of course, sensible modern people, though they believe a variety of strange things, do not believe in any such communion in emotion as this which seemed to be at work between Solly and his mother in the darkness of their house. That is why such things are never mentioned by those who have experienced them. (L, 259)

The third figure who experiences psychological release is Gloster Ridley. Curiously, he is at the center of the narrative action but not of the novel's emotional energy. Beyond his problems as editor of the *Bellman* and his hope of receiving an honorary doctorate from Waverley, what deeply concerns him is the guilt he feels concerning the condition of his wife. She is confined in a distant mental hospital, the victim of a car accident that occurred many years before when Ridley was driving and they were quarrelling. "Anxiety" is Ridley's nemesis (L, 4). He can't put to rest in his own mind the question of whether it was "really an accident, or whether [he] created it" (L, 264).

His problem is swept away all too rapidly and congenially through the sympathy of a married friend, Elspeth Fielding. An undeveloped character in the novel, she has that "infinitely superior emotional grasp" (L, 307) Davies locates in the best of women. Simply and sympathetically she clarifies Ridley's thinking by asking him, "What's the good of winning honours . . . if you can't live on good terms with yourself?" (L, 265). She relieves him of "his bugbear forever" by a wisdom "all rooted fast in love and womanly tenderness" (L, 265). Ever so quickly Ridley is "very much changed, very much cheered" (L, 265). He controls his worrying and takes firm command of the novel's climactic trial scene. The reader, however, may not be so convinced that Ridley has paid the "inordinate price" (L, 266) that, Davies asserts, is the cost of wisdom won from experience. At a point where dramatization is most required the novel lapses into rhetoric and wise pronouncements.

In *Leaven of Malice,* Davies pushes towards a depth that eluded him in *Tempest-Tost.* The satirist, lover of farce, and pundit in him are balanced by a surer sense of psychological direction. Humphrey Cobbler, who is in and out of so many scenes that he vies with Ridley for centrality, gives particular focus to the novel's salutary and comic outlook. His combination of "genuine raffishness" (L, 161), sardonicism, taste, and experience provides leavening insight into the psychological struggles of Pearl, Solly, and Ridley, even as it helps to put the follies of other characters into perspective.

At the same time, *Leaven of Malice* offers a disturbing picture of the Canadian social animal in action, of the meanness and malice beneath the quaint, decorous surface. It is a world in which people stalk and bully others. Browbeating of the sort Vambrace practises or more subtle kinds of manipulation are characteristic modes of behavior in Salterton. Mischief-making abounds. Self-knowledge is rare. The characters are full of plots against others. They act according to their positions vis-à-vis their opponents. One character, for instance, speaks authoritatively about the "psychological advantage" and domination to be gained by using a desk to establish position (L, 282). If Saltertonians are not being aggressive, they seem deeply driven by the need "never to lose face" (L, 281), a need that itself often leads to additional, if inadvertent, cruelty. Seen in this way, the quaint city is a minefield for the unwary. Its malice needs a leaven. That leaven lies in self-awareness and the psychological strength that comes from such awareness. In *Leaven of Malice,* Davies cautiously but effectively charted his future direction as a novelist.

A Mixture of Frailties: Beyond Pumpkin Center

In a letter dated 8 February 1955, Robertson Davies expressed a new resolve: "In my next novel, now a-brewing, I want to get into my bathysphere and go as deep as I can; it is about a girl who is trying to rise above a sordid home background." He worried, however, about certain critical responses to his satiric presentations of character. "I hesitate somewhat to [proceed]," he added, "if I really give the impression that I am sneering at my characters. Of course not everybody says I do; but some people get that impression, and I want to correct it if I can."[26] Davies did indeed go deeper in *A Mixture of Frailties,* particularly in his characterizations of Monica Gall and Giles Revelstoke; he takes, in MacPherson's words, "the step—so alien to the Marchbanksian side of his sensibility—which makes him a novelist, as distinct from a playwright."[27] Nevertheless, his struggle "to write about people as nearly as possible as I see them," to check a propensity for ridicule and crude burlesque, was, overall, not markedly successful. As a result *A Mixture of Frailties* seems an aesthetic contradiction, a book torn between the appeals of surface and depth, between the spirit of attack and the spirit of understanding, between cutting wit and psychological probing.

Leaven of Malice is a sustained and trenchant novel of social analysis, brilliantly, if sometimes grossly, debunking the modernizing and democratizing forces at work in postwar Canadian society. Having painted that picture, Davies returned to another subject of great interest to him—the artist in Canada. The qualities, training, and costs involved in the making of a Canadian artist, a subject touched on in *Fortune, My Foe* and *Hope Deferred,* is the substance of Davies's first focused *Bildungsroman.* He did not, however, turn his back upon his readers' expectations concerning Salterton. Nor did he show interest in working innovatively with the form of the novel of education. Rather, in *A Mixture of Frailties* he maintains the narrative omniscience that allows him to editorialize with impunity and to establish a confident, moral tone. He sets his portrait of the artist as a young girl in a Salterton frame, so that the continuing struggles of Pearl and Solly in a provincial context can counterpoint and inform Monica Gall's painful progress as an artist on an international scale.

Reviewers responded positively to the novel. For Don Wickenden it was "a far more solid and coherent narrative [than *Leaven of Malice*], and one possessing rather more specific gravity."[28] Edmund Fuller enthused that he had "never read a better novel about the training and rise of an artist."[29] Davies's "first serious novel"[30] garnered wide-ranging praise in both Canada and the United States, though in England the response was less enthusiastic. Geoffrey Nicholson argued that "The real trouble with the book is that after two false starts and frequent changes in tone, you are never sure how seriously Monica is to be regarded."[31] Norman Shrapnel, resisting Davies's show of knowledge about music and music training, called the author "a shade naive" and conventional in his treatment, though he allowed that "he knows his background and has given us a most entertaining and by no means trivial book."[32]

The novel begins with a new disruption of the old Salterton order. Mrs. Louisa Bridgetower is dead. The first paragraph precisely introduces one of the book's pervasive themes: for powerful, manipulative personalities, to be dead is not to be forgotten.

It was appropriate that Mrs. Bridgetower's funeral fell on a Thursday, for that had always been her At Home day. As she had dominated her drawing-room, so she dominated St. Nicholas' Cathedral on this frosty 23rd of December. She had planned her funeral, as she had planned all her social duties and observances, with care.[33]

That careful dominance takes the form of a quirky will by means of which Mrs. Bridgetower maintains her power over her son and closest friends. Publicly she wins favor by establishing a beneficent trust to sponsor a European education in the arts for a deserving young Salterton female. Privately, however, as a continuing sign of disapproval of Solly's marriage to Veronica Vambrace, she wields a powerful "Dead Hand," giving the couple a paltry $100 and harnessing them with the obligation of living in and maintaining her large house until such time as they produce a male child. Only then will the house and her million-dollar estate be theirs. In the meantime Solly, Puss Pottinger, Dean Knapp, and Matthew Snelgrove are to oversee the trust and, in so doing, feel her continuing presence in their lives.

The trust functions like the curse in a fairy tale, a wicked witch's curse that must be broken so that order and the possibility of happiness can be reestablished. Fairy tale and myth also inform the larger narrative of Monica Gall's education. As Clara Thomas has observed, Monica's story, at once that of a Canadian Cinderella and Galatea, comprises "a novel in itself."[34] It is her education that dominates, despite Davies's persistent effort to maintain a balance.

Her story begins most unpromisingly. Her world is entirely beyond Mrs. Bridgetower's, bearing no relation to the old woman's affluence, social prominence, and Edwardian habits. It is a world that Davies treats with a typically aggressive and satiric emphasis. Monica works in the local factory, Consolidated Adhesives and Abrasives (the Glue Works), where she is a secretary and her father a janitor and union man. Her church is the fundamentalist Thirteenth Apostle Tabernacle frequented by her parents. Under the guidance of Pastor Beamis, an oily ex-boxer, she sings soprano in the Thirteeners' Heart and Hope Gospel Quartet. It is only through the agency of Humphrey Cobbler, who follows the Gospel Quartet's radio broadcasts out of "perverse glee" (M, 38), that Monica is suddenly brought to the attention of the Bridgetower Trust and given the opportunity of an unusual education.

Needing a kitchen for his Cinderella, Davies resorted to the very kind of writing he was seeking to avoid. He shows little sympathy toward and virtually no ability to identify with the shabbiness or sordidness of Monica's world. Her "real natural talent" has been "overlaid" by what the English conductor Sir Benedict Domdaniel clinically labels "a stultifying home atmosphere and cultural malnutrition" (M, 54). To hammer home the point Davies presents a series of scenes that differ significantly in tone and quality from the satire directed, for instance, at the antics of Puss and Snelgrove in socially proper Salterton or "the menagerie," a group of Bohemian mediocrities in London who cluster about Monica's teacher, Giles Revelstoke. Showing little but cold disdain for fundamentalism, the union outlook, and the quest for upward mobility, Davies trivializes Monica's world, indulging in "broad contempt for the hick-Canadian" that Clara Thomas terms "both crude and cruel."[35] Ma Gall is presented as a bizarre manic-depressive whose moods are governed by excesses of sugar consumption, Alf Gall as a Jack Spratt figure distinguished only by his inertness, Beamis as "an unctuous gorilla" (M, 38), and Monica's boyfriend, George Medwell, as a young "realist" whose "whole moral system was rooted in his conception of economics" (M, 62). Add the kind of scene Davies describes with relish, Ma's going-away party for Monica, complete with the Beamis clan, a couple of theatrical homosexuals, and the mouthy local radio announcer, and the reader is grateful for the efficacy of Mrs. Bridgetower's trust fund. As Ivon Owen observed, the sequence involving Monica's family is "too wildly farcical to supply the commonplace atmosphere the pattern demands."[36]

Davies's desire to deal realistically and effectively with the Galls' world is evident in his comments on Jessie Fothergill's popular novel *The First Violin,* which has a strong influence on Monica and itself provides a mythic pattern for her story. "Girls in novels never seemed to have parents except when they were of some use in the plot, and then they were either picturesque or funny," he writes. "The Galls were neither; they were oppressively real and many-faceted" (M, 67). His purpose is, nevertheless, undermined by a presentation in which caricature and slapstick predominate. Monica's formative world is scarcely more forceful as oppressive reality than Marchbanks's Skunk's Misery. When at a later stage in the novel Davies seeks to present the strength of the relationship between Monica and her mother, the reader is hard pressed to forget the earlier burlesque.

Having provided Monica with a family, society, boyfriend, and religion she can readily cast aside, Davies takes her to England, a raw provincial equipped mostly with romantic ideas from *The First Violin.* And, as is often the case in Davies's writing, the popular writing of the nineteenth century, far from providing ridiculous models for behavior, is a source of illumination and analogue. Who, Monica wonders, will be her "First Violin," her "man of mystery" and who "the magnetic—but daemonic and sardonic—von Francius?" (M, 66). *A Mixture of Frailties* provides answers in Sir Benedict Domdaniel and Revelstoke. But as these patterns of romance work themselves out in the novel, Davies exposes Monica to a wide variety of experiences and challenges, all of which contribute to the impression of a detailed realism on the one hand and to the development of an accomplished singer and wiser human being on the other.

The key to that education is Domdaniel. An elegant, world-famous conductor who functions as professional advisor to the Bridgetower trust, he is the novel's Prospero or magus, Monica's paternal counselor and the subtle manipulator of experiences most valuable to her. Recalling Val Rich in *Tempest-Tost,* he is another instance of Davies's preoccupation with the clearly superior individual who knows himself, is without illusions, is above cheap cynicism and doubt, and who not only can see what is best for others but also is able to communicate that insight precisely. As Pygmalion he molds a singer and a woman who will, in the end, be an agreeable wife for himself, precisely attuned to his fine sense of professionalism. Davies makes it clear, however, that Domdaniel's position is hard won. He is a nobleman by merit, an English Jew who, realizing the nature and extent of his talents, has made the most of himself. His name suggests, among other things, blessedness (benediction), masterliness (dom), and vision (Daniel). Such, the novel implies, are the qualities awaiting those who respond fully to his remarkable tutelage.

For the most part Domdaniel stands back from the actual work. Murtagh Molloy, a fifty-year old Irishman, instructs Monica in voice control and command of emotion. More a teacher of the theater than music, his specialty is "muhd," the ability by means of voice and body to project powerful, convincing emotion. He initiates "the process of vocal and spiritual unbuttoning" (M, 116) that frees Monica from the musical and religious hell of her Salterton upbringing. Voice training, however, is not in itself enough. Domdaniel also appoints a "wise and capable woman" (M, 243), Amy Neilson, to introduce Monica to a cultivation of cosmopolitan breadth. In addition, he arranges as ingredients in her development language lessons and a visit to the Welsh countryside.

The most emotionally influential of her English teachers is Giles Revelstoke, whom Domdaniel appoints "to broaden her musical experience" (M, 143). Revelstoke also sets out "to take care of [her] style" (M, 156), to teach her the real glory of singing (singing is, for him, "a form of human eloquence, speech raised to the highest degree" [M, 157]), and "to nurture [her] spirit" (M, 158). Through sex and song he extends her education in ways she hadn't anticipated, leading her into the labyrinth of mixed motives and painful self-exploration. But what Monica undergoes with Revelstoke comes as no surprise to the worldly Domdaniel. Having sent her to Revelstoke for what he calls "excellent reasons" (M, 143), he tells her that "falling in love with one's master is recognized practice in the musical world" (M, 212). "Anything to broaden your range of feeling" (M, 213) is worthwhile, he further suggests. It is almost as if the elderly Domdaniel knows that she must sow her wild oats if she is to be prepared to wed him. In effect, Domdaniel plays Pygmalion and magus to both Monica and Revelstoke.[37] After Giles's death, he confesses to her that he was "[t]oo fond of him," too concerned with improving his musical fortune and with humanizing the egotist in him (M, 361). It would seem to be Domdaniel's sole failing that, in attempting to promote a creative miracle by encouraging Revelstoke to write his opera, *The Golden Asse,* he inadvertently sets in motion the events leading to the death of his protégé. Domdaniel's folly lies, he realizes, in trying "to mould somebody else's fate" (M, 361). What fails with Revelstoke succeeds, however, with Monica.

Giles Revelstoke is among Davies's most interesting characters. He is at once egotist and artist, a self-serving, perverse sensibility and a potential genius. Drawing upon the life and career of Peter Warlock [Philip Arnold Heseltine] (1894–1930), whose "suicide" occurred on Tite Street where Revelstoke resides in the novel and where Davies himself later lived, Davies probes in the character of Revelstoke the interrelation of the demonic and creative in the artistic temperament. He had read Cecil Gray's controversial study, *Peter Warlock: A Memoir of Philip Heseltine* (1934), and drew freely upon it in characterizing Revelstoke as a man of two distinctly different characters. Famed for his song cycles and his "lusty, roystering, swashbuckling, drinking, [and] wenching" activities, the bearded Warlock had been the basis for D. H. Lawrence's demeaning portrait of Halliday in *Women in Love* and Aldous Huxley's arresting characterization of Coleman in *Antic Hay*.[38] His reputation was extraordinary.

Gray's memoir sought to offer an explanation of Warlock's dual nature. The "Mild and Melancholy Philip," unsuccessful with women and music, transformed himself into "Peter Warlock, the Complete Man, masterful, compelling and Rabelaisian." What also emerges is the picture of a self-indulgent man who allowed his creative energies to lapse into venomous attacks upon others and self-loathing. This Warlock was the devilish sorcerer of his conscious renaming, a man who assailed critics and friends on impulse, revelling in antagonisms, doing what he wanted, and going on periodic binges that were the stuff of legend. To Gray, Warlock was a classic instance of a man who was at once a romantic and a cynic. Dogmatically innocent, he believed that art must be pure, that women were either "destroying vampire[s]" or "redeeming saints," and that the artist must consume himself in the intensity of his own inner fire. As cynic, however, he despised not only all that was not pure but the impurities in himself. "In this frustration of the real self and triumph of the *alter ego*," writes Gray, "we find the clue to the whole problem of his life." When his inner tensions became too great, he launched out upon "violent personal quarrels and public controversies," psychologically pursuing a desire to punish what he most hated in others and himself.[39]

The serious artist that Domdaniel recognizes is represented in

Revelstoke's confident opinions and in the evolution of his musical works. From song cycles like *The Discoverie of Witchcraft* to his opera, Revelstoke advances under Domdaniel's goading from musical journalism to "real composition." But he never ceases to be an unmitigated egotist, obsessively protective of his work and often condescending and cruel to those closest to him. On one level, such behavior is simply the freedom of the artist; as Domdaniel says, "creators must simply do what seems best to them" (M, 212). To embody other aspects of this freedom Davies associates Revelstoke with sexual appetite, Bohemian habits, and a magazine about music, the *Lantern*.[40] Such bohemianism, however, turns out to be a part of Revelstoke's personal failure in the novel, for it is presented as a kind of eccentric indulgence in what is, in the end, sordid and second-rate in itself. The *Lantern* is "an expense of spirit" (M, 211). But what most clearly signals Revelstoke's failure in the novel is his asperity and meanness of spirit. At his frankest he admits, "I've no time for charm" (M, 155). At his most characteristic, he is morose or vindictive, indulging increasingly, like Warlock, in critic baiting and nasty personal attacks. As Monica painfully realizes, his ego is so unyielding that "He could not bear to be crossed in anything" (M, 228). Childlike and unappeasable, he insists on dominance and power over others.

One of the problems with *A Mixture of Frailties* is that the teachers are more fascinating than the student. Revelstoke and Domdaniel are such powerful, talented, and clever figures that they tend to diminish Monica's presence. In falling under Revelstoke's thrall, she is hard pressed to avoid becoming, if not Galatea, then another of his "groupies." Deeply in love, she resolves to be "Patient Griselda," but her strategy is put to the test by Revelstoke's demands. Her real problem is, thus, to break his control. However brilliant, Revelstoke is not a model to be followed. Incident by incident the novel makes clear that his genius is hampered by a childish and perverse egotism that puts him at odds with virtually all aspects of society. Revelstoke is Monica's major test. The mark of her quality is her ability to extricate herself from her emotional involvement, and to do so in a way that is, if not morally correct, at least deeply felt and considered.

The learning of hypocrisy—what might better be called the acquisition of healthy adaptability—is a major theme of Monica's education. Having at first naively resolved never to be disloyal to family and home, she has hardly set foot in England before she finds herself "edit[ing]" her past history and discovering that "facts presented themselves, somehow, in a rather different guise" (M, 94). As the guest of a Canadian family in London, the McCorkills, who are heavyhandedly caricatured as homesick cultural chauvinists, she soon learns the "adult luxury" of social hypocrisy, the ability to deal convivially with people whose views she cannot agree with. Despite such adaptation, however, Monica's fundamentalist simplicity and puritanism die hard.

Her early English experiences pave the way for more difficult and important psychological accommodations. The narrative focusses its moral attention upon three difficult situations, two involving deaths. The first involves Monica's considered refusal to lend Solly and Veronica some of the extra money that the Bridgetower trust belatedly gives her. While Veronica's plaintive request reveals that the trust has effectively enslaved Solly and her, leaving them "terribly in debt," their marriage in the process of "being twisted out of shape" (M, 308-9), Monica turns them down in order to help finance Revelstoke's opera. Legality is on her side as is her prior commitment to Giles. It is, nevertheless, difficult for her to separate what she hopes to gain personally—a new sense of obligation in her lover—from her higher aspirations, her "longing for what was perhaps unattainable in this world, a longing for a fulfillment which was of the spirit and not of the flesh, but which was not specifically religious in its yearning" (M, 311). In aligning herself with Giles's creative genius she pledges herself to that goal of *Hiraeth,* despite other powerful claims upon her.

If Monica's patronage of *The Golden Asse* reveals a grand aspiration among mixed motives, the situations involving death are more troubling still. These crucial instances, which take up much of the novel's last third, in general lack the clarity of presentation and firmness of handling one associates with Davies's writing. In breaking complex, new ground, he struggled to formulate the moral issues Monica faced and to make them pertain to her artistic education. Later in the Deptford trilogy, writing with greater sureness, he would continue to address the problem of the personal priority an individual must recognize in dealing with moral and aesthetic claims.

The first death occurs in Salterton. Feeling increasingly the pressure of "keeping two sets of mental and moral books—one for inspection in the light of home, and another to contain her life with Revelstoke" (M, 266), Monica is suddenly summoned home because of her mother's illness. Medically, she learns, the problem is treatable. She opts, however, to support her mother's refusal to be hospitalized and operated on. Her instinct is to treat Ma's fears, however eccentric, as sacred, though in doing so she leaves herself open to charges—her sister makes them explicitly—of having killed her mother. But Monica is strong enough to trust her intuition and to put the claims of common sense and medical science into a secondary position. Her commitment to her mother's emotional need is her way of paying genuine tribute to the woman who, she feels, is the source of her life and her imagination. It is, in essence, her deepest, least hypocritical tribute to her Salterton experience.

For the reader, the moral difficulties in the situation are not so easily swept aside. Monica's response to the doctors—"My mother lives by the spirit as well as by the flesh; if I kill the spirit by delivering her, frightened and forsaken, into your hands, what makes you think that you can save the flesh?" (M, 276)—is a powerful challenge, but it involves a disturbingly dogmatic flaunting of common sense. Despite the fact that Davies has the doctors see the wisdom of Monica's decision, it is not clear that Ma Gall's fear is sufficient reason to condone nonaction. The issue at stake is personal, not religious. More important, in a novel, the fundamental ethic and "politics" of which is to proclaim Eros over Thanatos (M, 108), such a decision seems curiously chilling. Medical knowledge and the value of life are discounted in order that the plot can spiritually unite Monica and her mother; they are united, however, in such a way that Ma can be promptly eliminated from the action. In the process neither the Galls nor the medical authorities are given the kind of substantial voices that effectively develop the issue's many complexities.

The second death is Revelstoke's "death by misadventure" (M, 344). Based on the sensational events of, and the inquest into, Peter Warlock's death (the English coroner was unable to determine whether or not he had killed himself), the incident is presented so as to implicate Monica both factually and psychologically. Davies makes her position especially difficult. Not only had she written to Revelstoke breaking off their relationship but she was the first to enter his apartment, finding him apparently dead, the gas still on and her letter in his hand. Overcoming her panic, she seized the letter and left, turning the gas back on but not lighting it. When she later learns that he died not of asphyxiation but from choking on his own vomit, her feelings of guilt and complicity increase. "By her selfishness and littleness of spirit," she believes, "she had killed him" (M, 348).

She soon discovers, however, that others also feel guilty. Indeed, the question, "Who killed Giles Revelstoke?", looms so large as to anticipate that major enigma of *Fifth Business* and *The Manticore,* "Who killed Boy Staunton?" The "usual cabal" in *A Mixture of Frailties* includes Revelstoke himself, Giles's mother, his *Lantern* colleague Bun Eccles, Monica's rival Persis Kinwellmarshe, the music critic Stanhope Aspinwall, and Domdaniel. By comparison to the Deptford trilogy, Davies takes little advantage of the question's possibilities, his purpose being to spread the sense of guilt around and to put Monica's quandary in perspective. Predictably, it takes a wise man to show her how to "clarif[y] her thinking" (M, 365). Revealing his own feeling of guilt—"Morally, I killed him" (M, 362)—Domdaniel offers her the succor of confession; he becomes her "sin-eater" (M, 363) and an accessory to her crime (if such it be) by destroying her letter to Giles. He helps her to see the destructiveness of Giles's demanding egotism and encourages her to seek "a metamorphosis" (M, 367), some sustaining and healthy outlook by which to proceed "in the life that has somehow or other found [her] and claimed [her]" (M, 379).

As in Ma Gall's death, Davies strives to engage Monica in a dilemma that tests her strength as an individual and convincingly measures for the reader what she has gained in getting beyond "the surface of all the heavy-hearted dullness that seems to claim so many people" (M, 379). He develops an intricate pattern of moral complicity, stressing the inevitable involvement of many people in one's moral and emotional problems and the need to shift or adapt one's moral accounts, especially under pressure of significant change in life and outlook. Though the language of the novel is often didactic, *A Mixture of Frailties* strives to put the narrow, puritanical voice of conscience in perspective. "So often," thinks Monica, "[the cruel inner voice] put the worst construction on everything, and in that respect it was like a conscience. But it spoke no morality which Monica could associate with a conscience—unless, somewhere, she were developing a new conscience, suited to her new needs" (M, 285). Monica's "new conscience" is crucial to her romantic metamorphosis.

A Mixture of Frailties gives a special but cautious glamour to the life of an artist. Salterton's Dean Knapp speaks for Davies in stating that, "A career in art must often mean great changes in personality—much abandoned in the past, and much learned. I've sometimes thought we might all be the better for taking new names when we discover our vocations" (M, 292). Monica follows the prescription; though she does not choose a new name, she evolves a new personality, rising above both her hick background (Giles contemptuously calls Salterton "Pumpkin Centre") and the experience of passion that "sometimes drives her to serious dishonesty, not far from crime."[41]

The transformed Monica, no longer the plain Canadian provincial nor Giles's "clumsy pretence-enchantress" [M, 335] in *The Golden Asse,* is ready to engage in life on a new plateau. She is the Cinderella triumph of the imperialism of art. What is disconcerting about her metamorphosis is the dogmatism of Davies's celebration of such imperialism. His teacher-characters give her ordained knowledge of a kind that replaces her "nice simplicity."[42] He makes it clear that she couldn't receive an education of such quality except at the center—in England.

When a Canadian of talent goes abroad and discovers "how little his country means to the average person elsewhere,"[43] what are the consequences of that recognition? Does he try to take on the characteristics of another nation or does he discard his provinciality while discovering what Canada does mean to him? While it is the latter process that Davies presents in *A Mixture of Frailties,* what emerges is colored by the book's excessive homage to artistic imperialism. Like Chimène in *Hope Deferred,* when Monica loses her provinciality, she loses very little. Cinderella released from Pumpkin Centre, she seems not to have felt very strongly about many things until Cobbler unearthed her. Ma Gall, the one home link Davies seeks to make vital, is so withered by early satire that it is difficult to accept her as the genuine root of the artist in her daughter. When Monica feels love it is in London, when she feels awe and wonder she is in Paris, and when, uncharacteristically, she is moved by landscape it is in Wales. There is in *A Mixture of Frailties* a very strong sense that Monica is cast too definitively as raw material. She can only be stimulated abroad by proper teachers. Good taste, which is mostly foreign, and wealth, which Davies regularly defends, must play their crucial parts in her transformation.

A Mixture of Frailties holds tightly to its imperialism. Perhaps as a result it falters in giving Monica's roots the serious consideration necessary to convince the reader that they matter. Unlike Willa Cather's Thea Kronberg in *The Song of the Lark* or Alice Munro's Del Jordan in *Lives of Girls and Women,* Monica draws little strength from the old things—be they memories of family, places, or formative experiences. She is a mere vessel to be richly filled under Domdaniel's paternalistic guidance. It seems to matter very little— and this is a major blind spot in the novel—what shape the vessel originally takes. What matters more is the celebration (in Domdaniel's case, it seems to be a case of hero worship) of the wise and talented teacher and the culture out of which he springs.

Chapter Six
The Deptford Trilogy: Passwords to the Duke's Realm

Robertson Davies's second trilogy—*Fifth Business* (1970), *The Manticore* (1972), and *World of Wonders* (1975)—has occasioned an entirely new level of interest in the writer and his art. While not all of the critical responses have expressed sympathy with or admiration for the trilogy's underlying premises, it is evident that the majority of reviewers and critics have been deeply impressed, even surprised, by Davies's achievement. In particular, *Fifth Business* has been the subject of lavish attention. One of its most enthusiastic supporters, Wilfred Cude, has called it as "a miracle of art," a splendid comic novel comparable to Twain's *Adventures of Huckleberry Finn*.[1]

Neither have the subsequent novels lacked for praise. Anthony Burgess, for instance, termed *The Manticore* a "small masterpiece," "one of the most elegant novels to come out of North America in a very long time,"[2] while Brian Moore congratulated Davies for breathing fresh life into "the old [Victorian] Novel House."[3] Edmund Fuller applauded *World of Wonders* and the entire trilogy as "a brilliant literary accomplishment."[4]

It is from the perspective of Davies's career that one can best distinguish the special qualities of *Fifth Business* and the trilogy as a whole. I should like to emphasize three distinct ways in which the Deptford novels differ from and, for many readers, improve upon the Salterton books. The first concerns the relative density of references to be found in the two trilogies. Always an allusive writer with a keen eye for literary analogue, Davies creates in *Fifth Business* and its successors a more enriched and fascinating network of coded references, images, and symbols than one finds in the earlier novels. In such allusive gardens Cude and other critics have happily hunted in search of sources and of patterns of meaning to be located in Davies's uses of hagiography, archaeology, magic, clocks, Jungian psychology, law, heraldry, nineteenth-century English theater, carnivals, folklore, and mythology. Davies's irrepressible zeal for dispensing information, planting references, and establishing connections makes the Deptford trilogy, in Anthony Dawson's metaphor, a spider's parlor that draws the reader into an engagement with various threads of information, the filamentary clues and signifiers with which the novels abound.[5]

One senses a new level of confidence on Davies's part, an increased ability not only to interweave interesting patterns but also to arrange his narrative structure so as to evoke and sustain mystery by means of those patterns. Readers are challenged by the implicit mandate of the novels to see as the trilogy's central figure, Dunstan Ramsay, sees, to understand the ways in which poetry, mythology, and hagiography, for instance, relate to "psychological truth." At the same time, in a way that is an improvement on *A Mixture of Frailties,* Davies is able to make narrative mystery a powerful component. It matters far more "Who killed Boy Staunton?" than it does "Who killed Giles Revelstoke?" It matters precisely because the respective protagonists—Ramsay, David Staunton, and Magnus Eisengrim— are deeply concerned about the question. Davies is far more adventurous in the Deptford trilogy both in the narrative strategies he applies and in the complexity of the moral questions he investigates.

The second distinction between the Deptford trilogy and the Salterton novels concerns the axis of this enriched allusiveness and sense of mystery. There is, as Burgess noted of *The Manticore,* "a sense of new psychological vistas, undreamt of by Dickens, opening up all the time."[6] As has been often noted, especially since the appearance of *The Manticore,* Davies's recent writing has been strongly influenced by the healthful and individualistic "depth-psychology" of Carl Gustav Jung. Patricia Monk has in fact devoted an entire book to the subject of Davies's empathy with and debt, as novelist, to Jung. Jung is mentioned only once in *Fifth Business* but that reference is indicative of his importance to the novel as a whole. Describing the sexual obsessiveness of his "lifelong friend and enemy,"[7] Boy Staunton, Dunstan Ramsay writes:

If his social life interested me, his private life fascinated me. I have never known anyone in whose life sex played such a dominating part. He didn't think so. He once told me that he thought this fellow Freud must be a madman, bringing everything down to sex the way he did. I attempted no defence of Freud; by this time I was myself much concerned with that old fantastical duke of dark corners, C. G. Jung, but I had read a great deal of Freud and remembered his injunction against arguing in favour of psychoanalysis with those who clearly hated it."(F, 213)

Fifth Business suggests that Ramsay discovered Jung in the late 1930s. Judging by his own book reviews, Davies himself turned seriously to Jung sometime in 1958. In an early 1958 review, he was still proclaiming Freud "the greater man."[8] Three months later, however, he was celebrating Jung's methods as "both safer and more lastingly effective than Freud's."[9] In 1955, for instance, Davies analysed *Measure for Measure*, the source of his "duke of dark corners" image, in a distinctly Freudian way. Reading "by the light of Dr. [Ernest] Jones' torch," Davies was clearly fascinated by the Duke as one "who likes disguise and mystification" and who is "a man with a well-established God Complex." "It does not take any very remarkable insight," he continues, "to perceive that Isabella is in love with her father, and loves Claudio only insofar as he serves as a substitute for that father. She is affianced to God, it is true, but the alliance between the father-figure and the concept of God in the unconscious mind is widely recognized."[10]

"[T]hat old fantastical duke of dark corners" evolved from a Freudian to a Jungian image from 1955 to 1970. As father-figure operating behind the scenes, as confessor and interpreter, and as the dispenser of justice (like "the character of Divine Correction in the medieval morality plays"),[11] Sir Benedict Domdaniel belongs to Davies's Freudian phase. By contrast, Dunstan Ramsay's duke is the master of the mysterious. He holds a variety of keys to that "strange world that showed very little of itself on the surface" (F, 35). He leads Ramsay, David Staunton, and Paul Dempster (Magnus Eisengrim) into that world of wonders, the realm in which the animals speak, where patterns of destiny emerge from the muddle of experience, where the wise guides have about them a fantastical unconventionality.

The Deptford trilogy is experience interpreted by the light of Carl Jung and his disciples. It is, however, always Davies's sense of experience that is presented, and it is always Davies who selects what in the vast body of Jungian thought is useful to him.

Like Dunstan Ramsay, Davies found in Jung a view of psychological experience in which he could recognize much that was pertinent to his life. He found support for his own optimism about individual growth and special personal destiny, especially in middle age. In a 1983 review of *The Essential Jung,* Davies noted, that "Jung was convinced that 45 was roughly the period of life when its immensely important second development began, and that this second period was concerned with matters which were, in the broadest sense, religious." Jung helped Davies to shape and justify what he already felt about the importance in middle-age of self-development and the pursuit of healthful self-knowledge, the need to recognize the priorities of emotion and intuition, the actuality of evil, the overemphasis upon sex in the modern consciousness, and the interrelatedness of various aspects of human knowledge. He noted that "the richness and variety of Jung's thought" can lead serious readers to "a philosophy that is enlarging and supportive . . . a mode of thinking which encourages fullness of life, rather than . . . a system that seeks ultimate truth, without touching daily experience."[12] As the Deptford trilogy's "duke of dark corners," Jung watches over the proceedings of a fictional world in which zealous puritan values, untinctured by self-knowledge, let loose the forces of disorder. Such disorder is resolved only by recognition among the special few of the powerful, unseen world.

The third point of distinction is the fact that, unlike the Salterton novels, the books in the Deptford trilogy deal in lifetimes. More precisely, they deal in destinies. All three are built upon the premise that there are two worlds of experience available to human beings. One in the daily world of objects, places, and social interaction—of surfaces; this is the province of human order, institutionalized truth, scientific laws, practicality, and causality. The other is the world of mystery, awe, and wonder. As a boy Dunstan Ramsay intuitively links himself to this other world through his interest in forms of magic, the *Arabian Nights,* and *A Child's Book of Saints.* Later, despite his Scot Presbyterian reticence, he engages increasingly in the study of saints, poetry, and myth, pursuing answers to the question of what religion is "about" rather than what the adherents of a specific religion believe. The search for clues linking these worlds is at the heart of Dunstan Ramsay's story. Whether these two worlds are called the ordinary and the magical, the realistic and the transcendental, or the conscious and the unconscious, in Davies's Deptford vision, they interact constantly. The unseen world always informs the visible world. As one wise counselor comments, it is most important to struggle at each stage of life to "make some sense of this life of marvels, cruel circumstances, obscenities, and commonplaces" (F, 206).

Learned guides abound in the Deptford trilogy. As in the Salterton novels, Davies's protagonists need to be led to the larger truths. They must meet their mentors at the right psychological moment. Moreover, as befits his increasingly mysterious and fantastical emphasis, Davies with *Fifth Business* moves toward more unconventional, extravagant, and grotesque counselors. The teaching they undertake can be jovial or brutal, but it is always serious and authoritative. Whether its emphasis be psychological recognition or aesthetic credo, it is also essentially moralistic. Indeed, it is distinctly elitist.

This "life of marvels" is only for especially sensitive and rare people. To such individuals Davies's teacher figures like Padre Ignacio Blazon and the Swiss "autocrat" Liesl Vitzlipützli attach themselves as fellow (though superior) aristocrats of the spirit. Like the three magicians in J. B. Priestley's Jungian novel, *The Magicians,* they serve at once to deepen the aura of mystery and to function as the aging hero's "masters" of special insights and "ancient wisdom." They make it clear that to achieve such self-knowledge and wisdom is a rare experience. As one of Priestley's magicians declares, such knowing is "Not for most."[13]

Such wisdom is characterized by its awareness of the vast sweep of time. That sweep implies a cosmic organization that diminishes and humbles human pretensions. Once recognized, it evokes a feeling of awe and terror that is religious in the pure, uninstitutional sense. In the Deptford novels the reader is always in history, particularly in a psychological sense. Types and archetypes abound as do typical and archetypical relationships. The sweep of time is symbolized by "the stone," the piece of pink granite Boy Staunton threw at Ramsay in 1908 initiating the action of the trilogy. It becomes a paperweight that sits on Ramsay's desk until it is found in Boy Staunton's mouth after his suicide over fifty years later. The fatal stone becomes for Ramsay a symbol of guilt (acknowledged in his case and evaded in Boy's) and of the peculiar and unseen intricacies of human relationships. In *The Manticore* we learn that the stone was perhaps "a thousand million years old" and that in "the long, voiceless, inert history of the stone," "[n]one of us counts for much."[14] That Ramsay throws it away, freeing Boy's son, David, of the bondage it imposes on his mind, does not, however, free

David from a sense of the past. David's descent into the Swiss cave with Liesl is meant to put him in touch with his bear-worshipping "ancestors" and their primal religious feelings. To Liesl and to Davies it is crucial that David, a middle-aged man too given over to reason, recognize the legacy of awe and terror man shared in responding openly to "the great mysteries" (M, 272). Such lessons constitute Davies's attempt to put his narrators—Ramsay and David—in touch with what Jung called "the collective unconscious" of the human race.

The emergence of this historical view in Davies's fiction was doubtless the result of many influences, especially on a Jungian cast. One worth noting is J. B. Priestley's *Literature and Western Man* (1960), which Davies reviewed, having read it twice with undiminished enthusiasm. In his introduction Priestley emphasized that, while his study concerned itself with Western literature after the invention of the printing press, "we must still remember that the procession we lead in time is very long indeed." To study Western man, we have to recognize our ancestors in "the remote dusk of pre-history"; "the men who did those wonderful cave paintings, say, at Lascaux, so highly charged with vitality and magical feeling, might be said to be alive in us today."[15]

Dunstan Ramsay seems just such a man as Priestley imagined himself to be—"a sort of composite Western Man, to whom everything has been related" and for whom such recognitions are crucial.[16] In his review of Priestley's book, Davies paid particular attention to Priestley's long historical view and to his sustained treatment of "the failure of our society to find a religion truly adequate to its needs."[17] For both writers, "man has come down the eons a religious being, who must needs worship something."[18] In its emphasis upon modern man's need for religious inspiration, its equating of the Classical with the conscious mind and the Romantic with the unconscious, and its "humane, well-bred" good sense, *Literature and Western Man* was an important stimulus to Davies at a time when he was searching for a new direction. The Deptford trilogy shares many of its concerns, adapting them to the egocentric energy that distinguishes Davies's protagonists.

Fifth Business: Seeing the World Unseen

Dunstan Ramsay's private memoir abounds in mysteries within the narrative and problems of interpretation for the reader. Ostensibly, it is his account of his life and actions. Because his boyhood was rooted in the stern Presbyterianism and careful materialism of turn-of-the-century, small-town Canada, the memoir is much concerned with guilt, money, and success. But while Deptford measures success on the scales of institutional religion and the marketplace, Ramsay's lifelong experiences lead him to apply other criteria. Success for him must be measured in terms of what John Henry Newman called "the world unseen." Ramsay's fascination with this rich and ambiguous realm, his certainty of its actuality and power and his ability to evoke its presence, is perhaps the single major factor accounting for the power and popularity of *Fifth Business*.

Ramsay undertakes to write his memoir at the age of seventy. He addresses it to the incumbent Headmaster of Colborne College, a fashionable Toronto private school where he had taught history for many years, serving as Acting Headmaster during the years of World War II. His two reasons for writing seem at first unrelated. Specifically, he is offended by a platitudinous tribute written for his retirement by a young colleague, Lorne Packer. Appearing in the *College Chronicle* and entitled "Farewell to the Cork," the piece inadequately summarized Ramsay's career and commented condescendingly about his unscientific view of history, his concern with "the borderland between history and myth" (F, 7). Secondly, Ramsay has a private explanation to offer the Headmaster concerning the sensational demise of Boy Staunton, who at the time of his death was the school's Chairman of the Board of Governors, an illustrious "Old Boy," and a highly prominent Canadian corporate and political figure.

It is Ramsay's strong conviction that "the world unseen" is a far more significant factor in human lives than most people realize that impels him to present his story and take his stand. Just as "that ineffable jackass Lorne Packer, M.A." could not see the importance of Ramsay's life and achievements because he was blinded by his scientific view of history and his religious illiteracy, so the public is confined to mere journalistic facts about Boy Staunton's death. Ramsay has much to tell about what happened and why the "suicide" occurred.

In *Fifth Business*'s opening scene set in 1908, ten-year-old Dunstable Ramsay ducks a snowball aimed at him by his "lifelong friend and enemy" Percy Boyd Staunton. Ramsay so times his maneuver that the snowball hits the pregnant wife of Deptford's Baptist minister, Amasa Dempster. The result is far more serious than either boy intended. Staunton's snowball contained a stone. It strikes Mary Dempster on the head, triggering her labor and the premature birth of her son Paul. Thus begins Ramsay's lifelong relationship with Mrs. Dempster, one that opens up for him aspects of experience foreign both to Deptford's materialistic outlook and the tenacious, demanding Presbyterianism of his mother.

During Paul's prolonged battle to survive his early days, Ramsay finds that he must bear his guilt alone. His burden is compounded by evidence that Mrs. Dempster's apparently addled condition may be permanent. While Staunton adamantly refuses to acknowledge his part in the incident, Ramsay, suffering "greatly" within, sees himself as one "of the damned" (F, 19), noting retrospectively that, "It is living with these guilty secrets that exacts the price" (F, 20). His Protestant imagination inflamed by Doré's illustrations of Dante's *Inferno* responds almost hungrily to his mother's assertion that "the Devil guided [the thrower's] hand" (F, 20).

Fifth Business traces Ramsay's relations over six decades with Staunton on the one hand and Mary Dempster on the other. The first chapter concerns Deptford life prior to World War I, focussing upon Ramsay's early interest in magic and saints, his caretaker relationship to the Dempsters, and Staunton's privileged position in town. During World War I, Ramsay enlists, in part to escape his mother's smothering demands. At Passchendaele he singlehandedly breaks up a German machine-gun nest, only to be hit by an exploding bomb. The result is a deep coma, burns, and the loss of a leg. Nursed back to health and sexually initiated by an English nurse, Diana Marfleet, who renames him Dunstan after the saint, Ramsay recovers his strength and returns to Deptford, receiving a hero's welcome as the recipient of the Victoria Cross (an achievement ignored in Lorne Packer's tribute).

The coma, lasting five months, has a transforming effect upon him. He vaguely recalls "that splendid, carefree world" where "I had been wonderfully at ease and healingly at peace" (F, 86) and compares the experience to lines he later read in Coleridge's *Kubla Khan*. But if the coma opens up for him that strange, other world, it also has the effect of crystallising Mary Dempster's importance in his inner life. It was her face Ramsay had seen in a churchyard on a statue of the Virgin just before he lost consciousness at Passchendaele. Linking this to two other "miracles" he attributes to

Mary in Deptford, he makes it the passion of his postwar life to discover whether or not Mary Dempster is a genuine saint. *Fifth Business*'s remaining chapters parallel the careers of Ramsay, Staunton, and, to a lesser extent, Paul Dempster. Having completed his education, Ramsay takes up schoolteaching. So great is his interest in hagiography that he writes popular studies of saints and contributes occasionally to the prestigious journal of the Bollandists. Increasingly, his energies lead him, like William James, toward an interest less in religion per se than in "the psychology of religion" (F, 187). Meanwhile, he maintains his friendship with Staunton and watches over Mary Dempster, personally undertaking the financial burden when she is institutionalized.

Staunton, who renames himself "Boy," marries the belle of Deptford, Leola Cruikshank, and quickly establishes himself as a businessman. He parlays his father's sugarbeet operation into a vast corporation based on sweets and confectionaries. Keen for prestige, he connects himself in fact and spirit to the Prince of Wales, for whom he serves as aide-de-camp during the Prince's 1927 Canadian tour. Never, however, does he face certain realities about his own nature. As a result, over several years he in effect kills the spirit of his wife by ignoring her and has a disturbing effect on his growing children.

Paul Dempster plays a lesser role in *Fifth Business*. At age ten he disappears from Deptford, apparently a runaway with a travelling circus. Ramsay, who befriended him as a child and introduced him to magic, rediscovers him in a second-rate circus in the Tyrol in 1929. That brief and unsatisfactory reunion is followed in 1947 by a meeting in Guadalupe. There on a sabbatical, which is partpayment for his acceptance at Boy's hands of the loss of his Acting Headmaster's position, Ramsay attends a magic show. Its star is Paul, now named Magnus Eisengrim. Drawn into the company by Liesl Vitzlipützli who is its manager and "autocrat," Ramsay is commissioned to write Eisengrim's fictional autobiography. It is Liesl who takes the lead in this crucial part of Ramsay's life; indeed, over the novel's last two chapters he slowly becomes part of a triumvirate with Eisengrim and Liesl, accepting their toughness, selfcertainty, and knowledge as the best kind of wisdom and society that the world has to offer. These friendships lead directly to Boy Staunton's death for it is in Ramsay's room that Eisengrim meets Staunton; they also lead to Ramsay's subsequent heart attack in

Toronto's Royal Alexandra Theatre and his fatalistic interpretation of his role—as "Fifth Business"—in Staunton's death.
Fifth Business is told retrospectively. Ramsay has reached the age of wisdom—three score and ten—and gained the elevated perspective of Liesl's Swiss mansion, Sorgenfrei, which he describes as "a house that itself holds the truths behind many illusions" (F, 9). His memoir is based upon his mature understanding of himself and his lifelong relationships. Such insight, it is clear, came slowly. As a young soldier, for instance, he had "no vocabulary" to explain the significance of "psychological truth," though he could sense its importance (F, 77—78). In his Deptford youth he was not capable of pointing out "the mythical elements that . . . underlie our apparently ordinary lives" (F, 47). "[M]y historical sense," he stresses, "developed later" (F, 95).

Ramsay's historical-mythological-psychological "sense," what might be called his sixth sense, is crucial to *Fifth Business*. As autobiographer, Ramsay interprets his life from the particular perspective provided by his experience and reading. He puts his emphases where he thinks they belong (F, 10). In both his choice of events and his explanation of them, he is the selective artist. The reader must take his word. Only if the text provides the means by which the reader can grasp a patterned discrepancy between autobiographical assertion and actual fact can the reader, with reason, question the interpretation thus presented. Neither *Fifth Business* nor its successors provide sufficient grounds to doubt Ramsay's perception or integrity. He is in several ways a disagreeable character, but he is always the hero of his own story. He is at once a man to whom many astonishing things have happened and, more heroic still, a man who has struggled to comprehend and articulate the meaning of those events and his part in them.

It was Browning's *The Ring and the Book* that first made Davies aware of the aesthetic deployment of first-person narrators: "There we have a story told to us by a variety of people, each from his own point of view, each stressing what he thinks important, and each bringing his own understanding of life and his own store of wisdom and egotism to the problem."[19] In using first person-narration he was intensely interested in providing different views of various events as well as differing interpretations of the psychological components affecting each view. It would, however, be misleading to conclude that he was equally committed to the relativity of truth. In his plays and novels his goal is to prescribe, delineate, and celebrate his chosen vision of truth. Multiple points of view in the Deptford trilogy do not lead to ambiguity or confusion. One strongly individuated point of view gives way to another and certain areas of mystery are sustained in themselves for both narrative interest and psychological point. Seldom is there inconsistency in essential matters from view to view. If at times it is difficult to distinguish Ramsay's voice from David Staunton's in *The Manticore* or Magnus Eisengrim's in *World of Wonders*, it is because each voice gives us back a great deal of the author himself.

But in what ways is Ramsay heroic and how does his particular heroism relate to what I have called his "sixth sense"? In a solemn moment in *A Jig for the Gypsy,* Richard Roberts states that the true purpose of man is "the long, solitary task of perfecting himself." By "perfecting" Roberts means bringing to completion or fully realizing inner potential. Dunstan Ramsay accepts the fact that he is a man and as such one who is flawed. An experienced schoolmaster, he has few sentimental illusions about boys or men. For him, a child is "a man in miniature"; that is, one capable of "notable virtue" and charm but "also schemer, self-seeker, traitor Judas, crook, and villain—in short, a man" (F, 9). He refuses to posture or simper in his autobiography; he refuses also to engage in "that disgusting self-love which so often attaches itself to a man's idea of his youth" (F, 9–10).

The picture he presents of himself is in many ways uncomplimentary. He is very much the Scots-Presbyterian Canadian: tight with money, close-mouthed, solitary, aloof, obstinate, and manipulative. His actions are often characterized by "a generous measure of spite" (F, 114) and a certain perversity or tenacity in holding to his views in the face of recognized authority. He takes pleasure in what he secretly knows and delights in getting off "a good one" when he senses a vulnerability in a hostile acquaintance. He is seldom nonjudgmental. Of Boy Staunton, he comments, "I really liked him, in spite of his affectations and pomposities." Ramsay keeps the strictest accounts in his relationship with his successful friend.

Disagreeable characteristics, however, are not necessarily weaknesses or flaws. If *Fifth Business* offers an implicit formula for how to manage your life, it is that you should recognize what you are. Ramsay acknowledges the meaner aspects of his nature because, when all the stories are told, it is himself that he is concerned with.

His autobiography implies that it is impossible to change one's individual nature. Thus, it is crucial to the long, solitary task of perfecting oneself that a man face his own personality unevasively, probing into the often unseen patterns that determine and characterize its expression. Only then—and the emphasis is clearly Jungian—can a man know himself and have an enlarged sense of his capacities.

In Dunstan Ramsay's self-presentation, Davies eschews conventional Christian wisdom. To impose New Testament ethics upon personality might seem commendable but ethics in *Fifth Business* have little to do with actual human motivation. When Ramsay observes that, "Boy loved to defeat hostility by turning the other cheek," he adds, this "is by no means a purely Christian ploy, as Boy had shown me countless times" (F, 302). It is a measure of Ramsay's perspective that he is deeply concerned with "psychological truth," not socially acceptable forms of behavior. For Ramsay and for Davies, turning the other cheek, meekness, and the Golden Rule have little to do with human action. In crucial instances a man acts out of what he is, regardless of his socialized training. If life has about it the atmosphere of battle in which defensive ploys and offensive maneuvers characterize behavior, it would be folly, Davies seems to suggest, to respond passively. A man must husband the sources of his strength, not by trying to reform his instincts, but by recognizing and understanding their inevitable energy and expression. The "deep Presbyterian" (F, 104), close Scot, and careful Canadian in Ramsay are consistent throughout *Fifth Business*. For all his conviction about the truth of his account, he assures the Headmaster that he will not see the memoir until "after my own death," even as he warns him that, as a document, it cannot be used to "prove anything against anyone" (F, 299).

In many ways *Fifth Business* is a justification of personality as received. If a man has a cruel or mean streak it is his duty not to eradicate it but to recognize it and to understand the part it must play in his life. His moral obligation lies not in personal reform, which might be called a willed or rationalized suppression of instinct. It lies in a lifelong struggle to understand one's own "psychological truth" and the relation of that "truth" to the lives of others.

Ramsay's heroism in *Fifth Business* is moral and imaginative. It is far more significant than the swift action and luck that earned him the Victoria Cross in World War I. In an age in which religion has about it a "stricken, lifeless, unreal quality" (F, 55), Ramsay is alive with private conviction about the elusive mystery, potency, and wonder of the world. His entire life has fed his fascination. From his childhood experience of *Arabian Nights, A Child's Book of Saints,* and books on magic and conjuring, he gravitates, in what seems to him a fated way, to a sustaining interest in the psychology of religion and in the place of poetry and myth in a man's personal life. Truth, as he understands it, comes to him slowly, appearing only at moments when he is psychologically ready for revelation and by means of agents sufficiently unusual and powerful to influence him profoundly. It takes the experiences of seventy years before he can be "truthful" about his life.

John Henry Newman's *Apologia Pro Vita Sua* bears several interesting resemblances to *Fifth Business.* Both are intensely religious autobiographies. Both are apologies; that is, they are defenses or justifications of lives led in particular ways according to particular beliefs. Both arise in response to accusations. Accused of lying by Charles Kingsley, Newman set out to "give the true key to my whole life," organizing "a corresponding antagonist unity in my defense."[20] To be thus accused was to have his entire identity challenged—"[Kingsley] asks what I *mean,*" writes Newman; he asks "about my Mind and its Beliefs and its sentiments."[21] Protestant-bred and private by nature, Newman risks self-exposure in order to justify his conversion to Catholicism and to celebrate the community he has come to share with "my dearest brothers of this House."[22] Lorne Packer is the Charles Kingsley of *Fifth Business* and the psychology of religion and mythology is Ramsay's Catholicism. Eisengrim and Liesl are his "dearest brothers" at Sorgenfrei.

Similarities in the outlooks of Newman and Ramsay are apparent in several aspects of their autobiographies. Both men offer up the histories of their minds, dwelling upon the effects of books, teachers, and personal experiences. Both begin with the imaginative stimulus of "the Arabian Tales" (Newman notes that "my imagination ran on unknown influences, on magical powers, and talismans") and move toward serious study of the saints.[23] Each presents life as a journey for which the surest guide is personal conviction and opinion. Each is secretive about aspects of his private life. Each treats his specific attacker as the representative of the opinion of many. Against that collective opinion, each sets his ego in an antagonistic relation, ready to conduct "warfare" on his own behalf and to scorn those who resist the richness of his own views.

Ramsay and Newman share as well an egoistic attitude. As Avrom Fleishman has observed:

> It is not simply that Newman is more remote or guarded than others; he insists not only on the privacy but on the primacy of his individual soul, and perhaps it is this superb egocentrism that gives him reason for his apprehensions. Fortunately for him, his reputation as a pillar of the Church and as a Victorian sage has blunted the imputations of egotism, and Newman's self-manifestation in the *Apologia* has hardly been felt as its most striking revelation."

Fleishman, however, is "not inclined to accuse Newman of excessive egoism"; rather, he shows its primal place both in Newman's life and in his "self-manifestation."[24]

Most of the critics who have quarreled with *Fifth Business* have at the heart of their complaints a dissatisfaction with egoism as the novel celebrates it. Most notably, Stephen Bonnycastle's article, "Robertson Davies and the Ethics of Monologue," challenges the ways in which the novel "promotes a fierce aristocracy of spirit" and implies that "real education is a matter of rising into a tiny elite which possesses great authority and power" and which treats "culture and education as private—and jealously guarded—property."[25] For Anthony Dawson *Fifth Business* exerts strong and unquestioned ideological pressures by means of its affective rhetoric.[26] Both Bonnycastle and Dawson rightly worry that the craftsmanship, mysteries, and eloquence of *Fifth Business* have the power to suspend legitimate inquiry into the egocentric and exclusive values the novel solemnizes. They voice resistance to the dream of superiority enacted in the novel, realizing full well that it is a dream many are willing to share, perhaps for the wrong reasons.

Egoism manifests itself in many ways. Young Dunstan's desire to be a polymath is like a self-prophecy. His persistent, righteous piques and his capacity for nursing a desire for revenge are the characteristics of a man who takes himself very seriously. He shows remarkably little love for others and delights in excluding from his view those whose conceptions of reality displease him. He is so greatly enraptured by his spiritual and intellectual adventures that he finds it hypocritical to be unduly modest.

At the same time Ramsay presents his case under a convincing banner. My life, he insists, is special, not merely egocentric. It is special because Ramsay has been seized by a significant quest and has undergone experiences worth telling. With an intensity of egoism like Newman's, he also commits himself to higher goals such as revitalizing the possibility of the spiritual life, in his case in the twentieth century. Moreover, as an intellectual and historian, he consciously brings the rational and analytical to bear upon the spiritual, not only through historical research but also by means of the subtle implementation of Jungian language and principles. So compelling is Ramsay's approach that few readers have quibbled with the values underlying his story.

Always the egoist, Ramsay is slow to realize certain truths. As in his previous novels, Davies provides the wisdom through teachers of a superior and undemocratic cast. *Fifth Business*, like *A Mixture of Frailties*, has three; the teachers of the former, however, have a mediumistic quality one associates with figures like Priestley's three magicians and Iris Murdoch's Honor Klein in *A Severed Head*.

The first is Mary Dempster, who is so influential in Ramsay's adolescence. Her sole piece of advice—"it does no good to be afraid" (F, 71)—stands him in good stead throughout his life. What most affects him is her "wholly religious" (F, 55) nature. Hence, though in her addled state she is harshly judged by the good women of Deptford, her power is such that she takes the place of Ramsay's mother in his inner life. He thinks of her as his "greatest friend," adding that "the secret league between us [was] the tap-root that fed my life" (F, 55). His mother's fits of harshness and Mrs. Dempster's two Deptford "miracles"—saving Ramsay's brother's life when all seemed lost and allowing a crazed tramp to have sex with her (thereby initiating a spiritual transformation of the tramp)—confirm her importance to him. Guilt gives way to fascination and need. With the loss of his parents during the war and his vision of Mary's face when he fell unconscious in France, that commitment deepens. From Mary he learns, above all, that some people "lived by a light that arose from within." Thus, it is less the pursuit of an accredited sainthood for her than the search for further clues to that lighted world from which Mrs. Dempster seems "an exile" (F, 55) that impels Ramsay's postwar research.

Ramsay's second teacher, Padre Blazon, proves his most engaging guide. A great joker and epicure despite his hundred years, he seems more a Rabelaisian phenomenon than a believable Jesuit.[27] He appears twice in the novel, first to advise Ramsay, then, years later, to confirm the value of his advice and to congratulate Ramsay for following it according to his personal lights. Davies makes it clear that he is at once an "oddity" (F, 198) and a fossil of theatrical caricature: "He was, indeed, so farcical in appearance that no theatre director with a scrap of taste would have permitted him on the stage in such a make-up" (F, 198). As a novelist with a growing taste for the unusual and sensational, Davies felt no such compunction. Blazon is Humphrey Cobbler splendidly aged and tricked out in priestly attire; he breathes wit and raffishness into the Protestant sobriety of Ramsay's various quests just as Cobbler refreshes staid Salterton.

From "this learned chatterbox" (F, 201), Ramsay gains a new perspective on Mary Dempster and himself. Combining the wisdom of age with joie de vivre and irreverence, Blazon suggests that Ramsay concern himself less with the actuality of miracles and more with "the reality of the soul" (F, 203). Mary Dempster's significance lies in "psychological truth," in Ramsay's ability to locate her in his "personal mythology" (F, 207). With a Jungian emphasis upon life's phases and God's duality, he chastizes Ramsay about his "muddled Protestant mind," coaches him in enlightened self-interest, and pronounces him "something special" (F, 207). In their second meeting, Blazon's role is to congratulate Ramsay on his progress, not only in befriending the devil (who turns out to be Liesl) but also in the perspicacity and elegance of his recent writing about saints. In the eyes of this self-proclaimed wise man, Ramsay has achieved "the heroic life" (F, 294).

By contrast to this jolly counselor and dispenser of high compliments, Liesl Vitzlipützli is all seriousness, sobriety, and mystery. "Too much explanation of such a character would be a great mistake,"[28] noted Davies in commenting upon his treatment of her. Her presence is climactic in both *Fifth Business* and *The Manticore,* and her importance is signaled by her grotesque appearance, wealth, intelligence, autocratic spirit, and toughness. Combining the attributes of impresario, sage, and lover, she is the Domdaniel of *Fifth Business,* but one who gives Ramsay the opportunity he needs to test his religious insights and psychological mettle.

In *Fifth Business,* Liesl is a sort of psychological ringmaster, her authority having the snap of a whip. As Ramsay tells David Staunton in *The Manticore,* she "likes pushing people to extremes" (M, 279). Her major role is to urge Ramsay and David in their turns toward greater respect for their entire selves, toward deeper self-recognition and understanding. Having chosen her stage name from a minor devil figure in Goethe's *Faust,* Liesl makes it her business to play the devil to Ramsay's Saint Dunstan. While he wrestles with her and breaks her nose as in the Dunstan myth, Davies varies the pattern by having Ramsay profit greatly from the experience. The fighting is followed by lovemaking, friendship, and mutual respect. Liesl effectively awakens him to his "grim-mouthed and buttoned-up and hard-eyed and cruel" Scot-Protestant characteristics and challenges him not only to live his life but also to locate his place in "poetry and myth" (F, 255-56). It is Liesl who suggests that Ramsay is "Fifth Business." Out of her gnostic resources she provides him with a major clue to his lifelong relations to Boy Staunton. He takes her insights unquestioningly to heart.

Wise figures are essential to the educational process of Davies's novels. His characters can only go so far on their own resources. They need enlightened direction, stimulation, goading, browbeating, challenging. Typically, each teacher represents steps up a hierarchical staircase, the summit of which is on the one hand what Jung called individuation and on the other the development of talent and the achievement of wisdom. They signal the distinctive tendency in Davies to romantic hero worship as well as to the celebration of his autocratic worldview. Born to powerful parents and fascinated by formidable figures like Tyrone Guthrie, his is a view that delights in celebrating greatness as he conceives it and in condemning the pap of the masses. As Stephen Bonnycastle has emphasized, monologue not dialogue is the chief means of instruction in the wolfish world of the Deptford novels. One has to learn to be a wolf, to adjust conventional or learned moral axioms to fit darker realities. One has to be led into an explanation of mysteries not apparent on the surface. By contrast to earlier novels, the teachers in the Deptford trilogy become more mediumistic, more grotesque, and more extravagant to suit their gnostic functions. They are not criticized in essential matters; they are beyond criticism, like the wise men in fables and fairy tales.

Fifth Business owes much in this regard to J. B. Priestley's *The Magicians* (1954) and Iris Murdoch's *A Severed Head* (1961). In the former Sir Charles Ravenstreet, in seeking a new orientation for himself late in life, must choose between two kinds of elite, that of the power-wielding businessman Mervil—"a few men, who know their own minds, can dominate and use millions of people who have to have their minds made up for them"[29]—and that of the three mysterious magicians, Wayland, Marot, and Perperak, who represent gnostic wisdom. They have hypnotic and telepathic powers; their ancient wisdom springs from their freedom from both man's imprisonment in chronological time and the modern slavery to materialism.

Just as Ramsay finds himself between the materialistic world of Boy Staunton and the religious realm of Mary Dempster, Ravenstreet must choose. He opts for the religious realm, but not before he is witness to Mervil's striking exhibition of childishness (one thinks of Boy Staunton's immaturity) and the grim fate of a disgruntled chemist who is the pawn of Mervil's business power. In an incident that anticipates Staunton's death, the chemist drives his car at high speed into a quarry, drowning both his unfaithful wife and himself. The court's verdict, "Accidental Death," looks forward to the ordinary world's limited view of both Revelstoke's and Staunton's mysterious ends. As Perperak suggests, "Perhaps each man gets what he asks for. We see. You read magic fairy tales?"[30]

Though they have mastered extraordinary powers and are above the law in their actions, Priestley's magicians are gentle awakeners, kindly to Ravenstreet in their paternalism. Iris Murdoch's Honor Klein, a Cambridge anthropologist, is of a flamboyantly tougher mettle. In extricating the novel's protagonist, Martin Lynch-Gibbon, from his difficult relationships, she speaks for the wisdom of "the dark gods." Goyaesque and unpleasant looking, she counsels him "to become a centaur and kick [his] way out" of the snares that enchant and constrain him: "only lies and evil come from letting people off."[31] A Liesl-like figure, Honor first appears in a hellish setting; later she wrestles with Martin before finally offering him a companionship based upon acute awareness of the chanciness of life. It is also Honor who calls Martin's attention to Herodotus's myth of Gyges and Candaules, a psychological pattern much cherished by Dunstan Ramsay in explaining his relationship with Boy Staunton and his Deptford wife.[32]

Mary Dempster, Blazon, and Liesl carry an aura of mystery suggestive of the worlds of Priestley and Murdoch. They are, however, very much the products of Davies's own vision, imaginative expressions of a fierce romanticism that cherishes uncommonness, self-development, and toughness. More confidently than in the Salterton novels, Davies in *Fifth Business* places the self at the center of his concern while articulating his impatience with the range of narrow and life-denying moral views that fetter real growth.

The Manticore: Up the Down Staircase

Having attracted "a new public" eager for more along the lines of *Fifth Business*, Davies faced a major problem. The sequel's central character ought to be the boy who threw the snowball at Ramsay and who "succeeded in avoiding any feeling of guilt whatever." To adopt the outlook of a materialistic businessman was, however, uncongenial to Davies. Facing "a technical difficulty of substantial proportions," he chose to tell Boy Staunton's story indirectly: "I decided to write it from the point of view of his son, who was compelled, as children often are, to live out the unlived portion of his father's life and to be driven to an unwanted recognition of the kind of man his father truly was."[33] To measure Boy Staunton's effect upon his son, Davies chose to subject David to Jungian analysis in Zurich. The steps by which the son begins to face the condition of his inner life and to regain his psychological health parallel the process of his recognition of the various crimes of the spirit practised upon him in the name of a manly upbringing.

The novel begins with David's screening by the Director of the Jung Institute. A criminal lawyer, bachelor, and heavy drinker, David, now forty, has been deeply shocked by his father's sudden death, the grim comedy of the funeral, and the unpleasant disclosures of the will. On a bender shortly after these events, he attended Magnus Eisengrim's *Soirée of Illusions* in Toronto where he surprises himself by crying out in the midst of a mediumistic scene "Who killed Boy Staunton?" Alerted to his own instability and embarrassed by his action, he uncharacteristically seeks help. Protective of his considerable Toronto reputation, he goes abroad for analysis, though he holds doggedly to his rationalistic disdain for psychiatrists and their "higher hokum" (M, 3).

In Switzerland he finds help in two women and two kinds of therapy. The longest of the novel's three sections, "David Against the Trolls," documents the course of his analysis with Dr. Johanna von Haller. Despite his resistance both to analysis and to the fact she is a woman, she leads him on a technicolored tour of his personal unconscious, helping him to interpret his dreams and revealing to him the forms that various archetypes—Shadow, Friend, Anima, Magus, and Persona—have taken in his life: At first David is inclined to browbeat Dr. von Haller, treating her like a vulnerable witness. He resists any intrusions upon his protective image of his father as "a great man," though it is clear that Boy is his "Great Troll." What Dr. von Haller reveals to him does, however, have its salutary effects. After a year she tells him that he is "a much pleasanter, easier person" (M, 235). In his diary David himself philosophizes:

I am beginning to recognize the objectivity of the world, while knowing also that because I am who and what I am, I both perceive the world in terms of who and what I am and project onto the world a great deal of who and what I am. If I know this, I ought to be able to escape the stupider kinds of illusion. (M, 242–43)

In the Latin labels Davies applies, David is conscious of moving from the egotism of *esse in intellectu solo* to the life-sustaining outlook, *esse in anima*.

The novel's third section provides a large jolt. "My Sorgenfrei Diary" recounts David's experiences at Liesl's Gothic-Revival castle in the Swiss mountains. Enjoying a Christmas hiatus in his analysis, David journeys to St. Gall, where, by chance, he meets Ramsay and Liesl in a bookstore. The encounter is not, according to Ramsay, accidental: "As an historian, I simply don't believe in coincidence . . . ," he tells David; "I suppose you had to meet us, for some reason" (M, 252).

By means of shock tactics and dangerous challenges such as Dr. von Haller would never have risked, Liesl hastens David's recovery and growth. She does much to set him on his own feet psychologically; if she does not completely break him of his newfound reliance on analysis, she at least provides him with a sharp test of his own inner strength. At Sorgenfrei David is, thus, the initiate among wise, superior figures. The challenge offered him is to put psychologists and systems in perspective and to "get on with [his] own concerns" (M, 261). He is invited to live heroically and to explore his "inner labyrinth" alone (M, 263). Liesl's autocratic pronouncement is reminiscent of Samuel Marchbanks at his crustiest:

It isn't everybody who is triumphantly the hero of his own romance. . . . But just because you are not a roaring egotist, you needn't fall for the fashionable modern twaddle of the anti-hero and the mini-soul. That is what we might call the Shadow of democracy; it makes it so laudable, so cosy and right and easy to be a spiritual runt and lean on all the other runts for support and applause in a splendid apotheosis of runtdom. . . . But there are heroes, still. The modern hero is the man who conquers in the inner struggle. (M, 266–67)

Tough testing follows tough talk. In a remote Alpine cave near Sorgenfrei, David is forced by Liesl to ponder upon the aesthetic and spiritual remnants of an ancient bear-worshipping culture. Initially, he is unimpressed by her awe before these dramatic vestiges of "our ancestors." Angered by his superficiality of response, she then leads David to the inner sanctum of the cave, forcing him to crawl several hundred yards along a narrow black passage. It is in struggling out of the inner cave that he learns the meaning of fear and his own capacity for survival. Edging along in the dark he is startled by a horrific noise that turns his bowels to water. "I was at the lowest ebb, frightened, filthy, seemingly powerless" (M, 275). Facing death if he fails to move, he draws strength not from the memory of his father but of his great-grandmother, a spirited English prostitute appropriately named Maria Dymock. She provides him with the "guts" and "power" to reach the light. Meeting the challenge, he feels "renewed" and "reborn" (M, 276).

Modern man, Davies implies, needs to have the shit scared out of him. He must be released from the constipation of reason and the tyranny of living according to flattering self-images. Liesl's tough medicine is the superior laxative that purges David. She achieves what Jungian analysis could never do, because its procedures are intellectualized and professionalized. She deliberately provokes a gut reaction, depriving David of his usual rational defenses, throwing him entirely upon his elemental personal resources. The drama of this testing stands out vividly among Davies's novels. It stands out precisely because Davies is driven to make so much of it, as if he had suddenly, after so many years, become more aware of the body—man as body—lurking behind the heretofore dominant sense of man as social identity. In reaching for a dramatic climax, for a startling leap beyond Jungian analysis, Davies strained for significance. But while the scene he created completes a pattern of excremental imagery in the novel, one senses that the purgative metaphor gets the better of the author, usurping experience in the process. What David feels in the cave is, all the paraphernalia of the event notwithstanding, not so unusual an experience as Davies makes it appear.

A heavily didactic novel, *The Manticore* is a falling off from the achievement of *Fifth Business*. It suffers by comparison in several ways. In the first place there is little effective distinction between Ramsay's and David's voices. Though both books are told in the first-person and the two narrators are a generation apart, they share a sameness of voice and tone that is disconcerting. As lifelong bachelors and professionals, as men who are wealthy, secretive, tightfisted, and opinionated, their similarity of voice has some basis in character. Nevertheless, as Davies would inadvertently reveal when he undertook in *The Rebel Angels* to narrate part of the novel in a woman's voice, his particular skills are not those of a writer who can effectively differentiate—except in histrionic ways—among several narrative voices. A difficulty in his plays, this weakness, which must be seen as evidence of the strength of his personal voice, becomes increasingly clear in *World of Wonders* (where Liesl and Eisengrim often alternate as narrators), but is most troubling in his use of Maria Theotoky in *The Rebel Angels*.

Secondly, while *The Manticore* employs Jungian analysis as its framework and has often been praised for its clear presentation and explanation of analysis in operation, the pattern it reveals has the disadvantage, at least on repeated readings, of seeming oversimplified and contrived. What troubles is that, for all of David Staunton's implicit resistance to Jungian procedures,[34] Dr. von Haller's therapy works very well indeed. Artistic arrangement outstrips life in *The Manticore*. What is likely to be a long, uneven process is reduced to sessions lasting a single year. Virtually everything unfolds chronologically. The archetypes of David's unconscious appear like figures in a well-organized procession. His dreams, which readily reveal their meanings, are perfectly pitched to his psychological condition; he even remembers exact left and right-hand positioning in certain dreams. In short, the complexities of the psyche yield to David's— and Davies's—commitment to order and "the Plain Style" (M, 64) in *The Manticore*. Liesl's outré methods enjoy similar quick success in the final section.

Finally, there is the characterization of David Staunton himself. The wit and wisdom of Dunstan Ramsay is cumulative. He writes out of a wide experience and span of life. David Staunton is some thirty years younger and has undergone what might be called a midlife crisis of significant proportions. He is cast as a devotedly rational man, a fact Davies capitalizes upon in David's treatment of people as witnesses whose inconsistencies can be revealed and in his choice of presenting "a brief of [his] case" (M, 64), a lawyer's apologia, to Dr. von Haller as part of his treatment. David, is, however, far from a rational man. He regularly uses metaphors pertaining to literature, theater, myth, music, and religion. Unlike his analyst, who uses metaphor to spare him jargon, David uses it because it expresses his sensitivity. He precisely recalls such adolescent experiences as seeing Walter de la Mare's *Crossings* and Mendelssohn's opera, *Son and Stranger*. It is even given to him to explain to Dr. von Haller what "absalomism" means. In such instances his inability to relate the allusion to his own condition is meant to reflect both the state of his illness and the cap that reason places on his imaginative tendencies.

When, however, David is called upon to be a humorist, Davies strains the reader's credibility. That Staunton is able to recount his sexual initiation—arranged by his father and in forty years his sole sexual experience—with such gusto and comic timing suggests the degree to which Davies adjusts his narrator's capacities to meet his own authorial requirements. The yoking of troubled, resistant analysand with knowing narrator is a source of uneasiness in such instances. In well-constructed set pieces such as David's sexual initiation, one is aware of Davies, the comic writer, seizing a rich opportunity. When David remarks, "There is a point in a man's undressing when he looks stupid" (M, 174), it is comedy not analysis that is in the saddle, just as it is when David, with buoyant and baroque flourish, describes his successive encounters with Boy's mistress as vivace, andante, scherzo, and allegro con spirito. Pursuing unusual and comic presentations of sexual activity, Davies risks a pertinent question: given the relative pleasantness of the experience, why should sex have disappeared totally from Staunton's life? Pressing psychological reasons are given but they do not fully convince. The pursuit of comic tour de force and of psychological turning point are at times uneasily wed in the novel.

Taking as its point of reference the small Ontario town of Deptford, *The Manticore*, like *Fifth Business*, is very much a Canadian story. Together the two books constitute a history of sorts of twentieth-century Ontario and Canada. In a writer preoccupied for decades with the question of what it means as an artist or as a sensitive individual to stay in Canada, this ought not to be surprising. The two novels trace the kind of spiritual life possible in a Canada much in the grip first of a no-nonsense Presbyterianism, then of an ethic of materialism. They reveal the validity of Liesl's premise that Canada is not "a country where big spiritual adventures are possible" (F, 256), even as they demonstrate that Deptford is scarcely, in Boy Staunton's contemptuous phrase, "that hole."

Behind Liesl's pronouncement lies the cosmopolitan conviction that at least two kinds of education are necessary to develop the potential of a provincial. To cite the assessment of David Staunton by Pargetter, his Oxford tutor, "he made it clear that as a Canadian I started well behind scratch in the journey toward professional literacy and elegance" (M, 203). Just as Monica Gall is awakened, educated, and transformed in England, so Ramsay and David find their most intelligent mentors and their moments of enlightenment in Europe. The development of professional skill and knowledge is but one stage in Davies's exacting regimen of personal development. His heroes must go beyond this level toward spiritual awakening and wisdom. For Monica it is what she calls *Hiraeth;* for Ramsay it is to become a man like William James or Carl Jung, whose spiritual needs fed their intellectual curiosity about, and pioneering studies of, religion; for David it is to know himself more completely, accepting the heroic challenge, in Ramsay's words, of making "a working arrangement with the bear that lives with us" (M, 279).

To be a Canadian is to be raw material. It is also to be the victim of familial and social pressures that initiate the long, difficult process of spiritual growth. Both *Fifth Business* and *The Manticore* attend lovingly and feelingly to these pressures. In the case of *The Manticore* the treatment consistently addresses one of Davies's persistent interests, the life of the wealthy and privileged, which Ramsay in *Fifth Business* could only observe in a detached way, as Boy Staunton's special friend. On a simple level, *The Manticore* provides an account of the rise of the Staunton family from humble English origins to enormous wealth and prominence. "It is not easy to be the son of a very rich man," notes David in beginning his Zurich notebook. "This could stand as an epigraph for the whole case, for and against myself, as I shall offer it. Living in the midst of great wealth without being in any direct sense the possessor of it has coloured every aspect of my life and determined the form of all my experience" (M, 67).

The pressures upon David are those not so much of wealth per se, for he did not directly possess that wealth. They are the pressures of a rich father who flaunted his money and power in ways that the son was unwittingly taught to admire. Accordingly, *The Manticore* functions on one level as a defense of wealth and position. David is disdainful of "the orgulous self-esteem of the deserving poor" (M, 83) and eager to promote the advantages of money. Wealth in itself does no harm. It is not, however, sufficient in itself to stimulate growth. David and his sister find themselves in middle age evolving into "discriminating patrons" of the arts, but this, he sadly admits, is "the only spiritual life we have, and not a very satisfactory one when life is hard" (M, 131). In a novel so concerned with spiritual condition, this is a definitive admission.

In both *Fifth Business* and *The Manticore* an index of the possibilities of spiritual life in Canada is provided by William Lyon Mackenzie King, who served as Prime Minister most notably from 1935 to 1948. Boy Staunton was his Minister of Food during World War II. To the anglophile Boy, Mackenzie King represents all that is wrong in Canada. His worst faults include his dabbling in spiritualism and his "mistrust of England and his desire for greater autonomy for Canada." For David, he is "undoubtedly an odd man," yet "a political genius of an extraordinary order." It is Ramsay who reads deeply into King's spiritualist propensities: he tells Boy, "You'd better face it . . . ; Mackenzie King rules Canada because he himself is the embodiment of Canada—cold and cautious on the outside, dowdy and pussy in every overt action, but inside a mass of intuition and dark intimations. King is Destiny's child. He will probably always do the right thing for the wrong reasons" (M, 98–99).

Though David remembers Ramsay's pronouncement, he tries to rule his own existence in an orderly, independent way. As a lawyer he seeks a life separated from his father's flamboyance and business concerns; indeed, he sets out to be a vigilant opponent of evil. What *The Manticore* requires is that his reliable rationality be put to the test and found wanting. Analysis is but a start. "[A]fter a year with Jo," says Liesl, "you need something more lively" (M, 247). That liveliness consists of recognition of heroic individuality such as can not be learned by consultation. David is told to look to the examples of Jung, Freud, and Adler. Trust not the system but the example of heroism that created it, counsels Liesl:

Davey, did you ever think that these three men who were so splendid at understanding others had first to understand themselves? It was from their self-knowledge they spoke. They did not go trustingly to some doctor and follow his lead because they were too lazy or too scared to make the inward journey alone. They dared heroically. And it should never be forgotten that they made the inward journey while they were working like galley-slaves at their daily tasks, considering other people's troubles, raising families, living full lives. They were heroes, in a sense that no space-explorer can be a hero, because they went into the unknown absolutely alone. Was their heroism simply meant to raise a whole new crop of invalids? Why don't you go home and shoulder your yoke, and be a hero too? (M, 264)

There is no more important monologue in the novel. It declares at once Davies's romantic orientation as a psychological novelist even as it puts Jungianism in a perspective that is crucial to *The Manticore* and the trilogy itself.

What interests Davies is the beglamoring prospect of independent heroic journeying into the depths of self. If Liesl's terms are applied, David by *The Manticore*'s end has only begun to test and explore himself. It also remains unclear how far, measured against Liesl's great explorers, Ramsay himself has travelled, though clearly his progress is far greater than David's.

Constraining David's "inward journey" is the image of his father as a great man. Like Solly Bridgetower whose mother is his "Great Troll," he must at the right psychological moment lay his ghosts as best he can. As David's problem has lasted far longer than Solly's and as he is more resolutely alone in his life, its weight is the greater. A perfect candidate for analysis, he is allowed to recount and revise his experiences, to see the ways in which, especially in response to his father, he suppressed "Feeling" and, in so doing, wronged and alienated the better guides available to him.

The necessity of preserving an inviolate image of Boy leads him to evaluate others in blindly self-serving ways. He sees his mother as weak because his father assumes she is—"I even sank so low that I wanted my mother" (M, 50), he confesses at one point. He spitefully condemns the sensitive mentor of his adolescence, Father Knopwood, who felt obliged to speak out against his father's crudeness and vulgarity. He dismisses much of Ramsay's advice and commentary, thinking of him, unlike his father, as "a man who missed his way in life" (M, 208). He becomes uncharacteristically prejudiced in accounting for the way in which Louis Woolf, a cultivated Jewish surgeon, put an end to his romance with Woolf's daughter. In such recollections, however, David's sensitivity and vulnerability are as evident as his need to preserve his father's image. The reader measures the cost to David even as he feels the power he vests in the father.

In battles between parent and offspring, there is, for Robertson Davies, no clear victory in psychological terms. "To *live* is to battle with trolls / in the vaults of heart and brain" (M, 206). In *The Manticore* the object of the struggle is the freedom to pursue the heroic life. There must be positive gains; borders must be crossed; guides must be found; tests must be passed. David Staunton must learn more about himself through awareness of his archetypes and through elemental encounter. He must come to know his manticore self—man's head, lion's body, sting in the tail. He must learn what a cruel weapon his "razorlike ethical sense" can be, what "a miserable stinker" he becomes when his "shadow" prevails. Such self-knowledge constitutes a breakthrough. It is a major step on the road to perspective and balance. But still he must live with his trolls and particularly his "Great Troll." They do not go away.

In *The Manticore,* as in the other books in the Deptford trilogy, metaphors abound. As Dunstan Ramsay "liked metaphor better than reason" (F, 57), so does David Staunton. Metaphors are both links and clues, ways of drawing together realms of experience and of suggesting insights into mysteries. Two such patterns helping to draw together the novel are chess and defecation imagery.

Simply a game in David's boyhood, chess becomes something extraordinary in the hands of his Oxford tutor. A teacher of law and devoted to "[e]xactitude, calm appraisal, [and] close reasoning" (M, 195), the blind unmarried Pargetter is a highly skilled player who, from memory, carries on numerous long-distance games simultaneously. Just as David can never match him in his knowledge of the law, neither can he defeat him on the board. Seeking guidance from Pargetter in an attempt to make himself independent of his father, a man in his own right, he is susceptible to his tutor's advice to "put your emotions in cold storage at least until you are thirty" (M, 194). He accepts Pargetter as his master, "my ideal, my father in art" (M, 196). At the same time, he seems to welcome the browbeatings he receives at Pargetter's hands, for he realizes that his mind is being honed to a shrewd edge, that he is being forced to develop "the memory-trick" of retaining "what I had done six or eight moves back" (M, 194).

Dr. von Haller calls Pargetter "a very fine Magus indeed" (M,

207). He is, however, blind in more than sight. Though he cites Louis Saint Laurent's view that law is one of the humanities, he shows neither much humanity nor breadth of view. Like the chess he plays so well, his is entirely a horizontal outlook, given over exclusively to reason and memory. That David chooses this brilliant blind man as his "father in art" is a measure of his own incompleteness, of the linearity and backward-looking emphasis of his self-discipline.

The unusual chess game David discovers at Sorgenfrei clarifies Pargetter's limitations and helps to define the larger, heroic view that Liesl advocates as life's great adventure. Here he finds five transparent chessboards mounted one above the other. While each is played horizontally, the participant plays the five games simultaneously as one game, observing comparative positioning from above. It is, Liesl notes, "Not half so complicated as the game we all play for seventy or eighty years" (M, 263). To add complexity, the players use black and white on alternate boards. About this subtlety, Liesl remarks:

Didn't Jo von Haller show you that you can't play the white pieces on all the boards? Only people who play on one, flat board can do that, and then they are in agonies trying to figure out what black's next move will be. Far better to know what you are doing, and play from both sides." (M, 263)

Liesl's horizontal-vertical chess game is at once a kind of ultimate challenge as game—fit only for the most intellectually adept—and a metaphor for genuine heroic self-awareness. It is a game that the blind Pargetter, master of the horizontal board, could not play. Spatially, the vertical axis carries special meaning in *The Manticore.* It is linked to the circular staircase descending into the earth that David visualizes in his "anticipatory dream" (M, 12–15) for Dr. von Haller. At that early stage of his analysis, he forsook the challenge of descent, not realizing that a treasure lay below and not able to understand the advice of the gypsy woman at the entrance. By novel's end, however, fresh from Liesl's shock treatment, he recalls the dream clearly and rewrites its script. Now "free to go down if I pleased" (M, 280), he senses that there is a treasure below. He is now ready to meet the woman who will be his guide. Metaphorically, the horizontal axis is reason; the vertical axis is feeling, that mode of experience David has so long kept in cold storage. The stairs will take him "down the staircase to a strange land" but one to which he is "native" (M, 280). While one might take the chess metaphor further still it is perhaps sufficient to note that Liesl's library calls attention to the heroic life of the feelings in other ways—the telescope, the two globes, terrestrial and celestial, and the ceiling inscribed with the Ten Commandments are reminders of the wonder world of the vertical axis, a realm where metaphors are clues to the mysteries of the spiritual life.

In his use of Freud's thesis of the "functions of excretion in deciding and moulding character,"[35] Davies also builds into his characterization of David a motif of retention and purgation that prefigures his still more elaborate use of the metaphor and theme in *The Rebel Angels*. A product of a culture that waged active war on constipation, Davies gives to David powerful memories of "these terrible weekly aids" (M, 76) from Epsom salts to Dr. Tyrrell's Domestic Internal Bath. The latter device called for an impaling of the constipated child on a spike in "the service of the wildest nonsense and cruelty" (M, 77). It is as if such violations forced upon the sensitive David a kind of willful retentiveness that accentuates the "unusual regard for authority and the power of reason" (M, 77) he claims to have had from birth.

Defecation takes on added negativeness and horror for David in the episode involving Bill Unsworth. A summer-camp friend, the reckless Unsworth involves David in the mindless and haphazard destruction of an uninhabited summer cottage. The adventure ends with Unsworth's defecating upon a pile of photographs, straining himself, "a great stool dangling from his apelike rump" (M, 151). Waking as it were from a trance, David becomes conscious of the "dirty, animal act" and the meaningless, evil expression on Unsworth's face—he was "simply being as evil as his strong will and deficient imagination [would] permit" (M, 151).

In becoming a lawyer, David sets himself against the evil of Bill Unsworth, an evil he recognizes in himself as participant. Such negative feelings about defecation inform David's humiliation when in the bear cave he loses control. His condition stands as a humiliation of his sense of personal intactness and self-control. It takes him some time to realize his gain; much that he has kept locked up in him is released and he finds himself alerted at last to the miraculousness of the human spirit. The rationalistic man, having been freed from the grip of reason, is ready to get on with the healthy business of laying his ghosts to rest and of pursuing his own treasure, of cherishing his bear so that his bear will feed his inner fire.

World of Wonders: Portrait of the Artist as Wolfish Old Man

Confident and flamboyant, *World of Wonders* is the story of Paul Dempster, the child born prematurely as a result of Boy Staunton's snowball. It is a study in the strange and unusual, for nothing about Paul's life is ordinary. His peculiar education, which Davies delights in unfolding, accounts for his transformation into Magnus Eisengrim, the world's greatest magician and illusionist and, among magicians, the greatest actor. It is as if, in homage to those histrionic individuals who loomed largely in the English theater of Davies's formative years, he strove to make Eisengrim a contemporary tribute to their vanished splendor, courtesy, toughness, talent, and distinction of personality.

Davies's method of presentation in *World of Wonders* again involves monologue and discussion, though the discussion serves typically to amplify what the monologue reveals. Dunstan Ramsay, like Eisengrim a "permanent guest" (W, 7) at Sorgenfrei, is the narrator. As historian he claims to be pursuing "documents" that pertain to his old boyhood friend Eisengrim who, being "too clever for [Ramsay]" (W, 14), has kept much of his life and thoughts a mystery. Having ghostwritten Eisengrim's "poetic autobiography" (W, 15), *Phantasmata: the Life and Adventures of Magnus Eisengrim* to promote his magic show, the *Soirée of Illusions,* Ramsay is now bent upon discovering the real man, not only to understand the magician's psychological history but also to leave a second, clarifying record for posterity, thus assuring his own—the historian's—immortality.

The occasion is the shooting at Sorgenfrei of a BBC film about the nineteenth-century French illusionist, Robert-Houdin. Eisengrim has been engaged to play the role of Robert-Houdin and to duplicate one of the French magician's celebrated *Soirées Fantastiques.* The situation brings Eisengrim, Liesl, and Ramsay together with three prominent members of the film crew—the producer Roly Ingestree, the Swedish director Jurgen Lind, and the cameraman Harry Kinghovn.

What Davies offers in effect is the after-dinner talk of the six in response to stylized dollops of autobiographical monologue from Eisengrim. What the magician chooses to say and reveal quickly becomes the focus of discussion. Ramsay records all, turning up his "mental, wholly psychological historian's hearing-aid" (W, 21), and providing interpretive information where necessary. As monologue requires an occasion, Davies provides it in Ingestree's attempt to head off a quarrel between the two artistic "egotists," Lind and Eisengrim. Flatteringly, he challenges Eisengrim to provide a "subtext" (W, 14) out of his experience for Robert-Houdin's life as revealed in his "wretched" book, *Confidences d'un prestidigitateur.* Eisengrim in particular is scornful of the French illusionist's commonplace values, humility, and complacency. But as Robert-Houdin inadvertently revealed in himself "something savouring of the crook," so Ingestree suggests must Eisengrim draw upon "an enriching, but not necessarily edifying, background to what is seen" (W, 14). Nevertheless, it comes as a surprise to Ramsay that the magician accepts the challenge and uncharacteristically offers "to spill the beans" (W, 14).

Having in his early sixties reached what Liesl calls "the confessional moment in his life" (W, 15), Eisengrim parcels out his life story in richly detailed, carefully controlled sections. With the actual filming in process, he recounts evening by evening the early years of his life. The first of the novel's three sections, "A Bottle in the Smoke," describes the hard, unpleasant life of Paul's Baptist childhood in Deptford, his involvement with a cheap travelling circus called Wanless's World of Wonders, his sexual subservience and artistic apprenticeship to a sodomist and magician named Willard, his slow development within the motley family of the circus troupe, and his decamping for Europe with the dying Willard to escape the law. Paul Dempster, alias Cass Fletcher, alias Jules LeGrand, ends this sequence freed at last from Willard who dies a gruesome death, the victim of morphine addiction. "I thought I was the toughest thing going" (W, 148), Magnus summarizes at this point, noting among his strengths his ability to pick pockets, push dope, kick box, and fight with a broken bottle. He has also emerged from this hardening training as "an expert conjuror" and "a deft mechanic." Remembering the Book of Psalms he was forced to memorize as a boy, he characterizes himself at this stage in his life "like a bottle in the smoke," like goatskin "as hard as a warrior's boot" (W, 148–49).

Bearing the title "Merlin's Laugh" and set in London, section 2 shows the kind of wine that fills Eisengrim's toughened skin. Having come to England to view the film's rushes and to do final close-ups, the Sorgenfrei threesome set up in the Savoy. The pattern of monologue and discussion is thus continued as Eisengrim describes in fond detail his experiences as a junior member of the theater company of Sir John and Milady Tresize. The section allows Davies the occasion to express his affection for nineteenth-century romantic and melodramatic theater and to document his enthusiasm for the style and commitment of those few companies that followed in the grand wake of Sir Henry Irving (1838–1905). It begins near Irving's monument (behind London's National Portrait Gallery) and never, as it were, leaves its shadow. Eisengrim lovingly describes the company's various productions *(Scaramouche, The Master of Ballantrae, The Corsican Brothers)*, the cast members, the formidable Sir John and Milady, and a climactic Canadian tour undertaken by the company in 1932. Davies modelled the company and the Canadian tour on the accounts of and about Sir John Martin-Harvey and his wife, "Lady Nell," who made the last of seven successful Canadian tours in that same year. Davies of course had seen them in person on several occasions.

With the Tresizes, Eisengrim duplicates the anonymity imposed on him by his precarious place in Wanless's World of Wonders. He is renamed Mungo Fetch and required to be both an assistant stage manager and the double to Sir John. Despite the fact that he "seemed to be in a lowered state of consciousness," he "had to be everywhere and consequently [he] saw everything" (W, 210). Thus, though initially bereft of individuality, he absorbs all, honing the skills of staging, self-presentation, and projection that contribute to his later success. At the same time, he undergoes a transformation of a romantic, idealistic kind. He falls deeply—but not sexually—in love with the aging, overweight Nan Tresize. Stimulated by her kindness to and confidence in him, he gains "a new attitude to [him]self" (W, 177). The little tough becomes a chivalric gentleman, modeling himself on Sir John as a way both of endearing himself to Nan and of filling out the tabula rasa that she judges to be the condition of his personality (W, 186).

Also new to the company is a young, would-be playwright fresh from Cambridge. None other than Roly Ingestree, who has failed to recognize Eisengrim in his transformed state, he condescendingly sets himself in opposition to the uneducated little tough. Cast by

Davies as potential sons in art of the grand old actor, the one romantic and adulatory, the other cynical and mischievous, Eisengrim and Ingestree take turns as the section unfolds offering contrasting views of the company and each other. The sequence's climactic event, the Canadian tour, proves both the making of Eisengrim and Ingestree's "personal Gethsemane" (W, 248). The difference lies in quality of feeling (W, 249), for Eisengrim's commitment to the Tresizes—to the image of Nan, the talent of Sir John, and the pure idea of theater—is deeply emotional and total. It is not undermined by literary pretensions, personal insecurities, or the need to be clever. Thus, while Ingestree fails miserably both as playwright and in his sexual initiation (in a Medicine Hat bawdy house), Eisengrim learns his craft to the extent that he seems almost to become Sir John. Roly, however, has his revenge on the old man years later when, as organizer, he denies Sir John the opportunity to perform in a 1938 London gala celebrating the centenary of Sir Henry Irving's birth. The death of Sir John soon after the embarrassment of the gala leads Eisengrim, in a familiar Davies motif, to accuse Roly of being responsible for Tresize's demise. It is a grudge he has long borne and one of his primary reasons, it turns out, for telling his story as he does. He delights in catching Ingestree in what was a device of his own making.

Section 2 does not end neatly with the deaths of the Tresizes. Lacking a third distinctive venue for storytelling, Davies has Eisengrim and Liesl function as alternate narrators in recounting their meeting, developing relationship, and partnership in the *Soirée of Illusions*. Hired as an expert with clocks and mechanisms, Eisengrim comes to Jeremias Naegeli's Swiss estate during World War II to repair a rare collection of nineteenth-century mechanical toys. Here he meets the destroyer of the toys, Naegeli's grotesque daughter, Liesl, who is not long in attacking him while he is at work on the toys. As in her later fight with Ramsay, however, the results are positive for the long-term relationship: "we were destined," she asserts, "to be very good friends" (W, 328). In this case, it is Liesl who apprentices herself to Eisengrim whom she recognizes as "a truly original creature" (W, 16).

The novel's final section, "Le Lit de Justice," is a clever variation on the roundup chapter both for *World of Wonders* and the trilogy as a whole. Still at the Savoy but freed of the BBC crew, Eisengrim, Liesl, and Ramsay share a capacious bed—"a bed," says Ramsay, "is the best of all places for a philosophical discussion, an argument, and if necessary a showdown" (W, 336). As in the shared-bed scene in *Leaven of Malice* in which Solly receives advice and compassion from the Cobblers, Ramsay plays Solly to the higher wisdom of Eisengrim and Liesl. While certain matters (Who killed Boy Staunton?) are given final and apparently authoritative treatment, the nature of fate, of artistic greatness, of good and evil, and of God and the Devil are also discussed.

It is Eisengrim who, despite all he has endured, unreservedly declares that life is to him "pretty much like a World of Wonders. . . . Everything has its astonishing, wondrous aspect, if you bring a mind to it that's really your own—a mind that hasn't been smeared and blurred with half-understood muck from schools, or the daily papers, or any other ragbag of reach-me-down notions" (W, 355). The phrase "World of Wonders" links the tawdry circus of Eisengrim's apprenticeship to a passionate perception of a reality not apparent to most people. It is this view of reality, shared by Magnus and Liesl, that *World of Wonders* celebrates and explicates. Contemptuous of the bourgeois values that dominate education, the media, the theater, and family life, the two not only assert the validity of a higher and ultimate order of reality but live according to their knowledge of it. Before them, Ramsay is still something of a novitiate. Like the reader, he is made to stand in awe of the "gulf" that "lies between the reality of a magician with the Magian World View and such a pack of lies as Robert-Houdin's bland, bourgeois memoirs" (W, 332).

World of Wonders is a remarkably assertive, even swaggering, novel. With Ramsay clamoring for insight and Lind, Magnus, and Liesl prepared, in good time, to dispense it, the cumulative effect is heavily prescriptive, like listening to a lecture. What begins as a kind of forum involving six figures all committed to art and interested in speculative thinking about psychology, philosophy, and religion, is not long in evolving into the Magnus-Liesl show staged according to the requirements of their demanding values and sensibilities.

What is asserted above all is the autocratic egoism of the artist. *World of Wonders*, like *A Mixture of Frailties*, caps its particular trilogy by bringing matters down to the sustaining selfhood and values of the serious professional artist. The great artist, Davies implies, must be superior to conventional, middle-class notions and taboos. Art is not "the transformation and glorification of the commonplace"; rather it is "The revelation of the glory in the commonplace" (W, 12). What matters is the revelation, not the commonplace experience itself. Merging the skill and toughness of Eisengrim with the insights of Liesl, Davies creates a symbiotic image of such greatness. Experience has made the two what they are. Together they deplore modern education (Liesl comments that "We have paid a terrible price for our education, such as it is" [W, 324]), toss aside conventional attitudes to sexual roles, and mock the blandness of Christian values.

In Davies's romantic forge, transformations of character readily occur. The experience of being grotesque does not, as in Sherwood Anderson's *Winesburg, Ohio,* wound or incapacitate. Both Magnus and Liesl emerge from their experiences strengthened and enriched, far wiser and better off than those who have never known such deprivation, loneliness, and suffering.

The explication of the higher wisdom shared by Liesl and Magnus is Davies's intellectual trump card in the Deptford trilogy. The Dunstan Ramsay of *Fifth Business* had given over his life to the search for signs of that "strange world" beyond the surface of ordinary events and to his study of sainthood. David Staunton discovered something of that same "strange land" in his two-staged psychological initiation and therapy. *World of Wonders* has far less patience with the ordinary world than its predecessors. Harry Kinghovn, the cameraman, is Davies's straw man for the literalist view of reality. A tiresome quarreler who serves to bring a few sequences of talk to appropriate conclusions, Kinghovn's role is to speak for what the eye sees, "the appearance of everything" (W, 38). So devoted is he to what his camera can capture that he confidently asserts, "There is no God,. . . and I've never felt the least necessity to invent one" (W, 152). Jurgen Lind, however, puts his outlook in perspective by replying, "Probably that is why you have spent your life as a technician." The realist, the tough guy, the atheist, the literalist is a myopic in *World of Wonders.* No one will take him seriously because his vision is so pathetically limited.

The novel makes much of such distinctions. When Ingestree and Eisengrim disagree in their interpretations of what happened on the cross-Canada tour of the Tresize company, Kinghovn bursts out, "You two sound as if you had been on different tours" (W, 254).

The characters also acknowledge that for each idea there are two words, one that romanticizes or inflates and one that undercuts or deflates. *World of Wonders* relentlessly advocates the actuality of that "strange world" in which "the Great Justice" or "Poetic Justice" holds sway. Transcendental in its emphasis, this advocacy typically involves a persistent kind of moral and aesthetic bullying by dominant and domineering figures whose credentials are their successes in the undemocratic world of art and theater. Ramsay sets the mood for the reader by playing the keen spectator to the mystery of Eisengrim's greatness.

In essence, then, *World of Wonders* is alive with the kinds of romanticism Davies has always been impelled to assert. He presents not only the romance of nineteenth-century theater, magic shows, and carnivals—romance of the stage in variant forms—but also the romance of spiritual reality, the world of wonders beyond mere appearances, and the romance of the superiority of the great artist. It is on this extraordinary level alone, it would seem, that eminence is guaranteed. Perched as it were above the masses of men and their mundane, middle-class concerns, characters like Magnus and Liesl can speak authoritatively (if somewhat cryptically) to the things that really matter in life. They are sensitive to destiny's unseen ways, to what underlies outward forms of human behavior, and to the reality of abstractions. What they agree upon finds sympathetic response in Jurgen Lind, the chastened Ingestree, and Dunstan Ramsay. Only Kinghovn misses the disclosures of wonder.

Having used Jungian patterns so extensively in the first two novels, Davies sought a fresh authority for *World of Wonders*. He found it in Spengler's *Der Untergang des Abendlandes* which Liesl had read as an adolescent. It is "the banner" under which she first meets Eisengrim and it becomes her interpretative key to the wolfish magician. Her "Magian World View' is presented as a mature and serious reading of reality both within and without the novel. Assuming her major role as Magnus' intellectual voice toward the end of *World of Wonders*—"I knew about the Magian World View, and recognized it in my teacher. He knew nothing of it, because he knew nothing else" (W, 325)—she offers a reading of Spengler's "world outlook" that defines and justifies the roles that she and Magnus have chosen to play in life.

As Davies employs it, the Magian World View provides a reading of the invisible world that modern education, religion, and government have conspired to discredit and dismiss. Liesl's description is tinged with awe:

It was a sense of the unfathomable wonder of the invisible world that existed side by side with a hard recognition of the roughness and cruelty and day-to-day demands of the tangible world. It was a readiness to see demons where nowadays we see neuroses, and to see the hand of a guardian angel in what we are apt to shrug off ungratefully as a stroke of luck. It was religion, but a religion with a thousand gods, none of them all-powerful and most of them ambiguous in their attitude toward man. It was poetry and wonder which might reveal themselves in the dunghill, and it was an understanding of the dunghill that lurks in poetry and wonder. (W, 323)

Aligned to alchemy, gnosticism, and mythology, Davies's Magian World View, with its echo of Joseph Campbell and *The Manticore*'s cave scene, is essentially romantic and old fashioned. Davies adapts it to address not only his dissatisfaction with Freud but also his growing fascination with the revelatory properties of excrement. Anticipating the role of Ozy Froats in *The Rebel Angels* he has Liesl say that the Magian World View has in modern times "taken flight into science, and only the great scientists have it or understand where it leads; the lesser ones are merely clockmakers of a larger growth, just as so many of our humanist scholars are just cud-chewers or system-grinders" (W, 324).

Greatness of a romantic and heroic kind enthralls Davies in *World of Wonders*. Taking the best from his hard, unusual apprenticeship, Magnus has transformed himself into "a great master." That masterliness is to be found in his magician's craft, his manner, and his acting. It is there also in his teaching, for, as Liesl categorically asserts, "great things are not taught by blancmange methods" (W, 324). Above all else, he knows himself and is sustained by his self-knowledge, self-confidence, and self-love against whatever challenges or injuries the world may inflict.

The romantic worldview of *World of Wonders* is closely aligned to Davies's concern with healthful egoism. His pursuit of heroes distinguished by intellectual sophistication and artistic talent leads him to offer in Eisengrim and Liesl (the doer and the interpreter) his most forthright and outspoken celebration of self. Crucial to this presentation is a distinction between egotism and egoism offered by Magnus:

> An egotist is a self-absorbed creature, delighted with himself and ready to tell the world about his enthralling love affair. But an egoist, like Sir John [Tresize], is a much more serious being, who makes himself, his instincts, yearnings, and tastes the touchstone of every experience. The world, truly, is his creation. Outwardly he may be courteous, modest, and charming . . . but beneath the velvet is the steel; if anything comes along that will not yield to the steel, the steel will retreat from it and ignore its existence. The egotist is all surface; underneath is a pulpy mess and a lot of self-doubt. But the egoist may be yielding and even deferential in things he doesn't consider important; in anything that touches his core he is remorseless. (W, 191–92)

What sustains Eisengrim is what sustained Tresize—"an ideal of theatrical art that was contained—so far as he was concerned—within himself" (W, 193). *World of Wonders* is quick to admit that egoism has its inherent dangers; it can lead to isolation, outdatedness, even a kind of damnation. But it is the sine qua non of the great artist, especially one who is committed to a particular ideal and bears the responsibility of controlling others in the enterprise. *World of Wonders* is devoted to art in a way that neither *Fifth Business* nor *The Manticore* is. It makes no bones about laying down a kind of inviolate credo complete with romantic, cosmological rationalization. In *A Mixture of Frailties* aesthetic attention is focussed on learning and the flush of initiation; in *World of Wonders* it falls upon the tough knowledge of the initiated.

World of Wonders is perhaps best read as Davies's fullest celebration of artistic greatness. It is offered less in a spirit of apology or justification than of assertion. As such, the book is not so much a retrospective *Bildungsroman* as a controlled revelation of the outlook of the mature artist and the morality he must bring to his special calling. There is, thus, much in *World of Wonders* about the wolfishness of the artist, that "something black" (W, 12) in his nature that he brings to the service of his vocation. It is apparent in Eisengrim's attitude to Sir John Tresize, his "hunger not just to be like him but to BE him, whatever that might cost him" (W, 348). If Newman's *Apologia* provides something of a narrative model for *Fifth Business*, then Thomas Mann's *Confessions of Felix Krull* may well have been in Davies's mind in writing *World of Wonders*. There is much about what Patricia Monk calls "the morality of deception," those ways in which aspects of deception (sometimes shared with the audience) are essential to a performance or creation.[36] And there is much that invests the artist with heroic stature, whatever his necessary sins.

While *World of Wonders* seems to entertain other views, it does so merely to broaden its inquiry, not to question the importance of Eisengrim, his credo, and Liesl's Spenglerian interpretation of it. The forum that provides commentary upon Eisengrim's polished monologue is, not surprisingly, abandoned in the novel's final section. *World of Wonders* reveals Eisengrim to be a consummate storyteller whose authority and self-certainty suffer not at all from the questions and challenges he meets.

The sublime confidence that Eisengrim has gained from his dark, underworld education reflects Davies's own confidence in writing the novel. Both the author and his wolfish hero laugh with Merlin because they know what's coming next (W, 156). Both seem to bask in the "deeply satisfying" notion of Poetic Justice, notwithstanding their awareness that an individual can only "feel and serve and fear" it (W, 355).

It is, finally, one of the most disturbing aspects of *World of Wonders* that Davies shows so little inclination to bridle his artist-hero or to question seriously the premises he articulates so confidently. As Stephen Bonnycastle has argued of the Deptford trilogy, "the religion of these novels proposes a new ideal, something primitive and sublime, in which society and its institutions are insignificant, and dialogue and the reasoning powers of the mind are eliminated. When thinking, reasoning, and dialogue are undervalued, it is significant that chance, or destiny, should take on unusual importance."[37] Davies uses the Magian World View to clarify life in the present, but his outlook dismisses so much of the actual present that he seems subservient to a literary view of the past, a view at once autocratic, arbitrary, and romantic. Also taking on unusual importance is unabashed egoism, which, for Davies, makes most sense when wedded to artistic, intellectual, or spiritual endeavor. If Eisengrim in his outspokenness seems at times an extraordinary reincarnation of Samuel Marchbanks, it is because in the wolf-artist, in the man "goosed" so hard by life he won't stop climbing, Davies found a new and bracing expression of authority by means of which not only to satirize and criticize aspects of modernity that disturb him but also to pontificate upon what he most values. As James Neufeld has astutely noted, "the central egoism" in the Deptford trilogy is

the egoism of Robertson Davies as novelist. Davies is a tangible presence in each of these [Deptford] books and they seem to represent an important assertion of the values he holds dearest. Through these books, Davies has made the world his own creation. In them, he has asserted the importance of humble self-understanding in a world that threatens to crumble into hopeless relativity without the unifying, all-encompassing, vision of the egoist.[38]

Robertson Davies's Deptford trilogy is, without doubt, one of the most remarkable and fascinating achievements by a Canadian writer. In its outspokenness, its commitment to feeling, its insistence upon awe, it has a tremendous power. It is the work of a writer bent upon being at once romancer, social critic, and sage. Davies's comic vision is as irrepressible as it is serious. His opinions and tastes, firmly developed early in his career, have the temper of steel. From this essential core, so long in the nurturing, is now springing a new trilogy initiated by *The Rebel Angels*. Whether in its refreshing approach to universities and its renewed attention to familial tensions, it will break as much surprising ground as the Deptford trilogy did in the 1970s remains to be seen.

Chapter Seven
The Rebel Angels: Spelunking on Parnassus

"The modern writer," Davies wrote in 1960, "is too often a Theseus so enamored of the grotesque appearance and strange cavortings of the Minotaur that he has decided to make his permanent abode in the Labyrinth, and to accept the Minotaur's laws as his own."[1] He made it clear then that he deplores the kind of fiction that reflects a squalid, self-doubting outlook or displays "man as a derelict and irresponsible creature existing in a world where no moral values apply."[2] Since *Fifth Business,* however, he has been confronting the "Labyrinth" directly in his own fiction, but always with the clear moral purpose of celebrating man as a Theseus superior to its entrapments.

The Rebel Angels continues what *Fifth Business* began. In its range of ideas, its wit and erudition, and the grotesqueness and depravity of certain of its characters, it may seem to be an innovative "modern" work of the kind Davies earlier denounced. In fact, it is a remarkably conservative novel that breaks surprisingly little new ground. Most of its themes—the pursuit of wisdom and selfhood, the benefits of money, marriage as a community of interests, the importance of heredity, the wisdom that lies in alchemy and other forgotten or outlawed lore, the inescapable presence of malice and evil in all men's hearts—are standard fare. So too are such previously unrelated subject matter (or enthusiasms) as gypsies, defecation, and Rabelais. What is remarkable about *The Rebel Angels* is the renewed evidence it offers of Robertson Davies's inventiveness, intellectual curiosity, and durability. Settled in his outlook and distinguished by pronouncedly didactic inclinations, he nevertheless continues to attract and hold the reader's interest by means of his gifts as storyteller and weaver of patterns. He succeeds in the impression of offering a great range of life's experiences even as he arranges in striking, personalized designs the threads of what seems to be extraordinarily disparate material.

The Rebel Angels offers no less than "the house of intellect itself."[3]

Set in the university milieu that Davies peripherally satirized in his Salterton novels, it offers a rich tribute to that world. It is not the city of fools or youth in Davies's view, but the city of wisdom and the custodian of civilization.[4] One finds that great hope of *A Voice from the Attic*—the clerisy—transmuted here into the "Scholarly Elect" (R, 46) of devoted researchers, committed students, and lovers of knowledge for knowledge's sake. Such enthusiasm is the fruit of Davies's own eventful years at the University of Toronto and Massey College,[5] a manifestation of his respect for many of his colleagues, their often undervalued yet passionate pursuits, and the idea of the university itself. Its subject is the quest for the kinds of knowledge that bring wisdom to mankind; more specifically, as is typical of Davies, it investigates the kinds of knowledge that bring wisdom to man's struggle to understand his inner nature—in a new metaphor, his root and his crown—and to live comfortably with the range of propensities in himself.

The Rebel Angels interweaves three narrative threads. Three faculty members, Clement Hollier, an eminent paleopsychologist, Simon Darcourt, an Anglican priest who teaches New Testament Greek and is vice-warden of Ploughwright College, and Nasty McVarish, a disagreeable, egotistical Renaissance historian, are appointed advisers to the estate of Francis Cornish, a reclusive collector of art, books, and manuscripts. They work under the direction of Cornish's nephew, Arthur, a successful businessman who aspires to be a great patron. Prior to Cornish's death, McVarish had "borrowed" from him a previously unknown, extraordinarily important manuscript along with three autograph letters by Rabelais; his refusal to admit possession to the other trustees promotes the anger and hatred of Hollier, who craves the manuscript for academic and personal reasons.

The second thread is the story of Hollier's beautiful graduate student, Maria Magdalena Theotoky. Believing herself in love with her mentor, she works under his guidance hoping to win his attention. She is cast as an especially gifted student who wishes to escape her gypsy background and succeed as a modern, New World university woman. Much of *The Rebel Angels* is concerned with Maria's need to recognize the inescapable importance of her gypsy roots and to strike a balance between the claims of her heritage and her awareness of the university's high ideals. Taught by Hollier, McVarish, and Darcourt, she is well placed to observe their respective values, habits, and eccentricities.

The success of the narrative depends greatly, however, on its third thread, John Parlabane. The novel's most interesting character, Parlabane is a talkative, wayward scholar-philosopher who has led a random, dissolute life after losing his teaching job at his alma mater, the College of St. John and the Holy Ghost. *The Rebel Angels* begins with his return to the College and Hollier's helping hand from a monastery in England, and is brought full circle by his eloquent letter to Hollier and Maria in which he describes not only the way in which he murdered the deserving McVarish but also the method of his own suicide. He also returns the missing Rabelais papers, though Hollier, his friend since boyhood, is prevented from directly receiving them. In reviving earlier connections with Darcourt and McVarish and in establishing a bantering kind of intimacy with Maria, Parlabane involves himself in all aspects of the narrative.

While no plot summary adequately describes a novel as rich in information and allusion as *The Rebel Angels,* its most striking formal feature is its narrative structure. For the first time over a whole novel Davies uses two alternating narrators. Having struggled over his entire career to present a credible female protagonist, he set himself the challenge of writing half of *The Rebel Angels* from Maria Theotoky's point of view. Her sections, entitled "Second Paradise," take their text from Paracelsus's *"the striving for wisdom is the second paradise of the world"* (R, 39) and argue for the importance of the scholarly efforts that take place within the university realm. Maria's sections include long talks with Parlabane in which he describes in detail his sordid career; a closer look at Arthur Cornish, whose proposal of marriage she accepts near the novel's conclusion; and her complex response to the life of her mother and uncle, whose unusual occupation and outlook grow out of traditional gypsy lore. In these domestic scenes Maria is made to feel not only her mother's enormous power and conviction but also the way in which the gypsy *bomari* (the revitalization of stringed instruments in a bath of dung) provides a living example of Hollier's passionate research into the lost ideas by which people lived centuries ago.

Where Davies stumbles with Maria is in her voice. One is never convinced it is a woman speaking, let alone a twenty-five-year-old graduate student whose only experience of sex occurred the previous spring on Hollier's office couch. There is little difference in tone, vocabulary, idiom, or confidence of outlook between Maria and the middle-aged bachelor priest, Darcourt, who is the other narrator. Darcourt's sections, called "The New Aubrey," are, like hers, dedicated to the university's ideals. In response to the casual suggestion of a colleague, he has set himself to write a modern *Brief Lives*, committed to recording "a vagarious history [of the university] with all the odd ends and scraps in it that nobody ever thinks of recording but which are the real stuff of life" (R, 13). With his interest in idiosyncracy and his sense of the "topsy-turveydom" of living (R, 57), Darcourt provides both a convincing rationale for a wide-ranging presentation of university life and the necessary experience and knowledge to comment perceptively on what he observes. Maria, we are simply told, is a brilliant student, though this is nowhere convincingly demonstrated. While she undergoes certain personal struggles in the novel, Davies doesn't hesitate to grant her the wisdom of the ages.

Mitigating the problem of Maria as narrator (Davies wants the voice of youth and woman to be prominent within the modern university) is the lively, worldly, irrepressible voice of Parlabane. An extravagant descendant of Humphrey Cobbler's trickster and the genius-demon doubleness of Giles Revelstoke, he eloquently "put[s] some yeast into the unleavened Bread of Heaven" (R, 118), which is both the university and the novel. Taking Liesl Vitzlipützli's role as grotesque but engaging devil figure a step further, he is cast as an evil man who, though possessing "the big salutary humour" that allows him to recognize and discuss his state of mind, cannot save himself from indulging his appetites, whims, vanity, and "imp of perversity" (R, 66). An extraordinary egotist, he is not only "a gross old bugger" who likes his sex life rough and life itself messy and stinky (R, 67) but who also incarnates "that impatient, all-demanding child who wants love and power and can't get enough of either and who goes on raging and weeping in your spirit till at last your eyes are closed" (R, 32). His intelligence, wide experience, and elitist outlook, however, make him the source of much wisdom. Though he wrestles against the high evaluation of Rabelais offered by others throughout the novel, he is so much an authority about the light and dark sides of life that Maria includes him with Darcourt and Hollier among her "rebel angels," those apochryphal Prometheans who "people the universities and have established what Paracelsus calls The Second Paradise of Learning, and who are ready and willing to teach all manner of wisdom to the daughters of men" (R, 277).

In *The Rebel Angels* Davies makes an important distinction between the conscious, unmitigated malice of Nasty McVarish (the novel's convenient villain and scapegrace) and the wise, if inescapable, evil of Parlabane. *The Rebel Angels* emphasizes that "the soul of mankind" is larcenous, cruel, and inhumane (R, 183–84). It stresses that man, to be whole, must acknowledge the devil in himself and learn from him. At his best, Parlabane is such a guide. At his worst, which is often, he is a danger to others and to himself. Given such qualities and the gift of the gab, it is little wonder that the novel makes Parlabane, the devil's agent, its most interesting character. Why Davies did not make him a narrator (his monologues constitute a major part of the text) remains an anomaly that the unconvincing voice of Maria often brings into question.

Continuing the Jungian emphasis upon the light and dark sides of human experience, Davies strives in *The Rebel Angels* to embody and make articulate the dark side or devil's domain, the ever-present reality in human life of the seven deadly sins. In his celebration of the university he shows that neither genius nor love of learning is in itself a guarantee of moral wisdom. Each of his characters is tempted, and, to varying degrees, each reveals his vulnerability and weaknesses. But with Parlabane, who is both evil and aware of his evilness yet in his own mind committed to the goal of knowing and being himself, the reader is faced with a subtlety that plays an increasingly large part in Davies's writing. For all of his learning and insight, Parlabane is finally an egotist, not an egoist. His indulgent, autobiographical novel, *Be Not Another* constitutes a warning about the self that refuses to practice control, the soul that will not seek to save itself (R, 55). The distinction Magnus Eisengrim makes between the "self-absorbed" egotist and the "more serious" egoist serves as crucially for *The Rebel Angels* as for *World of Wonders* (W, 191–92). Egoistic wisdom necessitates the recognition of "the notion of religion as a mode of thought and feeling" (R, 55), which Davies, citing Einstein, links to the essential idea of the university. It constitutes not only a higher form of individuation but a moral perspective impossible if man indulges his animal appetites, perverse needs, or childish tendencies, or if he allows himself to succumb to the bleakness inherent in "the Minotaur's laws." Everything in Davies's writing and outlook hangs on the recognition of this distinction. The strongly romantic side of his temperament, so given over in *The Rebel Angels* to celebrating the university and its high goals, finds its justification in a commitment to self that is essentially religious and moral. That such commitment is selfish, undemocratic, and elitist does not bother Robertson Davies in the least. Indeed, that commitment, which is typically expressed in the form of didactic pronouncements, is the primary characteristic of his work as a whole.

Notes and References

Preface

1. Robert Kroetsch and Diane Bessai, "Death Is a Happy Ending," in *Figures in a Ground,* ed. Diane Bessai and David Jackel (Saskatoon: Western Producer Prairie Books, 1978), 213.
2. Anthony Burgess, "99 Novels: The Best in English since 1939: A Personal Choice," (New York: Summit Books, 1984), 130–31.
3. Jean Strouse, "Inventor of Gods," *Newsweek,* 8 February 1982, 78–80.
4. *The Rebel Angels* (Toronto, 1981), 55–56.

Chapter One

1. *Fifth Business* (Toronto, 1970), 121.
2. *Marchbanks' Almanack* (Toronto, 1967), 39.
3. Tyrone Guthrie, Introduction to *Eros at Breakfast and Other Plays* (Toronto, 1949), ix.
4. An interview with Professor Gordon Roper at Massey College in May 1967. Roper taped several extensive interviews at that time.
5. "A Rake for Reading," *Mosaic* 14, no. 2 (Spring 1981):2.
6. An interview with Michael Peterman at Massey College, 6 March 1980.
7. "A Rake for Reading," 1.
8. See note 4.
9. See "Kings and Cabbages," *Graduate* (University of Toronto) 4, no. 3 (1977):10–11.
10. See note 4; also "A Rake for Reading."
11. *One Half of Robertson Davies* (Toronto, 1977), 62.
12. See note 4.
13. See note 4.
14. *Times Literary Supplement* (London), 4 February 1939, 74.
15. Guthrie, Introduction to *Eros at Breakfast,* x.
16. See note 4.
17. Introduction to *The Diversions of Duchesstown and Other Essays,* by B. K. Sandwell (Toronto: Dent, 1955), xi.
18. Review of Oliver St. John Gogarty's *Mad Grandeur, Saturday Night,* 20 December 1941, 16.
19. "The Double Life of Robertson Davies," by Samuel Marchbanks,

Notes and References   161

in *Canadian Anthology,* rev. ed., eds. C. F. Klinck and R. E. Watters (Toronto: Gage, 1966), 399–400.
    20. Judith Skelton Grant, "Robertson Davies," in *Profiles in Canadian Literature,* vol. 2 (Toronto: Dundurn Press, 1980), 2.
    21. See note 4.

Chapter Two

    1. Gordon Roper, Introduction to *Marchbanks' Almanack* (Toronto, 1968), xi; Patricia Monk, *The Smaller Infinity: The Jungian Self in the Novels of Robertson Davies* (Toronto, 1982), 26; *The Well-Tempered Critic,* ed. Judith Skelton Grant (Toronto, 1981), 11.
    2. Variations of the pattern including the shift in 1949–50 from diary entries to Marchbanks's correspondence are described in John Ryrie's "Robertson Davies: An Annotated Bibliography," in *The Annotated Bibliography of Canada's Major Authors,* vol. 3 (Toronto, 1981), 70–71.
    3. "The Double Life of Robertson Davies," 397; hereafter cited as DL.
    4. Monk, *The Smaller Infinity,* 37.
    5. The column appeared simultaneously in the *Peterborough Examiner* and the *Kingston Whig-Standard.* Columns such as "The German and the Jew" (4 August 1943) and "Have We Ghosts in Canada?" (30 October 1943) did appear in the *Peterborough Examiner* under Marchbanks's name prior to the beginning of the diary.
    6. *The Diary of Samuel Marchbanks* (Toronto, 1947), 125; hereafter cited as D.
    7. *The Table Talk of Samuel Marchbanks* (Toronto, 1949), 95; hereafter cited as T.
    8. See *A Voice from the Attic* (New York, 1960), 5, 7.
    9. *The Diary of Samuel Marchbanks* (Toronto, 1966), n.p.
    10. Roper, Introduction to *Marchbanks' Almanack,* xii.
    11. *Marchbanks' Almanack* (Toronto, 1967), 110; hereafter cited as A.
    12. One of the negative aspects of this context is evidence of a complacent racism, the result in part of wartime attitudes.
    13. "Diary of a Hunted Man," *Peterborough Examiner,* 7 May 1949. See also *The Well-Tempered Critic,* ed. Judith Skelton Grant (Toronto, 1981), 30.
    14. This entry appeared in the *Peterborough Examiner,* 11 December 1943, but was not included in the three Marchbanks books. Marchbanks's political leanings, when expressed, are, like Davies's, Liberal.
    15. Simon Paynter, "The Diary of Samuel Marchbanks," *Canadian Forum,* March 1948, 284.

16. Hilda Kirkwood, "Robertson Davies," *Canadian Forum*, June 1950, 59.
17. "Zestful Table Talk by Robertson Davies," *Toronto Star*, 12 November 1949, 44, and W. L. Hurlow, "Under the Reading Lamp," *Ottawa Evening Citizen*, 19 November 1949, sec. 3, p. 2.
18. D. V. L., "From the Critic's Notebook," *Kingston Whig-Standard*, 9 November 1949, 4.
19. W. A. D[eacon], "A New Samuel Marchbanks," *Toronto Globe and Mail*, 10 December 1949, 13.
20. James Scott, "Take This Humor with a Grain of Salt," *Toronto Telegram*, 26 November 1949, 12.
21. *The Table Talk of Samuel Marchbanks* (London, 1951), vi.
22. Frederick Laws, "Essayist Hammers Humbugs," *News Chronicle*, 18 June 1951.
23. H. B., "Deipnosophism," *Punch*, 11 July 1951, 53.
24. William Plomer, "A Canadian Man of Letters," *Listener*, 12 June 1951, 1005.
25. Louis Dudek, "Almanacks Galore—Who Could Ask for More?", *Montreal Gazette*, 11 November 1967, 44.
26. J. M. Robson, "Light Prose," *University of Toronto Quarterly* 37 (July 1968):501–2.
27. Robert Fulford, "The Special Charm of Peanut Butter," *Toronto Star*, 17 October 1969, 21.
28. Roper, Introduction to *Marchbanks' Almanack*, xii.
29. Ibid., xi.
30. Monk, *The Smaller Infinity*, 39.

Chapter Three

1. Ann Saddlemyer, "A Conversation with Robertson Davies," *Canadian Drama* 7, no. 2 (1981):114.
2. "Ham and Tongue," in *One Half of Robertson Davies* (Toronto, 1977), 15.
3. Eric Nicol, *Vancouver Province*, 7 May 1955.
4. Saddlemyer, "A Conversation," 113. Susan Stone-Blackburn provides detailed treatments of all of Davies's plays, including *Pontiac and the Green Man*, in her recently published *Robertson Davies, Playwright* (Vancouver, 1985).
5. Richard Plant, "Cultural Redemption in the Work of Robertson Davies," *Canadian Drama* 7, no. 2 (1981):46.
6. Robertson Davies interviewed by Don Rubin, 8 June 1976. The Ontario Historical Studies Series, 12. See also Davies's tribute to Martin-Harvey in *The Enthusiasms of Robertson Davies*, ed. Judith Skelton Grant (Toronto, 1979), 27–29.

7. "Robertson Davies," in *Stage Voices*, ed. Geraldine Anthony (Toronto: Macmillan, 1976), 79.
8. Saddlemyer, "A Conversation," 116.
9. I am indebted to Gordon Roper's careful notes on *The King* for my description.
10. *Eros at Breakfast and Other Plays*, 72; hereafter cited as E.
11. Plant, "Cultural Redemption," 37.
12. Epilogue to *At My Heart's Core and Overlaid*, (Toronto, 1966), 115.
13. Elspeth Buitenhuis, *Robertson Davies* (Toronto, 1972), 28.
14. *Four Favourite Plays* (Toronto, 1968), vi.
15. Ibid., vi.
16. Introduction to *Hope Deferred*, in *Canada's Lost Plays*, vol. 3, 175.
17. Judith Skelton Grant, "The Rich Texture of Robertson Davies' *Fortune, My Foe*," *Canadian Drama* 7, no. 2 (1981):27.
18. B. K. Sandwell, "Foes to Fortune," *Saturday Night*, 13 December 1949, 23. Sandwell signed the review as Lucy Van Gogh.
19. *Four Favourite Plays*, 76; *Fortune, My Foe* hereafter cited as F.
20. Ibid., vii.
21. Szabo is a tribute to Tony Sang, the marionette master who died in 1942. See Grant, *The Enthusiasms of Robertson Davies*, 21.
22. Grant, "The Rich Texture," 27–35.
23. "*King Phoenix* Wins Canadian Drama Award," *Peterborough Examiner*, 19 January 1953. The adjudicator was John Allen.
24. An interview with Gordon Roper (1967).
25. *Hunting Stuart and Other Plays* (Toronto, 1972), 138; *King Phoenix* hereafter cited as K.

Chapter Four

1. Grant, *Robertson Davies*, (Toronto, 1978) 17.
2. Epilogue to *At My Heart's Core and Overlaid*, 112.
3. Susanna Moodie, *Roughing It in the Bush* (Toronto, 1962), 210.
4. Rod Willmot, "If Hearts are Trump: The National History Play," *Canadian Drama* 7, no. 2 (1981):50–61. Willmot contrasts Davies's political conservatism to the revolutionary zeal of Jean-Robert Rémillard's *Cérémonial funèbre sur le corps de Jean-Olivier Chénier* (1974).
5. *At My Heart's Core* (Toronto, 1950), 17; hereafter cited as A.
6. Sandwell, "Foes to Fortune," 23.
7. *Stage Voices*, 73.
8. Ibid., 71.
9. *A Jig for the Gypsy* (Toronto, 1954), v; hereafter cited as J.

10. *Fifth Business*, 35.
11. Author's note to *Hunting Stuart and Other Plays* (Toronto, 1972), 3; *Hunting Stuart* hereafter cited as H.
12. Saddlemyer, "A Conversation," 113.
13. "Casanova de Seingalt," *Toronto Star*, 12 December 1959. See also *The Enthusiasms of Robertson Davies*, 77–79.
14. *Hunting Stuart and Other Plays*, 197; *General Confession* hereafter cited as G.
15. Patricia Morley, *Robertson Davies* (Toronto, 1977), 54–55.
16. "Casanova de Seingalt," 77–79.
17. Morley, *Robertson Davies*, 42–49, and Rota Herzberg Lister, "Masques for Boy Actors: Aesop and Punch Restored," *Canadian Drama* 7, no. 2 (1981):63–79. Lister's is the fullest treatment of Davies's use of the masque form.
18. *A Masque of Aesop* (Toronto, 1952), 34.
19. *A Masque of Mr. Punch* (Toronto, 1963), 55; hereafter cited as P.
20. *Question Time* (Toronto, 1975), 35; hereafter cited as Q.
21. Patricia Monk, "Quike bookis: The Morality Plays of Robertson Davies," *Canadian Drama* 7, no. 2 (1981):80–93.
22. Frederick Radford, "Padre Blazon or Old King Cole—Robertson Davies: Novelist or Playwright?", *Canadian Drama* 7, no. 2 (1981): 23.
23. Urgo Kareda, "*Question Time* Is a Grand Disaster," *Toronto Star*, (26 February 1975), sec. E, p. 20.
24. Davies himself has described the inclusion of the beaver as "a naughty superfluity."
25. Morley, *Robertson Davies*, 56.
26. *Selections from Ralph Waldo Emerson*, ed. Stephen E. Whicher (Boston: Houghton Mifflin, 1957), 149.

Chapter Five

1. "Samuel Marchbanks Writes a Letter to Apollo Fishorn: 1950," in *The Well-Tempered Critic*, 32. The letter appeared in the *Peterborough Examiner*, 4 March 1950. See also *The Well-Tempered Critic*, 39–64.
2. Interview with Gordon Roper, May 1967.
3. Introduction to *A Mixture of Frailties* (New York, 1979), n.p.
4. Hugo McPherson, "The Mask of Satire," *Canadian Literature* 4 (Spring 1960):18.
5. *Tempest-Tost* (Toronto, 1951), 9; hereafter cited as T.
6. Simon Paynter, *Tempest-Tost, Canadian Forum*, November 1951, 187.
7. Margaret Stobie, "Critically Speaking," CBC Radio, 23 December 1951.

8. Glen Shortliffe, "La revue des arts et lettres," Radio Canada script, n.d.
9. B. K. Sandwell, "Civilized View of Canada," *Saturday Night,* 27 October 1951, 4–5.
10. Ibid., 5.
11. W. A. D[eacon], "Little Theatre Produces Play," *Globe and Mail,* 24 November 1951, 11.
12. McPherson, "The Mask of Satire," 22.
13. *Fifth Business,* 213. Davies here adapts a phrase from *Measure for Measure* to describe Carl Jung.
14. *The Manticore* (Toronto, 1972), 169.
15. Interview with Gordon Roper, May 1967.
16. Ibid.
17. D. J. Dooley, "The Satiric Novel in Canada Today: A Failure Too Frequent," *Queen's Quarterly* 64 (Winter 1958):588.
18. Eric Nicol, "Leaven of Malice," *Vancouver Province,* 27 November 1954, 15.
19. McPherson, "The Mask of Satire," 27.
20. Malcolm Ross, "Critically Speaking," CBC Radio, 14 November 1954.
21. Kingsley Amis, *Encounter* 4 (April 1955):77–78.
22. Edmund Fuller, "The Stirring and the Swelling," *Saturday Review,* 30 July 1955, 15.
23. Stuart Keate, "The Date was Nov. 31," *New York Times Book Review,* 10 July 1955, 6.
24. Claude T. Bissell, *University of Toronto Quarterly* 24 (April 1955):264–67.
25. *Leaven of Malice* (Toronto, 1954), 307; hereafter cited as L.
26. To Gordon Roper.
27. McPherson, "The Mask of Satire," 28.
28. Dan Wickenden, "Leisurely, Wry and Solid," *Herald Tribune Book Review,* 24 August 1958.
29. Edmund Fuller, "Money for Monica," *New York Times Book Review,* 31 August 1958, 6.
30. Claude Bissell, *University of Toronto Quarterly* 28 (July 1959): 370.
31. Geoffrey Nicholson, "Goodbye to New York," *Spectator* (London), 28 November 1958, 787.
32. Normal Shrapnel, *Manchester Guardian,* 9 January 1959, 6.
33. *A Mixture of Frailties* (Toronto, 1958), 1; hereafter cited as M.
34. Clara Thomas, "The Two Voices in *A Mixture of Frailties,*" *Journal of Canadian Studies* 12 (February 1977):82–84.
35. Ibid., 90.

36. Ivon Owen, "The Salterton Novels," *Tamarack Review* 9 (Autumn 1958):59.
37. Monk, *The Small Infinity*, 70.
38. Cecil Gray, *Peter Warlock: A Memoir of Philip Heseltine* (London: Cape 1934), 223–27, 228.
39. Ibid., 227–35.
40. Warlock briefly edited a musical periodical called *The Sackbut*. Cecil Gray writes of Warlock, "It was one of his greatest faults—by no means an uncommon one—that he tried every possible interpretation before it occurred to him to consider that he might have been in the wrong" (211).
41. Interview with Gordon Roper, May, 1967.
42. In *Tempest-Tost*, Nellis Forrester in describing Solly's English education reveals her naivete and insularity by saying, "There's a kind of nice simplicity about a Canadian that education abroad seems to destroy" (40).
43. Interview with Gordon Roper, May 1967.

Chapter Six

1. Wilfred Cude, *A Due Sense of Differences* (Lanham, Md., 1980), 81, 85–107.
2. Anthony Burgess, "A Small Masterpiece of Elegant Fiction," *Chicago Tribune*, 19 November 1972.
3. Brian Moore, "There's Life in the Old Novel House," *Book World {Washington Post}*, 26 November 1972, 8.
4. Edmund Fuller, "Illusion and the Theatrical Arts," *Wall Street Journal*, 18 March 1976, 16.
5. Anthony Dawson, "Davies, His Critics, and the Canadian Canon," *Canadian Literature* 96 (Spring 1982):134–38.
6. Burgess, "A Small Masterpiece."
7. *Fifth Business*, 1; hereafter cited as F.
8. "A Forward Look," *Saturday Night*, 15 February 1958, 21.
9. "The Individual and the Mass," *Saturday Night*, 24 May 1958, 26–28.
10. "Measure for Measure," in *Twice Have the Trumpets Sounded: A Record of the Stratford Shakespearean Festival in Canada, 1954* (Toronto, 1955), 67–74. Davies here uses the phrase "a fantastical duke of dark corners" often, playing with Lucio's words in the play itself.
11. Ibid., 71.
12. "A Definitive Jung in a Single Volume," *Globe and Mail* (Toronto) 18 June 1983, sec. E, p. 15.
13. J. B. Priestley, *The Magicians* (London: Heinemann, 1954), 70, 179. Davies reviewed the novel in *Saturday Night* on 1 May 1954. See *The Enthusiasms of Robertson Davies*, 141–44.

14. *The Manticore*, 262; hereafter cited as M.
15. J. B. Priestley, *Literature and Western Man* (London: Heinemann, 1960), ix–x.
16. Ibid., x–xi.
17. "Shrewd Judgements," "A Writer's Diary," *Peterborough Examiner*, 15 October 1960, 5.
18. Priestley, *Literature and Western Man*, 5.
19. Grant, *Robertson Davies* (Toronto, 1978), 35.
20. John Henry Newman, *Apologia Pro Vita Sua*, ed. David J. DeLaura (New York: Norton, 1968), 11–12.
21. Ibid., 11.
22. Ibid., 215.
23. Ibid., 14.
24. Avrom Fleishman, *Figures of Autobiography: The Language of Self-Writing* (Berkeley: University of California Press, 1983), 156. Fleishman's use of the word *egotism* I take to be similar to Davies's precise definition of egoism.
25. Stephen Bonnycastle, "Robertson Davies and the Ethics of Monologue," *Journal of Canadian Studies* 12 (February 1977):38.
26. Dawson, "Davies, His Critics," 134–38.
27. D. J. Dooley, *Moral Vision in the Canadian Novel* (Toronto: Clarke, Irwin, 1979), 120–21. Dooley terms Blazon "a very unJesuitical Jesuit" and suggests that, in his debt to Jung, Davies overlooked the degree of license he took in putting Jungian pronouncements about God's relation to the devil in a priest's mouth.
28. "Introductory Essay," in *Studies in Robertson Davies' Deptford Trilogy*, ed. Robert G. Lawrence and Samuel L. Macey (Victoria, B.C., 1980), 10.
29. Priestley, *The Magicians*, 47.
30. Ibid., 140.
31. Iris Murdoch, *A Severed Head* (London: Chatto & Windus, 1961), 81.
32. Ibid., 251–52.
33. "Introductory Essay," in *Studies*, 9.
34. Patricia Monk discusses Davies's "ambivalence" toward Jungian analysis in her chapter, "A Country and its Foreigners," in *The Smaller Infinity*, 105–46.
35. *World of Wonders* (Toronto, 1975), 34; hereafter cited as W.
36. Monk, *The Smaller Infinity*, 167. Monk's careful reading of the novel is the most extensive, detailed, and enlightening criticism thus far available.
37. Bonnycastle, "Robertson Davies and the Ethics," 35.
38. James Neufeld, "Structural Unity in 'The Deptford Trilogy': Robertson Davies as Egoist," *Journal of Canadian Studies* 12 (February

1977):74. My understanding of the Deptford trilogy owes much to the critical readings offered by both Bonnycastle and Neufeld.

Chapter Seven

1. *A Voice from the Attic*, 103–4.
2. Ibid., 343.
3. W. J. Keith. "The Not-so-divine Comedy of Robertson Davies," *Journal of Canadian Studies* 17 (Spring, 1982):135.
4. *The Rebel Angels*, 186–87; hereafter cited as R.
5. *The Rebel Angels* is in many ways a roman à clef. The college of the novel closely resembles the University of Toronto's Trinity College, while Ploughwright College is clearly modeled on Massey College. Massey's "High Tables" provides a model for two occasions of post-dinner discussion in the novel. Davies even includes a Warden, a position not unlike his own as Master, and at one point quotes one of his own characters from *A Mixture of Frailties*. More elusive but no less interesting are links between characters in the novel and recognizable members of the University of Toronto community over the past few decades.

Selected Bibliography

PRIMARY SOURCES

Listed in chronological order of first printing.

1. Plays

Overlaid: A Comedy. Toronto: French, 1948.
Eros at Breakfast and Other Plays. Introduction by Tyrone Guthrie. Toronto: Clarke, Irwin, 1949.
Fortune, My Foe. Toronto: Clarke, Irwin, 1949.
At My Heart's Core. Toronto: Clarke, Irwin, 1950.
A Masque of Aesop. Toronto: Clarke, Irwin, 1952; Toronto: Clarke, Irwin, 1955.
A Jig for the Gypsy. Toronto: Clarke, Irwin, 1954.
A Masque of Mr. Punch. Toronto: Oxford University Press, 1963.
At My Heart's Core and Overlaid. Toronto: Clarke, Irwin, 1966.
Centennial Play. Coauthored with Arthur Murphy, Yves Thériault, W. O. Mitchell, and Eric Nicol. Ottawa: Centennial Commission, 1967.
Four Favourite Plays. Toronto: Clarke, Irwin, 1968.
Hunting Stuart and Other Plays. Edited by Brian Parker. Toronto: new press, 1972.
Question Time. Toronto: Macmillan, 1975.
Brothers in the Black Art. Vancouver, B.C.: Alcuin Society, 1981.
Leaven of Malice: A Theatrical Extravaganza. Canadian Drama 7, no. 2 (1981): 117–90.

2. Sketches and Humor

The Diary of Samuel Marchbanks. Toronto: Clarke, Irwin, 1947; Toronto: Clarke, Irwin Canadian Paperback, 1966.
The Table Talk of Samuel Marchbanks. Toronto: Clarke, Irwin, 1949; *The Table Talk of Samuel Marchbanks.* Foreword by Norman Birkett. London: Chatto & Windus, 1951; Toronto: Clarke, Irwin Paperback, 1967.
Marchbanks' Almanack. Toronto: McClelland & Stewart, 1967; *Marchbanks' Almanack.* Introduction by Gordon Roper. Toronto: McClelland & Stewart, 1968.
High Spirits. Markham, Ont.: Penguin, 1982.
The Papers of Samuel Marchbanks, comprising the Diary, the Table Talk and

169

a *Garland of Miscellanea by Samuel Marchbanks*. . . . Toronto: Irwin, 1985.

3. Novels

Tempest-Tost. Toronto: Clarke, Irwin, 1951; London: Chatto & Windus, 1952; New York: Rinehart, 1952; Toronto: Clarke, Irwin, 1955; Markham, Ont.: Penguin, 1980; New York: Penguin, 1980.

Leaven of Malice. Toronto: Clarke, Irwin, 1954; London: Chatto & Windus, 1955; New York: Scribners, 1955; Toronto: Clarke, Irwin, 1964; New York: Curtis, 1973; Markham, Ont.: Penguin, 1980; New York: Penguin, 1980.

A Mixture of Frailties. Toronto: Macmillan, 1958; London: Weidenfeld & Nicolson, 1958; London: Macmillan, 1958; New York: Scribners, 1958: Toronto; Macmillan, 1969; New York: Curtis, 1972; Foreword by Robertson Davies. New York: Everest House, 1979; Markham, Ont.: Penguin, 1980; New York: Penguin, 1980.

Fifth Business. Toronto: Macmillan, 1970; New York: Viking, 1970; London: Macmillan, 1971; New York: New American Library, 1971; Harmondsworth, Eng.: Penguin, 1977; Markham, Ont.: Penguin, 1977.

The Manticore. Toronto: Macmillan, 1972; New York: Viking, 1972; London: Macmillan, 1973; Philadelphia: Curtis, 1974; Harmondsworth, Eng.: Penguin, 1976; Markham, Ont.: Penguin, 1976.

World of Wonders. Toronto: Macmillan, 1975; New York: Viking, 1976; Harmondsworth, Eng.: Penguin, 1977; London: W. H. Allen, 1977; Markham, Ont.: Penguin, 1977.

The Rebel Angels. Toronto: Macmillan, 1981; New York: Viking, 1982; London: Allen Lane, 1982; Markham, Ont.: Penguin, 1983.

What's Bred in the Bone. Toronto: Macmillan, 1985; New York: Viking, 1985.

4. Criticism and Essays

Shakespeare's Boy Actors. London: Dent, 1939; New York: William Salloch, 1941; New York: Russell & Russell, 1964.

Shakespeare for Young Players: A Junior Course. Toronto: Clarke, Irwin, 1942.

Renown at Stratford: A Record of the Shakespeare Festival in Canada 1953. Coauthored with Tyrone Guthrie. Toronto: Clarke, Irwin, 1953.

Twice Have the Trumpets Sounded: A Record of the Stratford Shakespearean Festival in Canada 1954. Coauthored with Tyrone Guthrie. Toronto: Clarke, Irwin, 1954; London: Blackie & Sons, 1955; London: J. Garnet Miller, 1955.

Thrice the Brinded Cat Hath Mew'd: A Record of the Stratford Shakespearean Festival in Canada 1955. Coauthored with Tyrone Guthrie, Boyd Neel, and Tanya Moiseiwitsch. Toronto: Clarke, Irwin, 1955.

A Voice from the Attic. New York: Knopf, 1960; Toronto: McClelland & Stewart, 1960; *The Personal Art: Reading to Good Purpose.* London: Secker & Warburg; Toronto: British Book Service, 1961; *A Voice from the Attic.* Introduction by Robert Cockburn. Toronto: McClelland & Stewart, 1972; *A Voice from the Attic.* New York: Viking, 1972.
Stephen Leacock. Toronto: McClelland & Stewart, 1970.
The Revels History of Drama in English. Vol. 6, *1750–1880.* Coauthored with Michael Booth, Richard Southern, Frederick Marker, and Lise-Lone Marker. London: Methuen, 1975.
One Half of Robertson Davies. Provocative Pronouncements on a Wide Range of Topics. Toronto: Macmillan, 1977; New York: Penguin, 1978; New York: Viking, 1978.
Grant, Judith Skelton, ed. with introduction. *The Enthusiasms of Robertson Davies.* Toronto: McClelland & Stewart, 1979.
Grant, Judith Skelton, ed. with introduction. *The Well-Tempered Critic: One Man's View of Theatre and Letters in Canada.* Toronto: McClelland & Stewart, 1981.
The Mirror of Nature. Toronto: University of Toronto Press, 1983.

SECONDARY SOURCES

Baltensperger, Peter. "Battle with the Trolls." *Canadian Literature,* no. 71 (Winter 1977):59–67. A study of the struggle between offspring and parents in Davies's fiction.
Benson, Eugene, ed. "Robertson Davies: Dramatist." *Canadian Drama* 7, no. 2 (1981). A special issue on Davies as dramatist. Includes seven essays, an interview, a chronology, and the text of the dramatization of *Leaven of Malice.*
Bonnycastle, Stephen. "Robertson Davies and the Ethics of Monologue." *Journal of Canadian Studies* 12 (February 1977):20–40. A revealing criticism of the values underlying Davies's thinking in the Deptford trilogy.
Bowen, Gail. "Guides to the Treasure of Self: The Function of Women in the Fiction of Robertson Davies." *Waves* 5 (Fall 1976):64–77. A study of Davies's evolving, but never satisfying, treatment of women as spiritual guides for his heroes.
Buitenhuis [Cameron], Elspeth. *Robertson Davies.* Toronto: Forum House, 1972. An early, useful study that appeared just after Davies broke new ground with *Fifth Business.*
Cluett, Robert. "Robertson Davies: The Tory Mode." *Journal of Canadian Studies* 12 (February 1977):41–46. An analysis of Davies's style by means of computer.

Cude, Wilfred. "The College Occasion as Rabelaisian Feast: Academe's Dark Side in *The Rebel Angels.*" *Studies in Canadian Literature* 7 (1982):184–99.

———. *A Due Sense of Differences: An Evaluative Approach to Canadian Literature.* Lanham, Md.: University Press of America, 1980. Cude devotes three previously published essays to *Fifth Business,* always taking an approach slightly aslant of prevailing views.

———. "Miracle and Art in *Fifth Business* or Who the Devil Is Liselotte Vitzliputzli?" *Journal of Canadian Studies* 9 (November 1974):3–16. Argues that *Fifth Business* is "a miracle of art" in which the real saint is not Mary Dempster but Dunstan Ramsay. Also in Cude, *A Due Sense of Differences,* 69–84.

Dawson, Anthony B. "Davies, His Critics, and the Canadian Canon." *Canadian Literature,* no. 92 (Spring 1982):154–58. An investigation of the exalted place of *Fifth Business* in Canadian literary criticism.

Dombrowski, Theo and Eileen Dombrowski. " 'Every Man's Judgment': Robertson Davies' Courtroom." *Studies in Canadian Literature* 3 (Winter 1978):47–61. A study of Davies's differing use of the court in his earlier and later novels.

Godard, Barbara. "World of Wonders: Robert Davies' Carnival." *Essays in Canadian Writing,* no. 30 (Winter 1984–85):239–86. A long essay reviewing Davies's fiction in the light of Mikhail Bakhtin's criticism.

Grant, Judith Skelton. "The Rich Texture of Robertson Davies' *Fortune, My Foe.*" *Canadian Drama* 7, no. 2 (1981):27–35. An examination of the detail with which Davies develops certain themes in *Fortune, My Foe.*

———. *Robertson Davies.* Toronto: McClelland & Stewart, 1978. A brief, informative monograph emphasizing Davies's multifacetedness as writer.

Guthrie, Tyrone. Introduction to *Eros at Breakfast and Other Plays,* by Robertson Davies. Toronto: Clarke, Irwin, 1949. A candid assessment of Davies and his early plays.

Heintzman, Ralph H., ed. *Journal of Canadian Studies* 12 (February 1977). A special Robertson Davies issue focussing particularly on the Deptford trilogy. Includes a Davies log, six essays, and Heintzman's thoughtful introduction, "The Virtues of Reverence."

Keith, W. J. "The Roots of Fantasy: Document and Invention in Robertson Davies' Fiction." *Journal of Canadian Studies* 20 (Spring 1985):109–19. A sweeping look at the interconnections between realism and "the realms of wonder and fantasy" from *Tempest-Tost* to *The Rebel Angels.*

Lawrence, Robert G. "Canadian Theatre in Robertson Davies' *World of*

Wonders." In *Studies in Robertson Davies' Deptford Trilogy,* 114–23. An examination of the influence of Sir John Martin-Harvey's career as it pertains to *World of Wonders.*

———— and Samuel L. Macey, eds. *Studies in Robertson Davies' Deptford Trilogy.* ELS, no. 20. Victoria, B.C.: University of Victoria, 1980. Includes nine essays on the Deptford trilogy, documenting particularly certain of Davies's sources and patterns of allusion, and Davies's own piece, "The Deptford Trilogy in Retrospect."

Lennox, John Watt. "Manawaka and Deptford: Place and Voice." *Journal of Canadian Studies* 13 (Fall 1978):23–30. A comparison of Davies's Deptford novels with Margaret Laurence's fiction set in Manawaka, Manitoba.

Lister, Rota Herzberg. "Masques for Boy Actors: Aesop and Punch Restored." *Canadian Drama* 7, no. 2 (1981):63–79. A detailed examination of Davies's serious treatment of the masque in *A Masque of Aesop* and *A Masque of Mr. Punch.*

Macey, Samuel L. "Time, Clockwork, and the Devil in Robertson Davies' Deptford Trilogy." In *Studies in Robertson Davies' Deptford Trilogy,* 32–44. Macey sees Davies's sense of evil increasingly tied to "the enslavement of modern man to Western technological progress."

McPherson, Hugo. "The Mask of Satire: Character and Symbolic Pattern in Robertson Davies' Fiction." *Canadian Literature,* no. 4 (Spring 1960):18–30. The best article on Davies's early fiction, it weighs the claims of satire and romance in the Salterton novels.

Merivale, Patricia. "The (Auto)-Biographical Compulsions of Dunstan Ramsay." In *Studies in Robertson Davies' Deptford Trilogy,* 57–65. Merivale looks skeptically at Davies's ability to integrate the private and public selves of Ramsay and Eisengrim. A stimulating essay.

Monaghan, David M. "Metaphors and Confusions." *Canadian Literature,* no. 67 (Winter 1976):64–73. Argues that Davies lets the metaphor of fifth business get out of hand, thus obscuring his concern with Ramsay's growth.

Monk, Patricia. "Davies and the Drachenloch: A Study of the Archaeological Background of *The Manticore.*" In *Robertson Davies' Deptford Trilogy,* 100–113.

————. *The Smaller Infinity: The Jungian Self in the Novels of Robertson Davies.* Toronto: University of Toronto Press, 1982. A detailed study of the influence of Jung's depth psychology upon Davies as novelist and thinker.

Morley, Patricia. "Davies' Salterton Trilogy: Where the Myth Touches Us." *Studies in Canadian Literature* 1 (Winter 1976):96–104. Growth of character in Davies's first three novels is seen as an index of Canada's cultural and spiritual maturation.

————. *Robertson Davies.* Toronto: Gage, 1977. A part of the Profiles in

Canadian Drama series, it provides plot summaries and brief analysis of most of Davies's plays.

Neufeld, James. "Structural Unity in 'The Deptford Trilogy': Robertson Davies as Egoist." *Journal of Canadian Studies* 12 (February 1977):68–74. A study of the distinction Davies makes between destructive egotism and healthful, productive egoism.

Oates, Joyce Carol. "Books Reconsidered." *New Republic*, 15 April 1978, 22–25. Ostensibly a review of *One Half of Robertson Davies*, the piece criticizes Davies as vain, overrated, and out of touch.

Owen, Ivon. "The Salterton Novels." *Tamarack Review*, no. 9 (August 1958):56–63. An early, perceptive article noting that Davies "stands curiously apart from the mainstream of contemporary fiction."

Peterman, Michael. "Bewitchments of Simplification." *Canadian Drama* 7, no. 2 (1981):94–109.

Plant, Richard. "Cultural Redemption in the Work of Robertson Davies." *Canadian Drama* 7, no. 2 (1981):36–49. An examination of Davies's response to Canada in his plays.

Radford, F. L. "The Apprentice Sorcerer: Davies' Salterton Trilogy." In *Studies in Robertson Davies' Deptford Trilogy*, 13–21. A look at ways in which the Salterton novels anticipate the Deptford trilogy.

———. "The Great Mother and the Boy: Jung, Davies, and *Fifth Business*." In *Studies in Robertson Davies' Deptford Trilogy*, 66–81. A detailed study of the relation between Dunstan Ramsay's growth and Jung's concept of individuation.

———. "Heinrich Heine, the Virgin, and the Hummingbird: *Fifth Business*—A Novel and Its Subconscious." *English Studies in Canada* 4 (Spring 1978):95–110. A study of the ways in which Davies adapts hero-myths to suit a Canadian context.

———. "Padre Blazon or Old King Cole—Robertson Davies: Novelist or Playwright?" *Canadian Drama* 7, no. 2 (1981):13–26. The article covers Davies's work as dramatist.

———. "Patricia Monk, *The Smaller Infinity*." *English Studies in Canada* 10 (December 1984):476–88. A trenchant review of Monk's Jungian study applying her views to *The Rebel Angels*.

Roper, Gordon. "A Davies Log." *Journal of Canadian Studies* 12 (February 1977):4–19.

———. "Robertson Davies, *Fifth Business* and 'That Old Fantastical Duke of Dark Corners, C. G. Jung.'" *Journal of Canadian Fiction* 1 (Winter 1972):33–39. Reprinted in *The Canadian Novel Here and Now*. Edited by John Moss. Toronto: NC Press, 1978, 1:53–66. First study of the influence of Jung on Davies as novelist.

Ryrie, John. "Robertson Davies: An Annotated Bibliography." In *The Annotated Bibliography of Canada's Major Authors*. Edited by Robert

Lecker and Jack David. Toronto: ECW Press, 1981, 3:57–279. An invaluable complete guide to writing by and about Robertson Davies.

Stone-Blackburn, Susan. *Robertson Davies, Playwright: A Search for the Self on the Canadian Stage.* Vancouver: University of British Columbia Press, 1985. A full and sympathetic study of Davies as dramatist including detailed commentary on his lesser known plays.

Sutherland, Ronald. "The Relevance of Robertson Davies." *Journal of Canadian Studies* 12 (February 1977):75–81. A brief study of the maturation of Davies as novelist from his early fiction to *Fifth Business.*

Thomas, Clara. "The Two Voices of *A Mixture of Frailties*." *Journal of Canadian Studies* 12 (February 1977):82–91. Thomas compares Davies's treatment of Monica Gall's education with his satirical omniscience in other parts of the novel.

Warwick, Ellen. "The Transformation of Robertson Davies." *Journal of Canadian Fiction* 3 (Summer 1974):46–51. Sees *The Manticore* as a clear-cut romance in which Davies's penchant for satire is minimized.

Index

Amis, Kingsley, 93
Anderson, Sherwood, 148
Apuleius, 106, 109, 112
Aubry's *Brief Lives*, 157

Beerbohm, Max, 9
Bissel, Claude, 15, 93, 102
Bonnycastle, Stephen, 127, 130, 152, 168–69
Browning, Robert, 123
Burgess, Anthony, 114, 115, 161

Callaghan, Morley, 25
Canada, 2, 6, 10, 11, 13, 24, 31, 35–41, 43, 44, 48, 50, 51, 57, 58, 60, 71, 75–78, 79, 81, 82, 84, 90, 93, 95, 97, 102, 103, 104, 109, 136–138, 145, 146, 148
Cather, Willa, 11, 113
Corsican Brothers, The, 36, 37, 145
Crest Theatre, 14, 62, 67, 70–71
Cude, Wilfred, 114

Davies, Brenda (Mathews), 10, 13, 70
Davies, Florence MacKay, 1, 2
Davies, Rupert, 1, 2, 3, 5, 6, 7, 8
Davies, William Robertson, academic career, 14–16; awards, 16; childhood and family, 1–6; education, 6–9; journalistic career, 10–14, 17–34

WORKS—NON-FICTION:
"Cap and Bells," 10, 18
Diary of Samuel Marchbanks, The, 12, 19, 21, 26–27, 28, 29, 30
"Double Life of Roberston Davies, The," by Samuel Marchbanks 12, 17, 32–34
Marchbanks' Almanack, 12, 21, 29–32
Mirror of Nature, The, 16
Papers of Samuel Marchbanks, The, 16
"Rake for Reading, A," 3
Shakespeare for Young Players: A Junior Course, 12
Shakespeare's Boy Actors, 9
Table Talk of Samuel Marchbanks, The, 12, 27–29, 30
Voice from the Attic, A, 14, 48, 154, 155
"Writer's Diary, A," 15

WORKS—FICTION:
Fifth Business, 1, 4, 15, 60, 74, 86, 111, 114, 115, 116, 118, 119–132, 135, 137, 138, 148, 151, 154
High Spirits, 16
Leaven of Malice, 2, 14, 31, 60, 61, 82, 83–84, 87, 91, 93–101, 102, 147
Manticore, The, 2, 5, 8, 15, 16, 60, 76, 87, 111, 114, 115, 118, 124, 129, 130, 132–143, 151
Mixture of Frailties, A, 2, 14, 44, 74, 82, 84, 101–113, 115, 128, 147, 169
Rebel Angels, The, 2, 16, 28, 74, 135, 142, 150, 153, 154–159, 162
Tempest-Tost, 6, 8, 14, 32, 33, 61, 81, 82, 83, 84–92, 93, 94, 95, 98, 101, 105
What's Bred in the Bone, 16
World of Wonders, 4, 15, 36, 74, 99, 114, 124, 135, 143–153, 158

WORKS—PLAYS:
At My Heart's Core, 13, 56–61, 66, 68
At the Gates of the Righteous, 45–47
Brothers in the Black Art, 3, 35
Eros at Breakfast, 13, 42–43
Fortune, My Foe, 13, 47–52, 53, 59, 60, 61, 81, 96, 102
General Confession, 14, 56, 70–74, 75, 77
Hope Deferred, 38–40, 41, 50, 102, 112
Hunting Stuart, 14, 38, 56, 66–70, 77, 96
Jig for the Gypsy, A, 14, 35, 38, 56, 61–66, 68, 77, 124
King Phoenix, 52–55, 63, 71
King Who Could Not Dream, The, 36–38, 52, 55, 70, 164
Love and Libel, 15
Masque of Aesop, A, 74–5
Masque of Mr. Punch, A, 74–5
Overlaid, 13, 40–42, 44, 60, 70, 88
Pontiac and the Green Man, 35
Question Time, 15, 35, 38, 56, 71, 75–78
Voice of the People, The, 43–44, 82

Index

Davies, Donald, Murray and Barbara (Chilcott), 14, 62, 67, 70, 71
Dawson, Anthony, 115, 127
Deacon, William Arthur, 29, 85
Dominion Drama Festival (DDF), 13, 28, 31, 38, 42, 47, 52
Dooley, D.J., 168

Edinburgh Festival, 13, 43
Eliot, T.S., 11
Emerson, Ralph Waldo, 79

Fleishman, Avrom, 127, 168
Freud, Sigmund, 10, 15, 69, 86, 96, 115, 116, 138, 142, 150, 167
Fuller, Edmund, 93, 102, 114

Gielgud, John, 9, 13, 36, 52
Grant, Judith Skelton, 50, 56, 162
Gray, Cecil, *Peter Warlock*, 107–108, 110, 167
Guthrie, Tyrone, 2, 9, 10, 13, 14, 41, 62, 90, 130

Hawthorne, Nathanial, 3
Hemingway, Ernest, 11
Holmes, Oliver Wendell, 27, 29
Huxley, Aldous, 7, 69, 107

Irving, Sir Henry, 10, 13, 36, 77, 145, 146

James, Henry, 99
James, William, 122, 137
Johnson, Samuel, 22, 27
Jonson, Ben, 13, 22, 27, 79
Joyce, James, 11
Jung, Carl, 15, 38, 55, 66, 73, 77–78, 79, 92, 114, 115–116, 117, 118, 119, 125, 128, 129, 130, 132, 133, 134, 135, 137, 138, 139, 140, 158, 167

Keith, W.J., 154
King, Mackenzie, 29, 77, 138
Kingsley, Charles, 3, 126
Kingston Whig-Standard, 6, 10, 12
Kingston, Ontario, 1, 6, 8, 13, 38, 47, 48, 81, 82
Knopf, Alfred, 14
Kroetsch, Robert, 161

Lawrence, D.H., 107
Leacock, Stephen, 4, 14, 15, 26, 27, 32, 63
Lewis, Sinclair, 2, 44

MacLennan, Hugh, 11
Mackenzie, William Lyon, 57
Mann, Thomas, 151
Martin-Harvey, Sir John, 7, 8, 13, 36, 145
Massey College, 1, 14, 15, 16, 155, 169
Massey Report, The, 13
Master of Ballantrae, The, 37, 145
McPherson, Hugo, 86, 93, 102
Mencken, H.L., 22, 27
Molière, 38, 39
Monk, Patricia, 33, 77, 115, 152, 162, 168
Moodie, Susanna, 56–59
Moore, Brian, 114
Morley, Patricia, 78
Munro, Alice, 113
Murdoch, Iris, 128, 130–131

Neufeld, James, 153, 168–169
Newman, John Henry, 120, 126, 127, 128, 151
Nicol, Eric, 35, 93

Old Vic Theatre, 9, 10, 12, 13, 36
Ontario, 1, 7, 19, 23, 24, 31, 40, 45, 89, 136
Ottawa Drama League, 13, 42, 47
Owen, Ivon, 104
Oxford University, 8, 9, 15, 137, 140

Paracelsus, 74, 156, 157
Pepys, Samuel, 18, 26, 27, 29
Peterborough, Ontario, 12, 13, 18, 32, 33, 56, 81
Peterborough Examiner, 10, 15, 17, 18, 30, 31, 162
Plant, Richard, 35, 39
Poe, Edgar Allan, 20
Powys, John Cowper, 11
Prestley, J.B., 14, 70, 71, 118, 119, 120, 130–31, 167

Queen's University, 6, 7, 8

Rabelais, François, 12, 22, 31, 107, 129, 154, 155, 156, 157
Renfrew, Ontario, 1, 4, 5
Renfrew Mercury 3, 5
Robert-Houdin, 114, 143, 144, 147
Roper, Gordon, 15, 32, 33, 161, 162, 164
Ross, Malcolm, 93
Ross, Sinclair, 11

Sandwell, B.K., 7, 11, 48, 50, 59, 85